The Formation of Husserl's Concept of Constitution

PHAENOMENOLOGICA

COLLECTION PUBLIÉE SOUS LE PATRONAGE DES CENTRES
D'ARCHIVES-HUSSERL

18

ROBERT SOKOLOWSKI

The Formation of Husserl's Concept of Constitution

ROBERT SOKOLOWSKI

The Formation of Husserl's Concept of Constitution

MARTINUS NIJHOFF / THE HAGUE / 1964

PREFACE

This work is conceived essentially as a historical study of the origin and development of one of the key concepts in Husserl's philosophy. It is not primarily meant to be an introduction to Husserl's thought, but can serve this purpose because of the nature of this concept. The doctrine of constitution deals with a philosophical problem that is fairly easy to grasp, and yet is central enough in the philosophy of Husserl to provide a convenient viewpoint from which other concepts and problems can be considered and understood. Husserl's thoughts on the phenomenological reduction, on temporality, on perception, on evidence, can all be integrated into a coherent pattern if we study them in their rapport with the concept of constitution. Furthermore, the concept of constitution is used by Husserl as an explanatory schema: in giving the constitution of an object, Husserl feels he is giving the philosophical explanation of such an object. Thus in our discussion of constitution, we are studying the explanatory power of phenomenology, and in relating other phenomenological concepts to the concept of constitution, we are studying what they contribute to the philosophical explanation that phenomenology attempts to furnish. To approach Husserl's philosophy in this way is to study it in its essential and most vital function.

I wish to express my thanks to the Catholic University of America for the assistance that made it possible for me to do the research leading to this volume. I am especially indebted to the Right Reverend Monsignor John K. Ryan and the Reverend John F. Smolko for the many ways they have helped me, philosophically and otherwise, during the past few years. I wish to make known my deep appreciation to Rudolf Boehm, of the Husserl Archives at Louvain, for the generosity with which he placed his time and his profound knowledge of Husserl at my service, and to Iso Kern, Assistant at the same Archives, for the many philosophical discussions which helped so much in my work. Above all, I wish to thank the Reverend H. L. Van Breda, O.F.M. for the friendly and careful direction he gave me in the composition of this work as a dissertation at the University of Louvain, and for inviting me to publish it in the *Phaenomenologica*. I would also like to thank all my professors at the University of Louvain for their kindness to me during the years I was a student there.

I wish finally to thank those publishers who have granted permission to quote from their publications, as indicated in the footnotes of this volume. These are Aubier, Editions Montaigne, Basil Blackwell, Desclée de Brouwer, Editions Gallimard, George Allen and Unwin, Librairie Philosophique J. Vrin, Max Niemeyer Verlag, Les Editions de Minuit, Presses Universitaires de France, and Verlag Anton Hain. I am especially grateful to the editors of *Philosophy and Phenomenological Research* for allowing me to reproduce some material that appeared as an article, "Immanent Constitution in Husserl's Lectures on Time," in the June, 1964 issue of their journal.

TABLE OF CONTENTS

INTRODUCTION

The concept of constitution is one of the key concepts which Husserl employs as a means of philosophical clarification. Through the use he makes of it, something which has been obscure is elucidated, something which was problematic becomes philosophically understandable. If philosophy has been conceived as *scientia certa per causas ultimas*, the "First Philosophy" which Husserl proposes could be called *scientia certa per constitutionem;* it is an apodictic, rigorous science that is supposed to clarify reality, and subjectivity as well, through constitution. But what is the nature of such clarification? What is the obscurity that is dissipated by arrival of the word "constitution," and what does this word do to reality and consciousness to make a phenomenologist feel satisfied that he understands? Is there any obscurity that still remains even after successful application of what Husserl calls constitutional analysis?

Our study hopes to shed some light on questions of this sort. In tracing the formation of Husserl's concept of constitution, we hope to further the understanding of what he considers a philosophical explanation. We do not intend to treat constitution in all the amplitude Husserl's phenomenology gives to it, a project which would be equivalent to a study of his entire philosophy, but to consider the formation of the concept itself. We will try to determine the first appearance it makes in Husserl's thought and the manner in which it gradually develops in the course of his philosophical reflection. We will attempt to examine the concept itself, and ask what images or schematism it involves, whether it appears first in any particular or restrictive form, and whether it is capable of being applied as universally as Husserl does apply it. It will be our concern to determine the contexts into which the concept of constitution is introduced, and the type of problem it is supposed to solve; to show, furthermore, how the clarification brought about by Husserl's first form of constitutional analysis provokes other regions of obscurity to appear, and thus calls forth a new type of analysis in genetic constitution. We hope to be able to outline the type of solution this concept gives and to pass judgment on its value.

Our study will not be concerned, however, with the problem of intersubjective constitution. We limit it to examination of the constitution Husserl attributes to individual subjectivity which, in his thought, is the more basic form of constitution. We do not wish to examine all the external influences which prompted Husserl's conception and development of this doctrine. Although we do mention some of the men and writings that exercised a decisive effect on his thought, we are chiefly interested in tracing the internal formation and development of Husserl's own concept of constitution. Finally, we are concerned with formation of the concept itself, and not with all its ramifications in Husserl's thought. As a result, some periods of his development are neglected; only those are treated which provide a distinct contribution to the formation of the concept itself. Husserl's early period, from the *Philosophy of Arithmetic* to *Ideas I*, is most extensively treated, and since the lines of development followed there cannot be appreciated and understood without some discussion of the terminus they reach in genetic constitution, a chapter on that subject, as it appears in *Formal and Transcendental Logic* and the *Cartesian Meditations*, is also included.

We have chosen to treat our subject in chronological order, following the sequence of books or published lectures that we have from Husserl. Such a format is almost unavoidable for a subject like ours, because it is important to situate Husserl's doctrine within the context and problems for which it was composed. Each of Husserl's works has an aim and characteristics proper to itself, and to treat his concept of constitution apart from these factors would be to falsify it to a significant degree. Each work, furthermore, furnishes an addition to what has been accomplished in earlier studies, so that each of our chapters is able to treat a distinct, important aspect of the concept of constitution.

In the first chapter, our study of Husserl's *Philosophy of Arithmetic* is geared to showing to what extent the concept of constitution is already operative in this work. It also examines certain themes and problems which are already in Husserl's thought but which are not incorporated into a systematic theory of intentionality and constitution, and thus must be considered only as anticipations of his subsequent thinking.

The chapter on the *Logical Investigations* studies Husserl's first thorough concept of intentionality, and the idea of constitution as related to it. The problem of the objectivity of knowledge, structural analysis of intentionality, the role of sensations, and the place of categorical and simple constitution, are all treated in this work, and definitions for elements in intentionality are reached which will be the basis for Husserl's later thought. As regards constitution, the predominant questions are: what precisely is it supposed to solve, and what "explanatory schema" is used in the solution? We will also stress the limitations on what Husserl's concept of constitution can achieve at this level.

Chapter three, devoted to the problem of inner temporality and the constitution performed in it, turns to an entirely different sphere. After having treated intentionality in the *Logical Investigations*, Husserl now turns to the factors which make intentionality itself possible. His reflections on inner time have far reaching effects on his concept of constitution. In a positive way, they form the remote basis for what will, after many years, emerge as genetic constitution; negatively, they shake the schematism which Husserl has used in the *Investigations* as the foundation for his idea and methodology of constitution.

The chapter devoted to *Ideas I* centers first on the relationship between constitution and the transcendental reduction, the procedure by which Husserl is to found his philosophy as a rigorous science. Relating constitution to the reduction will help us see the place that this concept has in the general structure of phenomenology as Husserl understands it, and to judge precisely how much is explained, and how much left unexplained, by a constitutional analysis. In addition, the *Ideas* are particularly interesting for our study of constitution because they retain the principle of intentional analysis as it has been outlined in the

Logical Investigations, but also admit the conclusions of the
lectures on time, which throw doubt on this principle. In *Ideas I,*
Husserl has not yet integrated his theory of temporality with his
entire phenomenology. Finally, the problems treated under the
rubric "Reason and Reality" provide an example of the value of
constitutional analysis.

Genetic constitution is treated in chapter five. *Formal and
Transcendental Logic* and the *Cartesian Meditations,* where genetic constitution appears in a definitive form, are the basis for
this chapter. We try to explain the sense of genetic constitution,
and to show how it provides a necessary complement to the
theory of constitution that marked Husserl's earlier period. In
particular, we indicate how genetic analysis makes it possible
for Husserl to integrate his theory of temporality with the concept
of intentional constitution. The limitations on what genetic
constitution is supposed to explain are also examined.

Finally, chapter six provides a discussion of the evolution
undergone by Husserl's doctrine of constitution, and examines
the basic motives which caused it to develop the way it did.
The concept is located within the general perspective of Husserl's
philosophy, and an attempt is made to evaluate its success as a
method of philosophical explanation.

Questions of terminology form an important problem in our
study, because many phenomenological terms have no philosophically accredited English counterparts. In Appendix III,
there is given a glossary of terms which governs our English
version of Husserl's expressions. We wish to make one important
remark about terminology, however, concerning the English
equivalent of Husserl's terms *Erfahrung,* which refers to our
consciousness of transcendent, "external" reality, and *Erlebnis,*
which refers to our consciousness of immanent objects, such as
sensations and intentional acts. Both terms are generally translated by "experience" in ordinary English usage, but to follow
this use would give us no convenient way of distinguishing
between "internal" and "external" experience. We will therefore use the term "experience" exclusively as the correlate for
Erlebnis, to express our consciousness of what is immanent to
subjectivity, while the term "encounter" will be used exclusively as correlate for *Erfahrung,* to name our consciousness

of what is transcendent to subjectivity. Our use of "encounter"
is not to be taken in the technical sense the French equivalent,
rencontre, has in some literature of existential philosophy, where
it refers to the consciousness we have of other persons. As we
use it, "encounter" means our awareness of anything in the
world, whether animate or inanimate, person or thing, outside
of our own subjectivity. Its scope of application is as wide as
that of the German term *Erfahrung*.

CHAPTER I

CONSTITUTION AND THE
ORIGINS OF NUMBERS

*1. Husserl's own judgment of the "Philosophy of Arithmetic." The
methodology he uses in it*

Some thirty-eight years after publication of the *Philosophy
of Arithmetic*,[1] Husserl wrote the following appraisal of it: "Thus
it was, expressed in my later way of speaking, a phenomenologi-
cal-constitutional study. It was also the first that attempted to
make 'categorical objectivities' ... understandable out of constituting intentional activity...." [2] In other places of his work,
Husserl criticizes his *Philosophy of Arithmetic* because it was
tainted with psychologism, but the judgment expressed in *Formal
and Transcendental Logic* shows that he never repudiated his
first work completely; rather, as regards the concept of constitution, he considered it quite in keeping with the type of investigation he was to develop in the years to follow.[3] But to what

[1] *Philosophie der Arithmetik. Psychologische und logische Untersuchungen.* Volume I
(Halle a. S.: C.E.M. Pfeffer, 1891).
[2] "Es war also, in meiner späteren Redeweise ausgedrückt, eine phänomenolo-
gische-konstitutive Untersuchung und es war zugleich die erste, die 'kategoriale
Gegenständlichkeiten'... verständlich zu machen suchte aus der 'konstituierenden'
intentionalen Aktivität..." *Formale und transzendentale Logik* (Halle a. S.: Max
Niemeyer, 1929), p. 76.
[3] Husserl's own judgment makes us inclined to accept the thesis of Walter Biemel,
who claims that the problem of constitution is already operative, in rudimentary
form, in Husserl's first published work. Cf. "Die entscheidende Phasen der Entfaltung von Husserls Philosophie," *Zeitschrift für philosophische Forschung*, 13 (1959),
pp. 189-195. Agreement with this position is voiced in: Ludwig Landgrebe, "Husserls Phänomenologie und die Motive zu ihrer Umbildung," *Revue internationale de
Philosophie*, 1 (1938-1939), pp. 282-285; Quentin Lauer, *Phénoménologie de Husserl*
(Paris: Presses Universitaires de France, 1955), pp. 55-56; Suzanne Bachelard, *La
logique de Husserl* (Paris: Presses Universitaires de France, 1957), p. 2. The opposing
view can be found in: Roman Ingarden's remarks concerning: Walter Biemel, "Les
phases décisives dans le développement de la philosophie de Husserl," in *Husserl*,
Cahiers de Royaumont, Philosophie III (Paris: Editions de Minuit, 1959), pp. 66-67;
Werner Illeman, *Husserls vor-phänomenologische Philosophie* (Leipzig: S. Hirzel,
1932), pp. 11-19.

does Husserl refer, when he says that the *Philosophy of Arithmetic* contains explanations of constitution?

The aim of this work, as Husserl states in his preface, is to find the "tenable foundations" [1] of the science of arithmetic. The studies given in it are only preparatory to a systematic, architectonic philosophy of arithmetic. They provide the building stones which the construction of such a theory presupposes by giving a clarification and explanation of the fundamental concepts used in arithmetic. [2]

The methodological principle that governs the work is the following: "As soon as we hit upon ultimate, elementary concepts, all defining comes to an end.... What one can do in such cases consists only in pointing out the concrete phenomena from which or through which they are abstracted, and clarifying the method of this abstraction process." [3] When we deal with the basic concepts of mathematics, all that can be given in the way of explanation is "to describe the manner in which we come to these concepts." [4] In explanation of such concepts as number, plurality, equality, the relationship of more and less, the processes of adding and subtracting, and the art of computing with symbols, "we deal truly with ultimate facts." [5] We are faced with the task of explaining "such concepts...which, because of their elementary character, are neither capable of a definition nor in need of one." [6] Explanation of such critical concepts does not consist in defining them, but rather in providing a description of the way in which they arise.

Thus the type of explanation Husserl wants is a description

---

[1] "Haltbare Fundamente," *Phil. Arith.*, p. v.

[2] Cf. Husserl's notice to his own *Philosophy of Arithmetic* in the *Vierteljahrsschrift für wissenschaftliche Philosophie*, 15 (1891), p. 360: "Für ein tieferes philosophisches Verständnis der Arithmetik tut gegenwärtig Zweierlei Not: Einerseits eine Analyse ihrer Grundbegriffe, andererseits eine logische Aufklärung ihrer symbolischen Methoden. In dieser doppelten Hinsicht versucht der Verfasser möglichst gesicherte Fundamente zu legen; nicht aber ein geschlossenes System einer Philosophie der Arithmetik aufzubauen."

[3] "Sobald wir auf die letzten, elementaren Begriffe stossen, hat alles Definieren ein Ende.... Was man in solchen Fällen tun kann, besteht nur darin, dass man die konkreten Phänomene aufweist, aus oder an denen sie abstrahiert sind, und die Art dieses Abstraktionsvorganges klarlegt...." *Phil. Arith.*, p. 130.

[4] "Die Weise beschreiben, wie man zu diesen Begriffen kommt..." *ibid.*, p. 131.

[5] "Wirklich handelt es sich hier um letzte Tatsachen." *ibid.*, p. 17.

[6] "Solche Begriffe,... die wegen ihres elementaren Charakters einer Definition weder fähig noch bedürftig sind." *ibid.*, p. 103.

of the coming-to-be of fundamental arithmetical concepts, and the determination of the source from which they arise. He describes this method of explanation as a way of clarifying the "logical and psychological" nature of basic concepts.[1] What is the sense and structure of such explanations, and to what extent can they be called studies of constitution?

2. *Husserl's analysis of number*

The first four chapters of his work are devoted to explanation of the concept of cardinal number (*Anzahl*) which Husserl assumes, for the sake of exposition, to be the basic concept in arithmetic.[2] Five different steps can be distinguished in his analysis, and the type of explanation used in them is not homogeneous. The reasons given and the purpose sought in each step differ from those in other steps, and only in one of them does the concept of constitution appear.

(A) *Step one: number and multiplicity*

In his first step, Husserl begins by indicating that the concept of number presupposes the concept of multiplicity, and that analysis of number can be achieved only when analysis of the latter has been carried out. A number can arise only when a multiplicity is given.[3] Thus Husserl begins by shifting his attention to the concept of multiplicity, and sets out to explain it.

Why does number presuppose multiplicity? Husserl claims that both concepts coincide essentially with one another. "The difference consists only in that the concept of number already presupposes discrimination among the abstract forms of multiplicity, whereas the concept of multiplicity does not."[4] The concept of multiplicity can assume various forms, and the concept of number involves the sharp distinction of each of

[1] Cf. *ibid.*, pp. 7, 201, 247, 301.
[2] Osborn points out that Husserl's acceptance of cardinal numbers as the basic elements in arithmetic comes from the theory of Weierstrass. Cf. Andrew Osborn, *The Philosophy of Edmund Husserl* (New York: Columbia University Press, 1934), p. 37. Husserl says he will examine this assumption on the basis of what he finds in the studies of his promised second volume of the *Philosophy of Arithmetic* (cf. p. 6). Since the second volume never appeared, the problem was not treated any further.
[3] Cf. *Phil. Arith.*, p. 8.
[4] "Der Unterschied besteht nur darin, dass der Begriff der Anzahl bereits eine Unterscheidung der abstrakten Vielheitsformen von einander voraussetzt, derjenige der Vielheit aber nicht." *ibid.*, p. 89.

these forms from the others. The concept of multiplicity, however, disregards the differences among its forms: "What it
lacks is that which alone perfects and marks the number characteristic: the sharply determined 'how much'." [1] "Numbers
are the distinct species of the universal concept of multiplicity." [2]
Numbers arise when we make distinctions among the various
forms of multitudes that can be given to us. Thus when we are
faced with a multitude, "we acquire the corresponding number
when we classify the constructed forms of multiplicity as a 'two,'
'three,' etc." [3] Number is a more refined concept, it represents
"a considerably deeper level of concept formation."[4]

This first step of analysis is not specifically an inquiry into
sources. All it does is include the concept of number within the
scope of a wider concept, that of multiplicity, and it shows what
number adds to simple multiplicity. It subsumes number as a
species under a genus. In an analogous way, one might begin to
explain the concept "red" by stating that it presupposes the
concept "color," and thus indicate that the concept of color has
to be examined first. The remaining four steps of analysis are
concerned with explaining the concept of multiplicity.

(B) Step two: the concept of multiplicity is abstracted from groups

The concept of multiplicity is an abstraction. In step two,
Husserl indicates the concrete phenomena, the "realities" which
are the basis for the process of abstraction leading to this concept.
He claims, obviously enough, that this abstract concept is based
on concrete groups of objects given to our consciousness. "In
no way is there any doubt about the concrete phenomena which
form the basis for the abstraction of the concepts in question.
They are groups, multiplicities of determined objects." [5] Husserl
does not give a rigorous argument for this step, but appeals to

[1] "Was ihm fehlt ist dasjenige, was den Zahlencharakter erst vollendet und ihn
auszeichnet: das scharf bestimmte *Wieviel*." *ibid.*, p. 89.
[2] "Die Zahlen sind die unterschiedenen Spezies des allgemeinen Begriffes der
Vielheit." *ibid.*, p. 250.
[3] " ...Wir erhalten die entsprechende Anzahl, indem wir die gebildete Vielheits-
form als eine Zwei, Drei, usw. klassifizieren." *ibid.*, p. 112.
[4] "eine erhebliche tiefere Stufe der Begriffsbildung." *ibid.*, p. 90.
[5] "In Betreff der konkreten Phänomene, welche für die Abstraktion der in Frage
stehende Begriffe die Grundlage bilden, besteht keinerlei Zweifel. Es sind Inbegriffe,
Vielheiten bestimmter Objekte." *ibid.*, p. 9.

ordinary experience to clarify and justify it: "Everyone knows
what is meant by this expression [of 'groups']."[1]

It is not surprising that Husserl does not take great pains to
justify this step, since all it involves is a shift of attention from
an abstract concept to the concrete instance of that concept.
Analogously, one might say that the abstract concept "color" is
abstracted from colored things. Nevertheless, it is not a superfluous move, since it focuses his investigation on concrete
groups as the phenomenon now to be explained in the analysis
of multiplicity. The problem of the origin of the concept of
multiplicity, and hence that of number, has become the problem
of the origin of concretely given groups.

In indicating the concrete phenomena from which the concept
of multiplicity is abstracted, Husserl has not yet described the
actual process of abstraction which goes from the concrete
phenomena to the abstract concept. We must wait for step five
before this is given, since it depends on the argument developed
in the intermediary steps three and four.

(C) Step three: groups are "psychic relationships"

The third step of analysis explains groups in terms of relationships. Each individual in a group is related to the group
as a whole; its status as member of an ensemble is due to the
fact of its relationship to the group as a whole. Furthermore,
the group itself appears only when the members are so related.
Both the concrete group and the individuals within it are established as group and members by a relationship which Husserl proposes to call by the name of "collective liaison." [2] The
problem of the origin of the concept of number has now been
developed into the problem of the origin of the relationship
called collective liaison.

(D) Step four: constitution of groups

The fourth step of Husserl's analysis is an explanation of
collective liaison. After criticizing a series of unacceptable theories,
which consist essentially in reducing the collective relationship
to some other sort of relation (such as temporal or spatial re-

---

[1] "Was mit diesem Ausdrucke gemeint ist, weisst jeder." *ibid.*, pp. 9-10.
[2] "Kollektive Verbindung" *ibid.*, p. 15.

lations, the simple co-presence of individuals in an act of consciousness, or the relationship of distinction between elements), Husserl concludes, "There seems to be nothing left but to take up a new class of relations, one well distinguished from all others, for the collective liaison." [1] The determination of this special type of relationship will provide the "source" of groups, and hence explain the ultimate source of the concepts of multiplicity and number.

Husserl's description of collective relations hinges on an original distinction he makes between two types of relationships, primary and psychic relations. Primary relations exist between elements whose very contents imply a relationship to one another. For example, color implies a relationship to surface, parts of a continuum imply a relationship to the continuum itself, "red" implies "color," and so forth. In such cases, the relationship is given together with the elements related and is inseparable from them. We cannot think of color without a surface.

Psychic relations are those whose elements do not have this relationship to one another immediately given in their contents. Instead, such a relation arises only through a mental act which refers one of the terms to the other. "Here, the contents are united only through the act. . . ." [2] The source of psychic relations is to be found in the mental act of relating elements which, by virture of their content alone, are wholly unrelated to one another.

Husserl places collective relationships among psychic ones. The only thing that makes a given series of objects collected into a group, he argues, is the mental act that so relates them. There is nothing in the content of the objects themselves that logically necessitates this grouping. This is quite unlike the relationship, for instance, between a substance and its properties, where one term must logically imply the other. The mutual relationship of this book, this lamp, and this radio as members of a group of three objects depends only on someone's mental activity of collecting them into a group. We are not logically forced, by the nature of the things involved, to collect them

---

[1] "Es scheint also nichts übrig zu bleiben, als für die kollektive Verbindung eine neue und von allen anderen wohlgeschiedene Relationklasse in Anspruch zu nehmen." *ibid.*, p. 69.

[2] "Die Inhalte sind hier eben nur duch den Akt geeinigt. . . ." *ibid.*, p. 73.

into this or that particular group, nor are we logically compelled to collect them into a group at all. The relationship of membership in a group is logically extrinsic to the content of the terms involved in the relationship. Thus Husserl's conclusion is, "The collective unification is not visibly given in the content of what is presented, but has its effective state only in certain psychic acts, which envelope and unite the contents...." [1]

(E) Excursus: the concepts "something" and "one"

Husserl makes use of the concept "something" (*etwas*) in describing how group relationships are formed. We have seen that when we collect several members into a group, this collecting is entirely independent, logically, of the nature of the members involved. A house, an angel, and patriotism can be collected by a mental act to form a group of three, despite the differences in their ontological status. The only condition required, according to Husserl, is that each member be thought of as a "something." All further determination in the content of the members is logically superfluous for the formation of the group, and we abstract from it when we relate the members of a group.

When we predicate the term "something" to an individual, what do we assert about it? As far as content goes, this predicate does not rank with other predicates such as "red," "large," "immaterial," "mythological," and so on. It is not a partial content, as Husserl says, ranked among other characteristics of things, but it does express something common to everything: anything so qualified can, directly or indirectly, be made an object of our consciousness. [2] Thus in forming a group of individuals, it suffices if each individual can be an object of our consciousness; if we can think about it, then we can collect it with other individuals and form a group.

---

[1] "... die kollektivische Einigung nicht im Vorstellungsinhalte anschaulich gegeben ist, sondern nur in gewissen psychischen Akten, welchen die Inhalte einigend umschliessen, ihren Bestand hat...." *ibid.*, p. 79. On the same page, Husserl continues: "Ein Inbegriff entsteht, indem ein einheitliches Interesse und in und mit ihm zugleich ein einheitliches Bemerken verschiedene Inhalte für sich heraushebt und umfasst."

[2] Cf. *ibid.*, p. 86: "Worin alle Gegenstände ... übereinkommen, ist nur dies, dass sie Vorstellungsinhalte sind oder durch Vorstellungsinhalte in unserem Bewusstsein vertreten werden."

The predicate "one" is closely related to that of "something." Whereas "something" does not necessarily connote the fact that the individual in question is a member of a group, the predicate "one" does connote this fact. "Now since the name 'one' came to be used exclusively in counting, there arose a certain distinction of meaning between 'one' and 'a thing' and 'something,' through the fact that 'one' acquired the connotation of a correlation to multiplicity." [1]

The argument presented in step four seems to be what Husserl has in mind when he refers to his *Philosophy of Arithmetic* as a study in phenomenological constitution. Before studying it in more detail, let us complete our exposition of Husserl's analysis of the concept of number by seeing what he accomplishes in step five.

(F) Step five: reflection and concepts of multiplicity

Thus far Husserl has explained how concrete groups arise, but he has not yet accounted for the abstract concept of multiplicity. Concrete groups are particulars. A group of men, a group of books, a group of colors are all individual concrete phenomena, arising from our mental acts of collecting. How do we get from these phenomena to the concept of multiplicity itself? The title of one of the sections in Chapter I indicates how this concept arises: "The origin of the concept of multiplicity through reflection on collective liaison." [2] Husserl says, "If our understanding is correct, then the concept of multiplicity arises through reflection on the peculiar manner in which contents are united." [3] The *concept* of multiplicity, and hence ultimately the concept of number, arises from reflection on the way in which members are related to the group as elements in a whole.

---

[1] "Indem nun der Name 'Eins' beim Zählen ausschliesslich in Gebrauch kam, trat ein gewisser Unterschied der Bedeutung zwischen Eins und 'ein Ding' und 'Etwas' dadurch hervor, dass Eins die Korrelation zur Vielheit als Mitbezeichnung erhielt." *ibid.*, p. 90. Concerning the function of the concept "something" in the formation of numbers, Husserl says, in his *Über den Begriff der Zahl* (Halle a. S.: Heynemann'-sche Buchdruckerei, 1887), pp. 62-3, that two different things comprise the concept of number: the concept of collective unity, and the concept "something."

[2] "Die Entstehung des Vielheitsbegriffes durch Reflexion auf die kollektive Verbindung." *Phil. Arith.*, p. 12.

[3] "Ist also unsere Auffassung richtig, dann ist der Begriff der Vielheit durch die Reflexion auf die besondere...Einigungsweise von Inhalten...entstanden." *ibid.*, p. 15.

How are we to find the way in which members are related in a group? "The collective liaison can be grasped only through reflection on the psychic acts through which the group comes about." [1] The concept of multiplicity belongs to that class of concepts whose "all-pervading characteristic finds its simple explanation in that they are concepts of attributes which arise in reflection on psychic acts." [2] We discover the relationship involved in groups by reflecting on the mental acts which form groups; the abstract concept of multiplicity, and hence that of number, arises from an act of reflection on our mental acts.

Husserl explains the concept "something" in parallel fashion: it arises as a result of "reflection on the psychic act of presentation." [3] This concept also comes, therefore, from reflection on a mental act.

It is important to keep steps four and five distinct. In step four, Husserl accounts for the origin of a concrete phenomenon; a particular group of objects arises from a psychic act of relating as from its source. In step five, he accounts for the origin of a concept, an abstraction, and does so by appealing to reflection on the mental act described in step four. Step four can be called constitutional explanation, but step five does not directly involve the use of constitution.

Husserl stresses that the concepts described in step five are purely formal and devoid of any material content. "We have every right to designate the concepts 'something' and 'one,' 'multiplicity' and 'number,' these most general and most empty, content-wise, of all concepts, as form-concepts or categories. What characterizes them as such is the condition that they are not concepts of contents of any determined species, but that they encompass, in a certain way, each and every content." [4] Such logical forms arise from our mental acts and can be applied

---

[1] "Es kann also die kollektive Verbindung auch nur erfasst werden durch Reflexion auf den psychischen Akt, durch welchen der Inbegriff zu Stande kommt." ibid., p. 79.

[2] "Ihr allumfassender Charakter findet seine einfache Erklärung darin, dass sie Begriffe von Attributen sind, welche in Reflexion auf psychische Akte entstehen...." ibid., p. 91.

[3] "Der Reflexion auf den psychischen Akt des Vorstellens." ibid., p. 86.

[4] "Man kann mit vollem Recht die Begriffe Etwas und Eins, Vielheit und Anzahl, diese allgemeinsten und inhaltleersten aller Begriffe, als Formbegriffe oder Kategorien bezeichnen. Was sie als solche charakterisiert, ist der Umstand, dass sie nicht Begriffe von Inhalten bestimmter Gattung sind, sondern in gewisser Art aller und jede Inhalte in sich befassen." ibid., p. 91.

to any material content whatsoever. As Husserl shows in his treatment of psychic relations, the structure of these logical categories is not something given in the material content of the things we experience, but arises purely from our mental activity. They are logical forms imposed on the material content of our experience.

Four examples of such formal concepts or categories are studied by Husserl: the concepts of "something," "one," "multiplicity," and "number." He says that other similar relation concepts exist, such as those of distinction and identity.[1] These too arise from reflection on mental acts. Husserl does not organize the categories in any hierarchy of importance or relative dependence, but the fact that the concept "something" was shown to be operative within the concepts of multiplicity shows that its scope is wider than that of the other categories. The others all presuppose the concept "something." In his later works, Husserl calls all possible categories derivative forms of the concept "something," and thus indicates that this category is logically prior to the rest.[2]

In all these cases, it is important to distinguish between the concrete occurrence of one of these logical forms and the abstract concept of the form. The concrete occurrence is, as Husserl says, a concrete phenomenon. It results from a mental act. The concept of the form is an abstraction, and it results from reflection on the mental act that gives rise to the concrete occurrence of the form.

3. Groups, and psychic relations in general, are phenomena that result from constitution

Husserl's analysis of the concept of number thus leads through the five steps we have distinguished, and the central point of his analysis is found in step four, where concrete groups are said to arise from mental acts. After he has presented the argument contained in this step, Husserl feels satisfied that he has reached the ultimate source of numbers, which was the original purpose of his investigation. He says, "Now that we have found the source out of which the collective liaison arises and have identi-

[1] Cf. *ibid.*, p. 91.
[2] Cf. *Form. trans. Log.*, p. 101.

fied it with certain psychic acts, there is hardly any further obscurity that can remain concerning our concept."[1]

The argument presented in step four is the point at which Husserl uses constitutional explanation. He explains the origin of groups by means of the mental acts which "constitute" them.

How can we characterize a group? Consider, for example, a group of books. The group has a certain objectivity. Husserl speaks of it as a concrete phenomenon, as something given to our consciousness. This group of books can be considered as a single whole, as a single entity of a sort. We can make reference to it, and in a sense we can perceive the group. The group relationship, the collective liaison, is a "concretum"[2] which has a special reality and objectivity that is added to the objectivity and reality of the individual members of the group. "It is a misunderstanding to say that groups consist only of their individual contents.... However easily one might overlook it, there is nonetheless something over and above the individual contents there, something that can be noticed and that is necessarily present in all cases where we speak of a group or multitude: the liaison of the individual elements to the whole."[3]

However, the objectivity of groups is different from that of ordinary things and individuals that we encounter in the world, because it arises entirely from subjective mental activity. A group does not exist *qua* group until it is formed by a mental act of collecting; its existence depends on a subjective process. There is a certain paradox in groups, the paradox of something objective which exists only by virtue of subjective mental activity.[4]

Husserl does not treat explicitly the status of groups, and in general of all psychic relationships, in the *Philosophy of A-*

---

[1] "Nachdem wir uns die Quelle, aus welcher die kollektive Verbindung entspringt, aufgefunden und sie mit gewissen psychischen Akten identifiziert haben, kann in Betreff unseres Begriffes kaum noch eine Unklarheit bestehen." *Phil. Arith*, p. 83.

[2] Cf. *ibid.*, p. 10.

[3] "Es ist misverständlich zu sagen, die Inbegriffe beständen bloss aus den Einzelinhalten. Wie leicht man es auch übersieht, so ist doch über die Einzelinhalte hinaus etwas da, was bemerkt werden kann und was in allen Fällen, wo wir von einem Inbegriff oder einer Vielheit sprechen, notwendig vorhanden ist: die Verbindung der einzelnen Elemente zu dem Ganzen." *ibid.*, p. 13.

[4] Cf. Walter Biemel, "Die entscheidende Phasen," p. 195: "Dass es Gebilde gibt, die im Denken erzeugt werden müssen, um zu existieren, die also nur existieren, insofern sie erzeugt werden, d.h. insofern bestimmte Denkprozesse in Gang gesetzt werden, das ist eigentlich in nuce der Konstitutionsgedanke, der Husserl am Versuch des Fassens des Wesens der Zahl aufgegangen ist."

rithmetic. He speaks both of their objective and subjective aspects, but does not clearly focus his attention on the paradox of such realities. It was this failure to treat in detail the problem of the status of such relationships that led Frege to complain that Husserl was inconsistent on this point, that he sometimes treated groups as "presentations" (*Vorstellungen*), sometimes as objective realities.[1] The double treatment is not due to inconsistency on Husserl's part, but to the nature of groups and of all psychic relationships. They have a certain objectivity, and yet exist only by virtue of subjective acts. The same paradox arises later in Husserl's treatment of categorical objects in the *Logical Investigations*, but there he discusses the problem more explicitly.

Not only the existence of such relationships, but also their structure depends on the act that gives rise to them. There is a correlation between their structures, as Husserl states in the course of some critical remarks concerning Wundt's number theory.[2] In discussing the concept "one," Husserl says that it cannot arise without the presence of a certain act that is proportioned to the content of this concept; a correlation exists between the act and the concept it establishes.[3] A study of the structure of the act would give us information about the structure of the concept, and vice versa. Such a correlation exists in the case of all psychic relationships, since they find their origins exclusively in mental acts. The type of act that forms them will result in a corresponding type of relationship: an act of collecting results in the group relationship, and an act of identifying two terms results in the relationship of identity.

There is a close similarity between the explanation Husserl

[1] Cf Frege's review of the *Philosophy of Arithmetic* in *Zeitschrift für Philosophie und philosophische Kritik*, 103 (1894), p. 27: "Dadurch nun, dass man Subjektives und Objektives unter dem Worte 'Vorstellungen' zusammenfasst, verwischt man die Grenze zwischen beiden so, dass bald eine Vorstellung im eigentlichen Sinne des Wortes wie etwas Objektives, bald etwas Objektives wie eine Vorstellung behandelt wird. So erscheint beim Verfasser der Inbegriff (die Menge, Vielheit) bald als Vorstellung (15, 17, 24, 82), bald als Objektives (10 und 11, 235)."

[2] Husserl's exposition becomes confusing here because he fails to keep distinct the concrete phenomenon of a psychic relationship and the abstract concept arising from reflection on the mental act that forms concrete phenomena. In other words, he mixes steps four and five of our analysis. However, the concept can be considered to arise indirectly from the mental act in question, so Husserl's lapse of expression does not involve any serious difficulty.

[3] Cf. *Phil. Arith.*, p. 94: "Der abstrakte Einheitsbegriff kann nicht entstehen, ohne einen ihn tragenden – nämlich einen gewissen zu seinem Inhalte gehörigen – Denkakt."

gives for the concrete phenomena described in the *Philosophy of Arithmetic* and the explanation given for the origin of categorical objects in the *Logical Investigations*. In both cases, we have a reality which is somehow objective, but which owes both its existence and its structure to subjective mental processes. Since the process that results in categorical objects is called constitution in the *Investigations*, it seems the same name could be given to the "mental activity" [1] described as the source of psychic relationships in the *Philosophy of Arithmetic*. In the latter, Husserl already calls the concepts of such relationships "categories," [2] and in his own reference to this work in *Formal and Transcendental Logic* he adds the phrase, "categorical objects as formed objects," to describe the concepts treated here.[3]

4. Objections to our interpretation

In opposition to this interpretation, it can be objected that the psychologism prevalent in Husserl's first work excludes the possibility of any constitutional explanation. Categorical constitution, as presented in Husserl's subsequent works, supposes the production of logical categories or forms, and distinguishes them sharply from psychological phenomena. The study of categorical objects is a science of ideal objects, whereas the study of psychological processes is a science of empirical facts. The objection would claim that Husserl's psychologism in the *Philosophy of Arithmetic* neglects this distinction, and reduces the logical to the psychological. It would claim that Husserl treats logical categories as ordinary psychological facts to be determined and explained by empirical inquiry.

In other terms, the objection would claim that Husserl's psychologism destroys the "objectivity" of logical categories by reducing them to merely subjective psychological phenomena. The objectivity of logical categories does not mean, of course, that such categories are really subsistent entities along with houses, men, and animals, but as Husserl uses it, it does imply

---

[1] Cf. *ibid.*, p. 44. The expression "geistiges Tun" is found in a citation from a work by Baumann, but Husserl quotes it with approval.

[2] Cf. *ibid.*, p. 91.

[3] "Kategoriale Gegenstände als Gebilde." *Form. trans. Log.*, p. 73, n. 3. Other passages where Husserl expresses a similar judgment of his earlier work are found on pages 68, 76-77, 87, 96.

THE ORIGINS OF NUMBERS

at least that we can identify a given logical (or mathematical) form or entity as identically the same individual in a series of different occurrences. It means, for example, that we can say that the same number "six" or the same syllogistic form "Barbara" can appear at different places and times. If Husserl reduces logical forms to psychological processes, then this objectivity is lost, because each psychological event is numerically different from every other one, and we can no longer speak of the same number or category recurring in different empirical situations.

It is true that if Husserl reduces the logical to the psychological, and thus destroys the objectivity of logical forms, there can be no constitution in the *Philosophy of Arithmetic*. If logical entities are dissolved into a stream of psychological events, there is nothing left to be constituted.[1] The concept of constitution, in the form in which it is developed in Husserl's first work, does suppose that a subjective process produces a form or category which is no longer subjective, but in some way transcends the subjectivity which produces it.[2]

Furthermore, Husserl's own opinion, expressed in the introduction to his *Prolegomena,* seems to confirm this objection. He says that while he was writing the first volume of his book on arithmetic, he was convinced that psychology could yield the philosophical explanation of logic and the deductive sciences in general. To a certain degree, the psychological studies of the *Philosophy of Arithmetic* bore fruit: "Where it concerned the quest for the origin of mathematical presentations, or the factual, psychologically determined formation of practical methods, the achievement of psychological analysis seemed to me clear and instructive." [3] But this success is in response to a psychological problem, namely the factual origin of mathematical concepts and methods. In the question of the objectivity of mathematical

---

[1] Cf. Suzanne Bachelard, *La logique de Husserl*, p. 286: "Paradoxalement, c'est quand on ne voit pas que les formations logiques se détachent de la subjectivité avec le sens d'objects qu'on n'arrive pas à poser à leur égard les vrais problèmes subjectifs, les problèmes de leur 'constitution' par une subjectivité transcendentale".

[2] This objection has been presented by Ingarden. See the reference above, p. 6, note 3.

[3] "Wo es sich um die Frage nach dem Ursprung der mathematischen Vorstellungen oder um die in der Tat psychologisch bestimmte Ausgestaltung der praktischen Methoden handelt, schien mir die Leistung der psychologischen Analyse klar und lehrreich." *Logische Untersuchungen. Erster Teil: Prolegomena zur reinen Logik* (Halle a. S.: Max Niemeyer, 1900), p. vii. Second edition, 1928, p. vii.

concepts, and the correct explanation of logical categories as
opposed to psychological facts, the analyses of the *Philosophy
of Arithmetic* were not so successful. "However, as soon as a
transfer from the psychological associations of thinking to the
logical unity of the content of thought . . . was effected, no real
continuity and clarity could be produced." [1] Husserl goes on to
say that he began to doubt the very possibility of "how the
objectivity of mathematics, and of all science in general, could
be reconciled with a psychological founding of the logical."[2]
These statements seem to indicate that Husserl did feel that the
Philosophy of Arithmetic destroys the specificity of logical categories by attempting to explain them in terms of psychological
processes.

We shall see that in his analyses of the symbolical use of
numbers, Husserl does employ some psychological methods; but
the question to be decided now is whether his analysis of the
origin of authentically (i.e. non-symbolically) given numbers
suffers from the same defect. Is the five step analysis we have
outlined guilty of reducing logical and mathematical entities to
psychological phenomena?

The main consideration which saves Husserl's analyses from
the objection of psychologism is that the collective relationship,
and psychic relationships in general, presuppose that the individuals related be thought of simply as "something" (*etwas*).
These relationships are applicable to anything that can be the
object of thought. In other words, Husserl describes here categories of thought in general. He does not deal with empirically
occurring mental processes, resulting from particular subjective
dispositions, but with the conditions of possibility of thinking
as such. In speaking about such categories, he says, "What
characterizes them as such is the condition that they are not
concepts of contents of any determined species, but that they
encompass, in a certain way, each and every content."[3] No

1 "Sowie aber ein Übergang von den psychologischen Zusammenhängen des Denkens zur logischen Einheit des Denkinhaltes . . . vollzogen wurde, wollte sich keine
rechte Kontinuität und Klarheit herausstellen lassen." *ibid.*, p. vii.
2 "wie sich die Objektivität der Mathematik und aller Wissenschaft überhaupt
mit einer psychologischen Begründung des Logischen vertrage." *ibid.*, p. vii.
3 "Was sie als solche charakterisiert, ist der Umstand, dass sie nicht Begriffe von
Inhalten bestimmter Gattung sind, sondern in gewisser Art alle und jede Inhalt in
sich befassen." *Phil. Arith.*, p. 91.

matter what objects we think about, the categories arising from psychic relationships are applicable to them; whatever can be thought is subject to these categories.

In view of this, we can say Husserl is concerned with the explanation of specifically logical categories, and not just with psychological facts. It is true that he does not sufficiently distinguish the two spheres in the *Philosophy of Arithmetic*, and by his own admission did not himself clearly see the distinction between them when he composed this work. Nevertheless, the nature of logical categories forced him to treat them as universal categories of thought, different from empirical psychological phenomena.

If Husserl does grant the distinction between the logical and psychological realms, can the objection be raised that his explanation of logical categories by means of mental acts destroys the logical nature of such categories? He says that they arise from psychic acts, and calls his description of such acts "a chapter of descriptive psychology."[1] In his treatment of mental acts he appeals to inner experience to justify his findings. Does this turn logical categories into mere elements in a psychological process? In Husserl's later terminology, does it reduce the transcendental subjectivity and its performances to empirical subjectivity?

The fact alone that Husserl says logical categories are produced by mental acts does not necessarily mean he psychologizes them. Even in his later works, he holds that the acts of transcendental subjectivity have a psychological side, which can be investigated by empirical science.[2] What is specific to the transcendental realm is that it is restricted to ideal, logical realities, whereas the psychological is concerned with empirical facts. Husserl maintains such a distinction, roughly at least, in the *Philosophy of Arithmetic*. Psychic acts of relating can be considered as empirical facts, but in their capacity as sources for the universal categories of thought, they have a value which transcends the merely factual.

We can say, therefore, that the explanation given by Husserl

---

[1] "Ein Kapitel der beschreibenden Psychologie." *ibid.*, p. 70.

[2] For example, cf. *Die Krisis der europäischen Wissenschaften und die transzendentale Phänomenologie* (The Hague: Martinus Nijhoff, 1954), pp. 207-214.

for the origin of authentically given number concepts, and the explanation given for all the categories treated in the first part of *Philosophy of Arithmetic*, is a constitutional explanation. It accounts for the origin of logical and mathematical categories by means of subjective mental acts. In comparison with his later works, however, Husserl's presentation is not clear. He does not explicitly distinguish between the study of empirical psychological facts and the explanation of logical categories of thought. His terminology is especially misleading, for he uses such terms as "psychic acts," "inner experience," and "concrete phenomena," all of which have a distinct psychological connotation, to express factors which belong in the logical, constitutional sphere. Indeed, it seems that he did not clearly perceive the distinction between the logical and psychological during the writing of the *Philosophy of Arithmetic*, but the nature of the categories he was trying to explain forced him to treat them differently from ordinary psychological facts.

How does this conclusion account for Husserl's own criticism of the *Philosophy of Arithmetic* in his introduction to the *Prolegomena*, where he criticizes the psychologism of his first book? As we shall see, other parts of the *Arithmetic* use psychological explanations in a more pronounced way than the section we have studied, and Husserl's remarks could be interpreted as referring chiefly to these other sections. Even in regard to the first section, Husserl could have objected to his failure to isolate explicitly the logical from the psychological. One glaring confusion along these lines arises in what we have distinguished as step five in the analysis of number concepts. Here, Husserl says we acquire a number concept (a logical entity) from reflection on our intentional acts (psychological events). This is an instance of psychologism: the logical, noematic form is confused with the psychological, noetic act that gives rise to it. The logical and the psychological are not properly distinguished. However, this is only a minor point in Husserl's explanation of number, and was easily corrected, as we shall see, in the *Logical Investigations*. In all other respects, the pattern of thought we have described in the *Philosophy of Arithmetic* is so similar to that found in the *Investigations* that it cannot be said that Husserl rejects the method of his first work. The difference is that in the *Investigations* he is more conscious of his method. He is clearly aware that he is handling mental acts not as psychological, empirical facts, but as sources for logical entities.

Husserl's explanation of categories by subjective acts, even in the rough form of the *Philosophy of Arithmetic*, already raises a problem concerning the very principle of such explanation. Is such an inquiry possible, and does the type of explanation it offers really explain anything? This is the question of the validity of constitution as a means of explanation, and can be studied only after we have seen more about Husserl's concept of constitution.

5. Reflection and constitution

There is an important difference between the *Philosophy of Arithmetic* and the *Logical Investigations* in regard to categorical objects. In the *Investigations*, Husserl no longer maintains the need for what we have distinguished as step five in the genesis of a logical or mathematical category. He no longer says that we must reflect on our mental acts in order to form a category. Instead he claims that a categorical form is given immediately in the exercise of a categorical act. "A group, for example, is given, and can only be given, in an actual act of gathering together.... But the concept of group does not grow out of reflection on this act. Rather than turn our attention to the act which gives the group to us, we must turn to that which the act gives: to the group which it brings into appearance *in concreto*."[1] This statement claims the opposite of what is held in the *Philosophy of Arithmetic*. In the *Investigations*, Husserl says that a logical form (in this case, the group relationship) is immediately given in an intentional act, and that we can conceptualize this form by focusing our attention on the concrete form which is produced. There is no need to reflect on the producing act.

The explanation given in the *Investigations* is more satisfying

[1] "Ein Inbegriff z.B. ist gegeben und kann nur gegeben sein in einem aktuellen Zusammenbegreifen... Aber der Begriff des Inbegriffes erwächst nicht durch Reflexion auf diesen Akt; statt auf den gebenden Akt haben wir vielmehr auf das, was er gibt, auf den Inbegriff, den er *in concreto* zu Erscheinung bringt, zu achten...." *Logische Untersuchungen, Zweiter Teil: Untersuchungen zur Phänomenologie und Theorie der Erkenntnis* (Halle a. S.: Max Niemeyer, 1901), pp. 613-14. Second edition, 1921, II, 2, pp. 141-42.

than that of Husserl's first book. In the *Arithmetic*, strictly
speaking, we cannot say that logical and mathematical categories are directly constituted by mental acts. Husserl applies
the term "category" to the concepts that arise from reflection
on mental acts, and not to the relationship that is present in
the concrete phenomena of groups produced by acts. Nevertheless, the difficulty is mainly one of terminology and is not a
serious inconsistency of thought, for even in his first work Husserl does say that some sort of logical form, produced by mental
acts, is present in what he calls the concrete phenomenon:
"Nevertheless, there is a special unification there...." [1] The
"special unification" can be considered as the logical form constituted by a mental act. In the *Logical Investigations*, it is more
properly called a category.

6. Temporality and the origin of number

Husserl devotes a chapter of the *Philosophy of Arithmetic* to
the critical discussion of several other theories of the origin of
numbers.[2] These theories try to explain numbers by reducing
them either to the phenomenon of co-presence in our consciousness, to temporal relations between units, to the relation of
succession between units, to spatial relationships, or to the relationships that arise when we simply distinguish units from one
another. The result of his study of these theories is chiefly negative; he concludes that none of them explain the origin of
numbers correctly.

However, Husserl does find some valuable points in these
theories. He notes that the first of them implies that a special
act of consciousness is required for the origin of numbers; this
implication hints at something similar to his own theory.[3] Another positive result which he stresses is that "we learned thereby
to acknowledge time as a psychological pre-condition for
number."[4] Time is a necessary condition for numbers, and in
two ways: "(1) It is indispensable that the partial presentations
united in the presentation of multiplicity or number be found

[1] "Aber wie auch immer, es ist eine besondere Einigung da..." *Phil. Arith.*, p. 15.
[2] Cf. *ibid.*, pp. 17-67.
[3] Cf. *ibid.*, p. 68.
[4] "Wir lernten hierbei die Zeit als psychologische Vorbedingung der Zahl kennen."
ibid., p. 68.

THE ORIGINS OF NUMBERS 25

simultaneously in our consciousness."[1] The members united in
a group or number must be present at the same time in our
consciousness. "(2) Almost all presentations of multiplicity and,
at any rate, all presentations of number are results of processes.
They are wholes which arise successively out of elements." [2]
Numbers arise as a result of processes which necessarily involve
temporal extension. Husserl goes on to insist that although
cotemporality and succession are necessary conditions for
numbers, they do not themselves enter into the content of
numbers and multitudes. As he says earlier, they do not affect
the meaning of these concepts.

Husserl's observations concerning time are not developed any
further in the *Philosophy of Arithmetic*, but it is interesting to
note that his conclusions already foreshadow, in a vague and
general fashion, the emphasis he places on time as the basis for
constitution in his later works. Both points he lists here are
central to his lectures on time; the problem of co-presence of
several elements at the same present instant of our consciousness anticipates the problem of the "now-instant," and, more
important for the study of constitution, his statements about
the temporal extension of mental processes and phenomena
foreshadow his later doctrine on the flow of time as the source
of all our acts and sensory data. In this lectures on time, the
subjective time stream becomes the locus for the most fundamental type of constitution in our intentionality. The role of
temporality in formation of numbers is only brushed in the
Philosophy of Arithmetic, but the problem does make itself felt.

7. The problem of the origin of symbolically given numbers

In the first part of the *Philosophy of Arithmetic*, with which we
have been concerned until now, Husserl has attempted to show
the origin of numbers as they are given to us in direct consciousness. He has dealt with "the authentic concepts of multiplicity,
unity, and number,"[3] and the way in which they are formed.

1 "(1) Es ist unerlässlich, dass die in der Vorstellung der Vielheit bzw. Anzahl
geeinigten Teilvorstellungen zugleich in unserem Bewusstsein vorhanden sind."
ibid., p. 29.
2 "(2) Fast alle Vielheitsvorstellungen und jedenfalls alle Zahlvorstellungen sind
Resultate von Prozessen, sind aus den Elementen sukzessive entstandene Ganze."
ibid., p. 29.
3 "Die eigentliche Begriffe von Vielheit, Einheit und Anzahl." *ibid.*, p. 1.

However, the same concepts can also be used symbolically, and
in arithmetic, the foundations of which this book is supposed to
clarify, numbers are handled only in a symbolic way. "Arithmetic
does not operate with 'authentic' number concepts."[1] Husserl
understands arithmetic as a science of calculating with symbols
that represent numbers, not as a science dealing with numbers
themselves.[2]

When we add 2135 to 759 and reach the sum 2894, we do not
operate with the concepts of these numbers. It is hardly possible
for us to have an authentic concept of the number 2135. Such a
concept would require, according to Husserl's analysis, the actual
grouping of 2135 elements and the formation of an abstract
concept of a multitude composed of so many units. In addition,
it would require that we clearly distinguish this concept from
others formed in a similarly laborious way, for example the
concepts of 2134 and 2136. Our powers of discernment, as well
as our patience, make such a process impossible, especially
when it would be necessary to repeat it for every single number,
for every form of multiplicity we should ever wish to name.
The process Husserl proposes for the formation of authentic
number concepts can operate only for the first few numbers. We
can perform the collection, form the proper abstraction, and
distinguish between the concepts of two and three, or three and
four. But unless we are to remain on this rudimentary level and
scarcely go beyond groups of ten or twelve, we must find another
way of treating numbers. Husserl's reply to this difficulty is,
"To this we must answer: if we do not have the concepts given
to us in an authentic way, then we have them given in a symbolic manner."[3]

What does Husserl understand by a number concept's being
given in a symbolic way? "A symbolic or inauthentic presentation is, as the name itself states, a presentation through

---

[1] "Die Arithmetik operiert nicht mit den 'eigentlichen' Zahlbegriffen." *ibid.*, p. 211.
[2] Cf. Husserl's own review of this work (supra, p. 7 note 2), pp. 360-61: "Der
zweite Teil betrachtet die symbolischen Vorstellungen von Vielheit und Anzahl, und
versucht in der Tatsache, dass wir fast durchgehends auf symbolische Anzahlvor-
stellungen eingeschränkt sind, den logischen Ursprung einer allgemeinen Arithmetik
nachzuweisen."
[3] "Darauf ist zu antworten: Wenn wir die Begriffe auch nicht in eigentlicher, so
haben wir sie doch in symbolischer Weise gegeben." *Phil. Arith.*, p. 214.

signs."[1] Instead of operating with the authentic concept, we operate with a sign. The problem now is, "radically to study the origin and meaning of symbolical presentations in the sphere of numbers."[2] This will lead to the ultimate aim of the book, "to make comprehensible, psychologically and logically, the origin of the art of reckoning which rests on these concepts." [3]

In his analysis of authentic number concepts, Husserl found it necessary to study first the concept of multitude, and he proceeds in a similar way in his treatment of symbolic representations of numbers. The investigation of the symbolic representation of multitudes must come first.[4]

8. Origin of the symbolical presentation of groups

A multitude is given to us authentically when we are faced with a concrete group and perform the act of collective liaison, but do not bother to discern exactly how many members there are in the group. The concept arising from reflection on this process is the authentic concept of multitude. When can we say that a multitude is only symbolically given? Suppose we look across a field of grass. We can say that there is a multitude of blades of grass in the field. How is the "multitude" that is present there given to us? "Are we, in one cursory glance, really supposed to perform this complicated psychic activity and then in addition make a special reflection on it?"[5] We have obviously not gone through the process of relating each blade of grass to form the group. The concrete group, and hence the concept associated with it, is not authentically given to us. "Certainly the successive individual conception of the members in the multitude is still possible, but not the collection that links them together; and since, in such cases, we still speak of a mass or multitude, this can obviously only happen in a sym-

---

[1] "Eine symbolische oder uneigentliche Vorstellung ist, wie schon der Name besagt, eine Vorstellung durch Zeichen." *ibid.*, p. 215.

[2] "die Entstehung und Bedeutung der symbolischen Vorstellungen auf dem Gebiete der Zahl gründlich zu studieren." *ibid.*, p. 217.

[3] "die Entstehung einer auf diesen Begriffen ruhenden Rechenkunst psychologisch und logisch begreiflich zu machen." *ibid.*, p. 201.

[4] Cf. *ibid.*, p. 250: "Die symbolische Mengenvorstellungen bilden das Fundament für die symbolische Zahlvorstellungen."

[5] "Sollten wir etwa in dem einen Überblick wirklich die komplizierte psychische Betätigung ausüben und zumal noch auf sie besonders reflektieren?" *ibid.*, p. 219.

bolical sense." [1] In such a case, the group is only symbolically presented to us. "But the question now is, where does the basis and support for symbolization lie?"[2]

The answer Husserl accepts states that a few steps in the process of collection symbolize the entire, complete process; however, these steps are tied together with certain sensory characteristics which we perceive in the group presented to us. "There must lie, in the intuition of sensory multitudes, certain immediately accessible signs by which the characteristic of multitude can be recognized, and in which an intuition can indirectly guarantee the completability of the process described above."[3] The sensory characteristics are to guarantee that the few steps of collecting can stand for the complete process. They are the factor that makes the few steps of liaison capable of acting as symbols, as signs for the full process.

The sensory characteristics in question are not qualities of the individual members of the group. They are characteristics that arise when the members are assembled. Husserl calls them "quasi-qualities"[4] or "second order sensory qualities." [5] What they would amount to, in a given group, is a pattern or gestalt which arises in connection with the particular type of members involved in the group. This is a sensory characteristic, and enables us to speak of a swarm of bees, a fleet of ships, a row of trees, a column of soldiers, etc. The number of examples could be continued indefinitely. In each case, says Husserl, we have a specific type of pattern formed, a sensory characteristic which is specific to the type of things grouped.

When such a pattern is perceived and a few steps of collective liaison are carried out on some of the members presented with the pattern, the acts of liaison can serve as a symbol for the

---

[1] "Wohl ist noch die sukzessive Einzelauffassung der Mengenglieder möglich, aber nicht mehr ihre zusammenfassende Kollektion, und insofern wir in derartigen Fällen noch von einer Menge oder Vielheit sprechen, kann dies offenbar nur in symbolischen Sinne geschehen." *ibid.*, p. 218.

[2] "Aber wo liegt, das ist nun die Frage, der Grund und Anhalt der Symbolisierung?" *ibid.*, p. 220.

[3] "Es müssen in der Anschauung der sinnlichen Menge umittelbar zu erfassende Anzeichen liegen, an welchen der Mengencharakter erkannt werden kann, in den sie die Vollziehbarkeit der oben beschriebenen Prozesse indirekt gewährleistet." *ibid.*, p. 225.

[4] *ibid.*, p. 227.

[5] "Sinnliche Qualitäten zweiter Ordnung," *ibid.*, p. 225.

full process of collecting the entire group. "The rudimentary
process then serves ... as a sign for the full, intended process
...." [1] Thus the symbol is the few collective liaison steps which
are actually carried out. They are established as a symbol by
the presence of the pattern which accompanies them.

The way in which the sensory pattern functions here requires
some more explanation. Its role is to serves as a "support for
association" [2] between the symbol and the thing signified. It
acts as an intermediary between the two. Two aspects can be
distinguished in the function performed by the sensory pattern:
first, there arises an association between the pattern and authentically formed groups.[3] Secondly, when the pattern is given
to us in connection with a few acts of collective liaison, we are
assured that a group is really present and that we could, theoretically, continue our liaison activity until it were authentically
given. But there is no need for this, and the few steps we have
performed can serve, with the assurance given us by the sensory
pattern, as a symbol for the full process. The nerve of this
argument lies in the association that is formed, as a result of
experience, between the pattern and the authentically given
group, or the concept abstracted from it.

Husserl observes that sometimes, in symbolical presentation
of a group, no steps of collective liaison are made at all, and the
pattern alone serves as the sign for the group. "In the course of
swift thinking, often the external intuition alone, without any
rudimentary process and simply because of its figural character,
can become the symbolical representative of authentic presentations of multitudes." [4] Husserl does not explain this any
further, and we can suppose that his argument rests, once again,
on the principle of association.

1 "Das Prozessrudiment dient dann ... als Zeichen für den intendierten vollen
Prozess..." *ibid.*, p. 239.
2 "Anhalt für die Assoziation." *ibid.*, p. 225.
3 Cf. *ibid.*, p. 227: "Indem wir... die durchlaufende Einzelauffassung bei den
verschiedenartigsten sinnlichen Mengen übten, mussten sich notwendig diese Kenn-
zeichnen... mit dem Begriff solcher Prozesse und in weiter Folge mit dem Mengen-
begriffe assozieren und so jeweilig die Brücken herstellen für die unmittelbare Aner-
kenntnis einer zunächst einheitlichen sinnlichen Anschauung der hier betrachteten
Art, als eine Menge."
4 "...Im Verlaufe des rascheren Denkens, [kann] häufig auch die äussere Anschauung ohne irgend welche rudimentäre Prozesse, bloss vermöge ihres figuralen
Charakters zum symbolischen Vertreter der eigentlichen Mengenvorstellung werden..." *ibid.*, p. 240.

In closing, Husserl makes the following remarks: "The change that presentations of multitudes undergo throughout all the symbolization we have described do not affect their logical content."[1] The logical nature of groups and the concept of multiplicity is not changed when symbols instead of real groups are involved. The only difference is the way in which the group is presented to us, and the way in which we operate with it.

In explaining the psychological origin of symbolical presentations of groups and concepts of multitudes, Husserl's argument is different from that used in explaining authentically given groups. It is much more psychological, in the sense he was to repudiate in the *Prolegomena*. He bases his arguments on such factors as the weakness of memory, the inability of our imagination to handle immensely large groups, and our own incapacity to go through the entire process of collecting large groups. He appeals to associations which arise as a result of our previous experience. Even his use of sensory patterns as an intermediary for symbols of groups is an investigation of what empirically is the case, but not of what must be the case for a thinking being. These are all arguments which the *Prolegomena* would reject as not directly relevant to the sphere of phenomenology.

9. The explanation of group and multiplicity symbolism is not a constitutional explanation

Nevertheless, such arguments do try to explain how symbols arise for groups and concepts of multiplicity; do they explain the "constitution" of such symbols? They do not, because Husserl does not get to the root of their explanation. He fails to give a constitutional analysis of signs in general. He lacks a foundation for the specific type of symbolism used for groups; if he does not explain symbols as such, he cannot explain a specific type of symbol.

The use Husserl makes of association, which plays such an extensive part in his analysis of symbols, does not serve to explain or resolve the problem we are faced with now. Association expresses the fact that a sign is related to a thing, but it does not explain how this relation comes about.

---

[1] "...Die Veränderungen, welche die Vielheitsvorstellung durch all die beschriebenen Symbolisierungen erfährt, [betreffen] nicht ihren logischen Gehalt..." *ibid.*, p. 245.

Husserl was well aware of the need for explanation of such a central point. In his introduction to the *Philosophy of Arithmetic*, he says, "Entirely outside the frame of a philosophy of arithmetic appear the studies towards a general logic of symbolic method, to be discussed in the appendix to volume two...."[1] These studies never appeared, but we can discover how Husserl conceived the problem of symbols by his remarks in an article published in 1894, only three years after publication of the *Philosophy of Arithmetic*.[2] He gives the following example. Suppose we perceive a set of marks on paper, which we consider at first to be simply lines, with a certain form and elegance. Suddenly there dawns on us the thought that they might be signs, symbols in a language we do not know. What happens to make the change? "In that moment when the arabesque becomes a sign, and thus acquires the character of a representing content, the psychic situation has completely changed."[3] Something happens in our subjectivity to change the marks into signs. Husserl continues, "The considerations we have before us, no matter how much they may need completion, have surely aroused or strengthened the conviction that in intuition and representation we deal with two characteristically different states of consciousness. But solution of the question, what sort of states of consciousness they are, is still open."[4]

Thus there is a problem of constitution for symbols and it is essential as a basis for group symbolism. It must be explained by something that occurs in subjectivity, just as groups are explained by subjective acts, but Husserl is quite ready to admit that he does not yet have the solution; what kind of state of consciousness brings about symbolism is still an open question. In the *Logical Investigations*, where Husserl will have

[1] "Ganz aus dem Rahmen einer Philosophie der Arithmetik treten aber nun die im Anhange des II Bandes mitzuteilenden Untersuchungen zur allgemeinen Logik der symbolischen Methoden...." *ibid.*, p. vi.
[2] "Psychologische Studien zur elementaren Logik," *Philosophische Monatshefte*, 30 (1894), pp. 159-191.
[3] "In dem Augenblick, wo die Arabeske zum Zeichen wird, also den Charakter eines repräsentierenden Inhalt gewinnt, hat sich die psychische Lage total geändert." *ibid.*, pp. 183-84.
[4] "Die vorstehende Betrachtungen, so sehr sie der Vervollständigung bedürften, haben wohl die Überzeugung erweckt oder bekräftigt, dass wir es bei Anschauung und Repräsentation mit charakteristische verschiedener Bewusstseinszustände zu tun haben: aber die Lösung der Frage, was für Bewusstseinszustände es sind, steht noch aus." *ibid.*, p. 185.

a systematic theory of intentionality at his service, the question will receive its answer.[1]

The explanation which Husserl gives for group symbolism cannot be considered a constitutional analysis because it lacks its necessary foundation, the constitution of symbols in general. He would have to explain first what subjective performance constitutes signs as such, and then show what modifications or additions are operative in constitution of those particular symbols which stand for groups and concepts of multiplicity. Since he fails to do this, he cannot say whether or not the processes he describes are logically necessary activities in the production of such symbols.

10. Constitution and the source of symbolic systems of numbers

Husserl then goes on to describe how our number system, which is based on repeating cycles of ten units each, arises.[2] He stresses that the production of number symbols is not merely a question of nomenclature, of devising signs for concepts which we already have. "It is not as though the sequence of natural numbers were given to us first, and that we were to look afterwards for appropriate signs for their conceptual forms." [3] We are given only a few numbers in an authentic way. All the rest are given to us only through symbols, so that the formation of symbols is also a production of the numerical concepts they are associated with. "And so the number system we have acquired ...is not simply a method to sign concepts which are already given, but rather a method of constructing concepts, and of

---

[1] Illeman notes that Husserl neglects to explain the origins of symbolism, which should be treated as the central problem in a discussion of symbolically given numbers. Cf. *Husserls vor-phänomenologische Philosophie*, p. 24: "Wir vermissen aber nicht nur eine befriedigende Auskunft über den Zusammenhang von 'symbolischer Vielheits-' und 'Zahlvorstellung,' sondern auch eine befriedigende Klärung des Symbolbegriffes selber." The fact that Husserl has to go beyond mathematics to find a foundation for it is brought out by Bachelard, *La logique de Husserl*, p. 3: "Mais une critique de la science, si délimitée soit-elle, quand elle se veut radicale, doit vite briser les cadres où elle s'inscrivait primitivement. C'est bien l'infortune de tous ceux qui se livrent à une activité de fondation radicale qu'elle ne peut être localisée."

[2] We summarize Husserl's theory of number symbols in Appendix I.

[3] "Die Sache liegt doch nicht so, dass uns zuerst die natürliche Zahlenreihe gegeben wäre, und wir hinterher für ihre Begriffsbildung nach einer passenden Signatur suchten." *Phil. Arith.*, p. 264.

signing them as we construct them." [1] The formation of symbols becomes the formation of concepts as well. Symbols are not as extrinsic to concepts, in this case at least, as it might appear at first.

The question arises whether or not we can speak of constitution here. Can this be considered an explanation of the way in which numbers are constituted? The answer is negative again; Husserl's explanation is not directly a treatment of the constitution of number concepts. The explanation of a system of symbols does not, in itself, explain the sense of these symbols, nor does it explain the sense of the concepts they stand for, no matter how closely the concepts and their formation are tied to the symbolism. It is only when we explain authentically given numbers that the sense of numbers in general is reached. As Husserl remarks, "Every answer means pushing the question back another step, and only when we come into the field of authentic number concepts can we stand satisfied." [2] In itself, the system of symbols is neutral as regards interpretation, and only when related to authentic numbers does it acquire significance. Hence the explanation of the logical nature and source of numbers is incomplete if it neglects authentic numbers. The basic problem of constitution lies therefore with the problem of the origins of authentically given numbers.

Even if Husserl's treatment of symbols is tied in with authentic numbers, his exposition, as given in the *Philosophy of Arithmetic*, still does not give us a constitutional explanation, because he does not provide an explanation of symbols in general. This is the same weakness that arises in connection with symbols and groups. Husserl's exposition lacks the foundation it needs to be a study in constitution.

11. Sensory factors and the constitution of logical entities

In discussing the type of symbols to be used in arithmetic, Husserl says that their sensory characteristics are relevant to

---

[1] "Und so ist denn die gewonnene Zahlsystematik ... nicht eine blosse Methode, gegebene Begriffe zu signieren, als vielmehr Begriffe zu konstruieren und mit der Konstruktion zugleich zu bezeichnen." *ibid.*, p. 264.

[2] "Jede Antwort bedeutet eine Zurückschiebung der Frage um einen neuen Schritt, und erst wenn wir in das Gebiet der eigentlichen Zahlbegriffe gekommen sind, können wir befriedigt stehen bleiben." *ibid.*, p. 258.

the formation of the concepts they represent. Such sensory characteristics as whether the symbols are sounds or written signs, the appearance they have, and so forth, are called by Husserl "logical" factors. Even apparently unimportant sensory aspects deserve this name. "Indeed, later we will find occasion to show how even such apparently trifling distinctions as whether one writes with ink and pen on paper or with a stylus on a dust covered board can influence, in an essential way, the progress of arithmetical methods. And are these not supposed to be logical distinctions?" [1]

It seems strange to see Husserl using the term "logical" in this sense. It would seem more natural to use the term "psychological" instead, since the factors in question seem to serve the purpose of facilitating actual mental processes. They appear to belong to the type of factors that influence our reaction to a stimulus, such as light intensity, discrimination thresholds, and the like, all of which belong properly in experimental psychology. Is it only Husserl's lack of a clear distinction between logical and psychological investigation, during his early period, that causes him to use the term "logical" here?

This need not be the only reason. There is a sense in which such factors, which appear chiefly psychological, can be considered relevant to logical investigation as well. Husserl implies this in the definition he gives immediately after the passage we have just quoted: "Any distinction at all that influences the methodological domination of a field of knowledge is certainly a logical distinction." [2] The "domination of a field of knowledge" involves building up a series of logical structures, of judgments, inferences, and proofs, with the help of symbols. Whatever factors influence this process can be called "logical." They are so called because of their import in the rationalization of a given field of knowledge; when looked at from this point of view, they deserve the name. In a sense, they contribute to and thus share in the rationalization, the intellectualization, of a certain

[1] "Ja später werden wir sogar Gelegenheit finden zu zeigen, wie selbst scheinbar so nichtige Unterschiede wie die, ob man mit Tinte und Feder auf Papier oder mit Griffel auf staubbedecktem Täfelchen schreibt, den Gang arithmetischer Methoden wesentlich beeinflussen kann. Und das sollten nicht logische Unterschiede sein?" *ibid.*, p. 275.

[2] "Ein logischer Unterschied ist doch wohl ein jeder, welcher die kunstmässige Beherrschung eines Erkenntnisgebietes beeinflusst." *ibid.*, p. 275.

sphere of objects of consciousness. When considered as simple psychic phenomena, as factors in psychic causal laws, they can be treated as psychological events, but when considered as relevant and even necessary elements in the process of forming logical structures, they can justly be called logical.

The problem of sensory characteristics is not developed any further in the *Philosophy of Arithmetic,* but these remarks show that Husserl was aware of the influence sensory factors can have even in the logical sphere. In his later thought, the role attributed to sensations is placed in the context of a theory of intentionality, and their part in the constitution of logical entities is more thoroughly investigated. Even at this early stage of his thought, however, the problem appears.

12. Conclusion

Although the *Philosophy of Arithmetic* fails to make a clear distinction between psychological and logical studies, the concept of constitution is operative in that work. It is clearly used by Husserl in the explanation of the origins of groups, one of the steps in his treatment of numbers and their sources. Groups are concrete phenomena whose existence and structure are a result of subjective mental activity. Constitution is also operative in the explanation of other categories which Husserl treats, such as the concepts of something, identity, the relations of more and less, distinction, and, in general, all psychic relationships. Despite some psychological elements, the treatment given by Husserl does not fall into pure psychologism, and constitution does appear in the form Husserl would later call categorical constitution. In the *Philosophy of Arithmetic,* however, Husserl never uses the term "constitution" in his technical sense, to name the subjective process by which objective categories come to be.

Husserl's treatment of symbolically represented numbers and groups should not be called constitutional analysis. These studies are much more psychological and, even more important, they lack an explanation of what is central and presupposed by all of them, the constitution of symbols as such. Because this is not given, Husserl lacks the framework for treatment of the constitution of the specific type of symbols used in arithmetic.

Of secondary interest for the problem of constitution are Husserl's incidental remarks about the roles of temporality and sensory characteristics in the logical sphere. Even in the *Philosophy of Arithmetic*, he notes that all mental activity involves temporality, and that sensory data function in the formation of concepts. Both these themes are extensively developed in Husserl's later studies of constitution, although they are given only passing mention in his first work. Husserl's theory of intentionality, as introduced in the *Logical Investigations*, provides an overall structure in which these elements can be integrated and their function in constitution explicitly treated.

CHAPTER II

CONSTITUTION OF MEANING AND OBJECTS
IN THE *LOGICAL INVESTIGATIONS*

1. Constitution and the aim of the "Logical Investigations"

In his attempt to develop fully the foundations of arithmetic, Husserl was led to see that the problems raised in this study could be resolved only in a much wider philosophical context. He interrupted his mathematical inquiries "until I might succeed in arriving at certain clarity in the basic questions of epistemology and in the critical understanding of logic as a science." [1] The result of his new interests was the *Logical Investigations.*

The problem and concept of constitution hold a key position in this work. Its aim is to furnish a study of what makes up theoretical thought. It proposes to fashion "the theory of theories, the science of sciences." [2] Husserl attempts to elaborate a "pure logic" that will describe the structure of theoretical thought. Its aim is to determine the "more important concepts, and especially all the primitive ones" [3] of which theoretical thought is composed, together with the fundamental combinations those basic concepts form, and the laws which govern their grouping and manipulation in such combinations. By determining these elements, combinations, and rules, Husserl hopes to describe the skeletal form that governs the structure of all theory and reasonable thought. This part of his study will

---

[1] "...bis es mir gelungen sei, in den Grundfragen der Erkenntnistheorie und in dem kritischen Verständnis der Logik als Wissenschaft zu sicherer Klarheit vorzudringen," *Prolegomena*, p. vii; 2nd ed., p. vii. Our citations from the *Logical Investigations* are taken from the first edition. However, because it is so difficult to obtain, we will also give reference to the corresponding page in the second edition, and indicate if there are any changes in the latter. For dates of these editions, see *supra*, p. 23.

[2] "Die Theorie der Theorien, die Wissenschaft der Wissenschaften." *ibid.*, p. 243; 2nd ed., p. 242.

[3] "Die wichtigeren und zumal die sämtlichen primitiven Begriffe." *ibid.*, p. 243; 2nd ed., p. 243.

elaborate a *mathesis universalis*. The parts of the *Logical Investigations* which are devoted explicitly and exclusively to this aim are sections III and IV, entitled respectively, "Towards the Doctrine of Wholes and Parts," and "The Distinction between Independent and Dependent Meanings and the Idea of a Pure Grammar."

A *mathesis universalis* is only the first step in Husserl's project. It must be followed by another inquiry that will explain where all these logical elements and rules come from. "All these concepts must now be fixed, their 'origins' must be individually sought out." [1] "On the other hand, phenomenology discloses the 'sources' out of which the basic concepts and the ideal laws of pure logic arise, and to which they must in turn be traced back, that we might provide them with the 'clarity and distinctness' required for an epistemological understanding of pure logic." [2] This new investigation will be the "philosophical supplement to the pure *mathesis*." [3] It is in connection with inquiry into the sources of primitive concepts and forms that the problem of constitution makes itself known in the *Logical Investigations;* the study of their sources becomes the study of their constitution.

What are precisely the elements whose sources are to be studied? The clearest case is that of logical forms or, as Husserl calls them, categorical forms.[4] They are logical entities that are constituted in categorical acts, and Husserl gives an extensive description of their origins, a description that was to remain essentially the same throughout all his later works. In addition, he speaks about the constitution of meanings, which also qualify as logical entities. This second type of constitution is more basic than the categorical one, because it is operative in all forms of intentionality, whereas categorical constitution is found only in a certain class of intentional acts. Husserl expounds his general

---

[1] "Alle diese Begriffe sind nun zu fixieren, ihr 'Ursprung' ist einzelweise zu erforschen." *ibid.,* p. 245; 2nd ed., p. 244.

[2] "Anderseits erschliesst die Phänomenologie die 'Quellen,' aus denen die Grundbegriffe und die idealen Gesetze der reinen Logik 'etspringen' und bis zu welchen sie wieder zurückverfolgt werden müssen, um ihnen die für ein erkenntniskritisches Verständnis der reinen Logik erforderliche 'Klarheit und Deutlichkeit' zu verschaffen." *Log. Unt.,* p. 4; 2nd ed., II, 1, p. 3.

[3] "die philosophische Ergänzung zur reinen Mathesis." *ibid.,* p. 20; 2nd ed., II, 1, p. 21.

[4] Cf. *Prolegomena,* p. 244; 2nd ed., pp. 243-44.

theory of the structure of intentionality in connection with the constitution of meaning. Finally, he treats the constitution of an object of reference. Thus there are three distinct forms of constitution to be found in the *Investigations:* that of categorical forms, that of meaning, and that of objects of reference.

The main problem which occupies Husserl in the *Investigations*, however, is even more fundamental than that of the origins of logic. It is the explanation of "the relationship between the subjectivity of knowing and the objectivity of the content of knowledge." [1] Somehow, in our subjective awareness, we are able to encounter objectivity. We are able to be conscious of things, objective meanings, and logical laws which transcend our subjectivity. How is this possible? This is the basis for the "principle doubt" [2] which Husserl felt in consequence of his study of mathematics: can objectivity be explained by a psychological study of subjectivity? Husserl asks "how the *an sich* of objectivity can come to presentation, and thus in a certain extent become subjective; what it means, that the object is *an sich* and yet 'given' in knowledge; how the ideality of the universal (as a concept or law) can enter into the flow of real psychic experiences and become something possessed in the knowledge of the man who thinks...." [3] Husserl does not want to *prove* that we encounter objectivity; he accepts this as a patent fact, but he does want to explain how it is possible, how it can be understood. In other words, he wants to explain how subjectivity "constitutes" objectivity. This problem will be the crux of his phenomenology, not only in the *Investigations* but also in all his later works, and the ways in which he answers it will determine the evolution of his phenomenology and, more specifically, his concept of constitution.

---

[1] "Das Verhältnis zwischen der Subjektivität des Erkennens und der Objektivität des Erkenntnisinhaltes." *ibid.*, p. vii; 2nd p. vii.

[2] "Der prinzipielle Zweifel." *ibid.*

[3] "...wie denn das 'an sich' der Objektivität zur Vorstellung kommen, also gewissermassen doch wieder subjektiv werden mag; was das heisst, der Gegenstand sei 'an sich' und in der Erkenntnis 'gegeben'; wie die Idealität des Allgemeinen als Begriff oder Gesetz in den Fluss der realen psychischen Erlebnisse eingehen und zum Erkenntnisbesitz des Denkenden werden kann...." *Log. Unt.*, p. 9; 2nd ed., II, I, p. 8. (with slight changes).

2. The "Logical Investigations" and the "Philosophy of Arithmetic"

The aim of the *Investigations* is similar to that of Husserl's book on arithmetic, except that its scope is wider. Both are concerned with determining the primitive concepts of their respective sciences, and with showing the origins of these concepts.

There are, nevertheless, important differences between the two works. The most striking of these is Husserl's explicit treatment of the peculiar status of logic and logical entities in the *Investigations*. In the *Philosophy of Arithmetic*, he does not sharply distinguish logical entities from psychological events, and his search for sources consequently becomes, in some cases, genetic psychology. No such confusion is possible in the *Investigations*, thanks to the extensive critical studies carried out in the *Prolegomena*. In response to the criticism of Frege [1] and as a result of his study of Natorp,[2] Husserl argues at great length that logic and psychology form two specifically distinct disciplines, and that logic cannot be explained by an empirical psychological study. This implies that it must be explained by some other sort of inquiry, the method and rules of which remain to be determined.[3]

3. Definitions of elements in intentionality

Most of Husserl's treatment of constitution in the *Investigations* consists in structural analyses of intentionality. In order

[1] Cf. Dagfinn Follesdal, *Husserl und Frege* (Oslo: I Kommisjon Hos H. Aschehoug & Co., 1958), pp. 26-44. Follesdal shows that Husserl tried, in the *Prolegomena*, to accommodate his ideas to the essential points in Frege's criticism. He goes on to say that Husserl never succeeded in incorporating Frege's remarks into his work. For the reference to Frege's critique, see *supra*, p. 17.

[2] An indication of how deeply Husserl was influenced in his early thought by Natorp can be had by reading the latter's *Einleitung in die Psychologie nach kritischer Methode* (Freiburg: J.C.B. Mohr, 1888). Husserl read this book and quoted it in his *Investigations;* many of his central problems are taken from it. Husserl's connection with the neo-Kantians is amply treated in: Iso Kern, *Husserl und Kant* (The Hague: Martinus Nijhoff, 1964).

[3] Osborn says, in *The Philosophy of Edmund Husserl*, p. 57: "The *Prolegomena to Pure Logic* therefore was something more than a mere attack on psychologism. It was unexpectedly an attack on anti-psychologism as well." Husserl's attempt to find a middle way between psychologism and pure logicism is also described in Theodore Celms, *Der phänomenologische Idealismus Husserls* (Riga: Acta Universitatis Latviensis XIX, 1928), p. 279: "Es sind aber höchst originelle logische Untersuchungen, die mit keinen früheren verglichen werden können. In den bis jetzt bekannten Untersuchungen über die Logik sind entweder bloss die logischen Gebilde behandelt worden, oder es ist der Versuch bewagt, diese als bloss psychische Gebilde

to understand these analyses, some definitions of elements in or related to intentionality must be studied. The immediate application of these definitions will be in our discussion of the *Investigations*, but they will also provide a base for concepts we must use in treating constitution in Husserl's later works.

When he introduces a concept, Husserl rarely gives an explicit and precise definition. The meaning he attributes to it is often determined more by the use he makes of a term than by what he expressly says about it, and therefore the context into which it is introduced, the manner in which it is treated, and the problems it is supposed to solve, all must be considered if we are to recover the meaning of his terms. This must be kept in mind during our study of the following definitions.

(A) *Word meanings and meanings in general*

Husserl begins the *Investigations* with an analysis of "Expression and Meaning." Since logic is built up of a series of meanings[1] and since every science and theory is "an ideal complex of meanings *in specie*," [2] this study is the first necessary step in his pure logic. It will determine some of the primitive elements that go into the formation of logic and theoretical thought.

In addition, Husserl's interest in meaning stems from a more fundamental cause. The fact that he begins his study with an investigation of meaning is not accidental, for acts of meaning do not comprise only a partial area of theoretical thought. All theoretical acts must be meaningful. This study thus provides the background which the others all presuppose and without which they cannot be understood. In treating the problem of meaning, Husserl treats the structure of intentionality in general and thereby builds the framework in which he will handle the far reaching philosophical questions he has set out to solve.

Our introductory remarks have spoken of "meaning" in a general, undifferentiated sense. They affirm little more than that a large and very important part of human behavior is "meaning-

zu fassen. Die Problemstellung Husserls hat in der ganzen logischen Literatur nicht ihresgleichen."

[1] Cf, *Log. Unt.*, p. 93; 2nd ed., II, 1, p. 92.

[2] "Eine ideale Komplexion von Bedeutungen *in specie*." *ibid.*, p. 95; 2nd ed., II, 1, p. 95 (with slight changes).

ful," and that an understanding of what meaningfulness is, is the indispensable beginning for Husserl's studies. He proceeds to introduce distinctions and definitions into this problem.

The point of departure is the meaningful use of words. Husserl takes a commonplace activity, the meaningful utterance of a word or a series of words, and analyzes it to see what subjective operations go to make it up. He claims that two distinct acts must be present. There is one act which forms the word and another which contributes meaning to the word; every meaningful utterance involves "the unity of those acts in which an expression, taken physically, is constituted, with those entirely different acts in which the meaning is constituted." [1] Of these two types of acts, those which result in the physical word are of very secondary importance in communication and thought. Our attention goes through them and focuses on those which contribute meaning to the word: "When an expression functions as such, we do not 'live' in the acts that constitute it as a physical object, our 'interest' does not belong to this object; rather, we live in the acts that contribute sense...." [2]

The two acts are very tightly joined together: "They build an internally fused unity of peculiar character." [3] Husserl even calls the composition of the two an "act-totality." [4]

Husserl thus distinguishes two acts which must be present in the meaningful use of words. His next step is to state that the two acts can be separated. Despite their close unity, he claims that the act of meaning can sometimes occur even when no word-forming act accompanies it. There can be meaning without words. "The physical expression, the word sound, might be taken as unessential in this unity. And it is, since any other word sound might be there instead of it in a similar function; indeed

---

[1] "die Einheit der Akte, in denen sich ein Ausdruck, physisch genommen, konstituiert, mit den ganz anderen Akten, in denen sich die Bedeutung konstituiert." *ibid.*, p. 381; 2nd ed., II, 1, p. 406 (with slight changes).

[2] "Indem ein Ausdruck als solcher fungiert, 'leben wir' nicht in den Akten, die ihn als physisches Objekt konstituieren; nicht diesem Objekt gehört unser 'Interesse,' vielmehr leben wir in den sinngebenden Akten...." *ibid.*, p. 384; 2nd ed., II, 1, pp. 408-9 (with slight changes).

[3] "Sie bilden...eine innig verschmolzene Einheit von eigentümlicher Charakter." *ibid.*, p. 39; 2nd ed., II, 1, p. 39.

[4] "Gesamtakt." *ibid.*, p. 382; 2nd ed., II, 1, p. 406.

it might even be omitted entirely." [1] In making this separation, Husserl leaves the limited area of word meanings with which he introduced this subject, and moves into the wider field of meanings or senses in general.

Husserl thus feels that he has isolated acts of meaning and given them an ostensive definition. He takes it as a fact of ordinary experience that there is a difference between meaningful and meaningless utterance of words. He attributes the difference to the presence or absence of an act of meaning; the term "act of meaning" thus becomes the name of something we encounter in everyday experience. He then asserts that such an act can also appear unaccompanied by words. This leaves him with the notion of an act of meaning in general, and makes it possible for him to speak of it in relation to other types of acts, to analyze its structure, and to investigate how it operates.

(B) Meanings as ideal entities are distinct from acts of meaning

Husserl then makes a distinction which is of capital importance for his phenomenology, that between meaning and acts of meaning. The basis of this distinction lies in the fact that one identical meaning can be repeated in several numerically distinct acts of meaning. Thus in the case of word meanings, a proposition or word uttered a dozen times remains the same proposition or word throughout, although each act of utterance is different from every other one. The meaning can be treated as something identical, numerically the same, every time it is given expression. It becomes an "object" of its own type; an ideal object, it is true, but one that preserves an identity of its own. Husserl says, "As identical, it is itself in turn an object in reference to various new meanings – all this exactly like other objects that are not meanings, such as horses, stones, psychic acts, etc. Only because the meaning is something identical, can it be treated as something identical. We hold this as an unas-

---

[1] "Mag immerhin der physische Ausdruck, der Wortlaut, in dieser Einheit als unwesentlich gelten. Das ist er auch insofern, als anstatt seiner ein beliebiger anderer Wortlaut und in gleicher Funktion hätte stehen können; ja er könnte sogar gänzlich in Fortfall kommen." *ibid.*, p. 382; 2nd ed., II, 1, p. 407. For similar ideas, cf. *ibid.*, pp. 104-5, 532, 564; 2nd ed., II, 1, pp. 104-5, part 2, pp. 60, 92. Husserl's radical separation of language and thought betrays a naive conception of the function of language and symbolism in thinking.

sailable argument. . . ." [1] He also states, "We have distinguished, from 'to mean' as an act, the meaning itself, the ideal unity as opposed to the multiplicity of possible acts." [2]

What is affirmed for word meanings is also true of meanings in general. Let us suppose an act of meaning in which no words occur, for instance, focusing our attention on and thus intending "this red house" in an act of perception. I can do this several times. Each act of intending or meaning is distinct from every other act, but the meaning, the "sense" carried by the acts, is the same in each case.

Husserl's hypostatization of meaning does not imply that he classes meanings with the real things we meet in the world. The objectivity of meanings is ideal, not real. Meanings have their existence only within human acts, but one and the same meaning can be realized in a multitude of numerically distinct acts.

Husserl makes some more distinctions in order to bring the unity and objectivity of meaning into sharper focus. Many of his remarks are prompted by the philosophical and psychological theories prevalent at his time. Thus meaning is distinguished from objects of reference and from the "mental image" that may accompany meaningful discourse. The meaning of a word or statement is distinguished from the state of mind or mental acts which the word announces. For example, to utter a judgment announces that a mental act of judging takes place in the speaker's mind, but the meaning of the utterance is not this mental act. Finally, the act of meaning is distinguished from other mental acts, and in particular from acts of perceiving. Acts of meaning are orientated towards perceiving and receive their fulfillment in it, but the two types of acts are specifically distinct.[3]

---

[1] ". . . Als identisches ist sie [die Bedeutung] selbst wieder Gegenstand in Bezug auf mannigfaltige neue Bedeutungen – all das genau so wie andere Gegenstände, die nicht Bedeutungen sind, wie Pferde, Steine, psychische Akte, usf. Nur weil die Bedeutung ein Identisches ist, kann sie wie ein Identisches behandelt werden. Dies gilt uns als ein unanfechtbares Argument. . . ." *ibid.*, pp. 111-12; 2nd ed., II, 1, pp. 111-12.
[2] ". . . Unterschieden wir aber vom Bedeuten als Akt, die Bedeutung selbst, die ideale Einheit gegenüber der Mannigfaltigkeit möglicher Akte." *ibid.*, p. 77; 2nd ed., II, 1, p. 77.
[3] Cf. *ibid.*, pp. 46, 66-7, 78, 396-98, 486-88; 2nd ed., II, 1, pp. 46, 66-7, 78, 421-24; II, 2, pp. 14-16.

(C) *The relationship between meaning and objects of reference.*
Intentionality

Although meaning is distinct from the object meant, there is,
claims Husserl, a close liaison between the two. "Every expression not only states something, but it also speaks about
something; it not only has its meaning, but it is also referred to
certain objects." [1] The structure of an act of meaning is such
that it involves both a meaning and a reference to an object.
In fact, reference to an object is made through the meaning of
the act. "The expression indicates (names) the object by virtue
of its meaning. . . ." [2] The meaning implies reference to an object;
if an intentional act possesses a meaning, it is likewise directed
to an object that is meant. The meaning is what indicates how
the object is meant, it specifies the point of view from which
we refer to the object. Yet despite this close interaction between
meaning and reference, Husserl insists, "But the object never
. . . coincides with the meaning." [3]

An object of reference, according to Husserl, need not be a
really existing thing. When we read fiction or mythology, we
refer to fictional persons or events as the objects of our intentions. When I think about Falstaff, he is the object of reference of my intentional acts, even though he does not exist as a
real entity. Objects of reference are elements demanded by the
nature of intentional acts, and are not necessarily real, concrete
things.

The problem of objects of reference leads us into the concept
of intentionality. Every conscious act, according to Husserl, is
referred to an object, and another way of saying this is that
every act is by nature intentional. Consciousness is not a self-
enclosed island, but essentially involves reference to an object.
It is always consciousness *of* something. By such assertions,
Husserl excludes the concept of a consciousness that is locked
within itself and knows only its own immanent elements or
states.

[1] "Jeder Ausdruck besagt nicht nur etwas, sondern er sagt auch über etwas; er
hat nicht nur seine Bedeutung, sondern er bezieht sich auch auf irgendwelche Gegenstände." *ibid.*, p. 46; 2nd ed., II, 1, p. 46.
[2] ". . . Der Ausdruck bezeichne (nenne) den Gegenstand mittels seiner Bedeutung. . . ." *ibid.*, p. 49; 2nd ed., II, 1, p. 49.
[3] "Niemals fällt aber . . . der Gegenstand mit der Bedeutung zusammen." *ibid.*, p.
46; 2nd ed., II, 1, p. 46.

In other words, consciousness always involves the presentation (*Vorstellung*) of an object. This is the other side of the coin: intentionality means that consciousness is related to objects, but also that it relates objects to itself. Furthermore, the objects *themselves* are so related to us. We are not simply aware of an effect made by them on our senses (as Kant or the British empiricists would have it), but are aware of the object in itself. Consciousness is not insular, but puts us into a real intentional contact with things. How intentionality achieves this, how objectivity becomes present to consciousness, is precisely the problem of constitution.

(D) Objectivating acts

The relationship between meaning and reference is first developed in connection with words and signs and the intentional acts of meaning associated with them. The principle remains the same, however, in the case of intentional acts that are not associated with words. All intentional acts refer to an object, and do so under a certain aspect or sense. This is true of perceiving, remembering, evaluating, imagining, and so on. More fundamentally, it is true of all the acts which Husserl calls "objectivating" acts.

This is a type of intentional act which holds a privileged position in regard to the question of sense and reference in Husserl's thought. His reasoning leading up to it is intricate, chiefly because most of it is negative and shows what an objectivating act is not.[1] His conclusion is that an objectivating act is an act in which an object (with a given sense) is referred to, and to which nothing further is added, no further act is adjoined. An objectivating act sets up the sense-reference relationship to an object and stops there; it brings it about that something acquires objectivity (and meaning as well) for a knowing subject. It is a purely contemplative act. Nothing further is added, that is, there is no evaluation, no volition, no emotion, no further act of any sort adjoined to the purely contemplative objectivating act. The objectivating act establishes an intentional relationship to an object under a given aspect or sense, and thus establishes the object as an object of consciousness.

[1] Cf. *ibid.*, pp. 445-62; 2nd ed., II, 1, pp. 477-99.

This type of act is important because it serves as a basis for every other type of intentional act. Acts of evaluation, volition, emotion, and all other intentional acts *are* intentional only because they are built upon objectivating acts. Husserl says, "Every intentional experience is either an objectivating act or has such an act as 'foundation,' i.e. in the latter case, it necessarily has an objectivating act as a component part in itself. . . ." [1] All such acts acquire their reference to objects from the objectivating act that they are built upon. It can be said that they acquire rationality only in virtue of their objectivating component. The presence of objectivation is, in Husserl's theory, what differentiates a rational act of emotion or evaluation from blind instinct, from a stimulus-response type of reaction. It is only because of the objectivating act that someone can, for instance, recognize the object of his emotion as a reality apart from himself, with a meaning or sense of its own.

Thus as a result of his analyses, Husserl finds objectivating acts as the basic form of intentionality, intentionality *par excellence*. Since he is interested in describing a "thinking being," it is natural that his analyses of act structure will be geared primarily towards objectivating acts, which are specifically the acts of contemplation and rationality. As regards the problem of constitution, the constitution of meaning and objects of reference takes place within objectivating acts.

(E) The "quality" and "material" of objectivating acts

Husserl analyzes in more detail the structure of objectivating acts. Reflection shows, he claims, that an intentional act is composed of two elements, "quality" and "material." The quality of an act is that which makes an act to be the *type* of act that it is. Seeing a house, imagining the same house, and remembering it are three different types of acts. They all have different act qualities.

Each of these acts refers to the same object, however, and let us suppose that each considers the house from the same point of view. Then each refers to the same object under the same

---

[1] "Jedes intentionale Erlebnis ist entweder ein objektivierender Akt oder hat einen solchen Akt zur 'Grundlage,' d.h. er hat in letzteren Falle einen objektivierenden Akt notwendig als Bestandstück in sich..." *ibid.*, p. 458; 2nd ed., II, 1, pp. 493-94.

aspect. The element in intentional acts which refers them to an object, under a certain aspect or sense, is called the material of acts. "Therefore we must take the material as that element in an act which first and foremost grants it reference to something objective. It grants this reference in such complete exactness that through the material, there is firmly determined not simply the objective thing which the act intends, but also the manner in which the act intends it." [1] The quality and material taken together comprise what Husserl calls the "intentional essence" of an act. [2]

Husserl claims, in the *Logical Investigations*, that only objectivating acts have act materials; other acts, such as emotive ones for example, have an act quality, but are grafted onto the act material of an objectivating act. They have no independent material of their own. "Reference to an objectivity is constituted in general in the material. Each material, however (so says our law), is the material of an objectivating act and only through such an act can it become the material of a new act quality, founded on the first act." [3] Thus the quality-material structure applies primarily to objectivating acts.

(F) Intentionality and sensory content

In the *Philosophy of Arithmetic*, Husserl already intimated that sensory data play a role in formation of concepts when he

---

[1] "Danach muss uns die Materie als dasjenige im Akte gelten, was ihm allererst die Beziehung auf ein Gegenständliches verleiht, und zwar diese Beziehung in so vollkommener Bestimmtheit, dass durch die Materie nicht nur das Gegenständliche überhaupt, welches der Akt meint, sondern auch die Weise, in welcher er es meint, fest bestimmt ist." *ibid.*, p. 390; 2nd ed., II, 1, p. 415.

[2] Cf. *ibid.*, p. 392; 2nd ed., II, 1, p. 417.

[3] "Die Beziehung auf eine Gegenständlichkeit konstituiert sich überhaupt in der Materie. Jede Materie ist aber, so sagt unser Gesetz, Materie eines objektivierenden Aktes und kann nur mittelst eines solchen zur Materie einer neuen, in ihm fundierten Aktqualität werden." *ibid.*, p. 459; 2nd ed., II, 1, p. 494. At this point, it will be helpful to show the differences between act-material, as described in the *Investigations*, and noemas, which are presented in *Ideas*. The two concepts are basically the same, but there are some important differences which are related to some of the points now under discussion. The differences we wish to emphasize can be expressed as follows: (1) The *entire* "sense" or meaning carried by an intentional act is located in the noema, but in the *Investigations*, senses or meanings are located both in the act-material and act-quality. (2) Complex acts, such as acts of evaluation, have one noema, but it is different from that in the simple act of objectivation on which the complex act is founded. This means that the evaluational act deposits a new layer of sense into the noema. This is not the case for act-materials in the *Investigations*. The act-material is impervious to any change in its corresponding quality.

stated that variations in sensory material can be equivalent to "logical distinctions." However, he could not show how this comes about because he did not elaborate a comprehensive theory of intentionality in that work, and consequently could not state with any precision how sensory data function. Such a description of their role in intentionality is possible in the *Logical Investigations,* and is given in Husserl's treatment of what the calls the "sensory content" (*Inhalt*) of intentional acts.

Husserl's analysis of acts has so far revealed their intentional essence, their quality and material. In the concrete performance of an act, however, a third element appears. Every intentional act is performed in association with sensations; it is directed towards its object through such sensory data.[1] The sensory content serves as a carrier for intentional acts. In listening to someone speak or in looking at a landscape, certain sensations, real psychic events, occur in my consciousness, and "through" them I perceive the person or the landscape.[2] The auditory disturbances or visual psychic events that occur when I listen to or look at something are carriers of my intentional acts. Husserl calls sensory contents which function in such a way "intentional" sensations.

Husserl also raises the question whether or not we experience anything that could be called "non-intentional" sensations. Would a pain, a contented mood, or a buzzing in one's ear be correctly called non-intentional sensations? They are real psychic events, but are they really deprived of intentionality? Are they completely devoid of any function as carriers of intentional acts? Husserl gives arguments pro and con, but leaves the question unanswered.[3]

In the case of intentional sensations, what happens to make it possible for them to carry an intentional act? What does it

[1] Cf. *ibid.*, p. 655; 2nd ed., II, 2, p. 183: "Die Idee eines 'reinen Intellekts,' interpretiert als ein 'Vermögen' reinen Denkens (hier: kategorialer Aktion) und völlig abgelöst von jedem 'Vermögen der Sinnlichkeit,' konnte nur konzipiert werden vor einer Elementaranalyse der Erkenntnis nach ihrem evident unaufhebbaren Bestande."

[2] On what Husserl means by a "real" element in consciousness, cf. *ibid.*, pp. 374-75; 2nd ed., II, 1, pp. 397-99.

[3] Cf. *ibid.*, pp. 369-74; 2nd ed., II, 1, pp. 391-97. The question is also left open in *Ideen* I, p. 208. It is clear, however, that Husserl considers sensations non-intentional in themselves, even though they can (and perhaps must) function in intentional acts. Cf. *Log. Unt.*, P. 370; 2nd ed., II, 1, p. 392; and *Ideen* I, pp. 81 and 208.

mean to say that we perceive an object "through" sensations? Suppose, for instance, that what I first consider to be only a buzzing sensation in my ear turns out to be the hum of high tension wires; what occurs in the auditory sensation? Husserl explains: "The presentation (*Vorstellung*) in perception comes about through the following: the experienced complex of sensations is animated by a certain act character, by a certain apprehending or intending. When this happens, the perceived object appears...."[1] He also says, "The case is rather that the sensations function here as the representing contents of acts of perception, or... that the sensations undergo an objective 'interpretation' or 'apprehension'."[2] Sensations are animated, says Husserl, in an intentional act. They undergo an apprehension, which results in the fact that we can know an object (in our example, the electrical wires) through them. There is a reciprocal activity here; the intention animates sensory data, and the data are thereby enabled to carry the intentional act.

Husserl goes on to claim that one and the same intention performs the two functions of being directed towards an object and animating sensory data. "It will be immediately understood that the same thing that, in reference to the intentional object, is called presentation (a perceiving, imagining, or representing intention towards it), is called apprehension, interpretation, or apperception in reference to the sensations which really belong to the act."[3] This point will be useful in interpreting some of Husserl's statements concerning inner temporality and immanent objects.

The intentional essence of an act, its quality and material, when joined to the sensory content, forms a complete, concrete intentional act. "Every concrete, complete objectivating act has

[1] "Die Wahrnehmungsvorstellung kommt dadurch zu Stande, dass die erlebte Empfindungskomplexion von einem gewissen Aktcharakter, einem gewissen Auffassen, Meinen beseelt ist; und indem sie es ist, erscheint der wahrgenommene Gegenstand...." *Log. Unt.*,p. 75; 2nd ed., II, 1, p. 75.
[2] "Die Sachlage ist vielmehr die, dass die Empfindungen hier als präsentierende Inhalte von Wahrnehmungsakten fungieren, oder...dass die Empfindungen hier eine gegenständliche 'Deutung' oder 'Auffassung' erfahren." *ibid.*,p. 370; 2nd ed., II, 1, p. 392 (with slight changes).
[3] "Man versteht zugleich, dass dasselbe, was in Beziehung auf den intentionalen Gegenstand Vorstellung (wahrnehmende, einbildende, abbildende Intention auf ihn) heisst, in Beziehung auf die zum Akte reel gehörigen Empfindungen Auffassung, Deutung, Apperzeption heisst." *ibid.*, p. 364; 2nd ed., II, 1, p. 385 (with slight changes).

three components: the quality, material, and the representing content." [1]

When treating the sensory contents of intentional acts, Husserl often calls them "representants," a term which stresses their function in manifesting things or qualities of things to our consciousness. [2] In the case of acts of perception, when the object is directly intuited, Husserl even says that qualities of a material thing each have counterparts in our sensations: "Although the color which one sees. . . certainly does not exist as an experience of the person seeing, still there corresponds to it a real component in this experience, i.e. in the perception-appearance. There corresponds to it a color sensation, the qualitatively determined subjective color moment, which undergoes an objectivating 'apprehension' . . . in perception." [3]

(G) Sensory contents are "experienced" and not "perceived"

Husserl describes the way we are aware of sensory contents by distinguishing it from the way in which we are aware of transcendent objects of consciousness. When an intentional act takes place, I am said to perceive an object or, conversely, the object is said to appear to me. I do not, however, perceive the sensations which serve as carriers for the act in the same way as I perceive the object; conversely, they cannot be said to appear to my consciousness in the same way as the object appears to me. When a set of sensory data are animated by an intention, says Husserl, "then the perceived object appears, although it [the complex of sensations] does not appear, no more than the act in which the perceived object is constituted as such." [4] "I

---

[1] "Jeder konkret vollständige objektivierende Akt hat drei Komponenten: die Qualität, die Materie, und den repräsentierenden Inhalt." *ibid.*, p. 562; 2nd ed., II, 2, p. 90.

[2] Husserl speaks of *Repräsentaten.* Cf. *ibid.*, p. 372; 2nd ed., II, 1, p. 395.

[3] "Während die gesehene Farbe...gewiss nicht als Erlebnis des Sehenden existiert, so entspricht ihr in diesem Erlebnis, d.i. in der Wahrnehmungserscheinung, ein reelles Bestandstück. Es entspricht ihr die Farbenempfindung, das qualitativ bestimmte subjektive Farbemoment, welches in der Wahrnehmung...objektivierende 'Auffassung' erfährt." *ibid.*, p. 327; 2nd ed., II, 1, pp. 348-49 (with slight changes).

[4] "...[dann] erscheint der wahrgenommene Gegenstand, während sie selbst so wenig erscheint wie der Akt, in dem sich der wahrgenommene Gegenstand als solcher konstituiert." *ibid.*, p. 75; 2nd ed., II, 1, p. 75.

see a thing, v.g. this box; I do not see my sensations."[1] Husserl
prefers to say that sensory data are experienced (*erlebt*), whereas
objects are perceived or appear. "Thus the sensations, and
likewise the acts which 'apprehend' or 'apperceive' them, are
experienced, but they do not appear objectively; they are not
seen, heard, or perceived with some 'sense.' On the other hand,
the objects appear, they are perceived, but not experienced." [2]
Thus there are two different ways in which we are aware of
elements presented to our consciousness. We perceive (or "encounter") objects, and we experience sensations. Conversely,
objects appear to consciousness, while sensations are experienced
in it. This is a distinction that Husserl exploits in his lectures on
time.

Sensations are not the only things that are experienced but
not perceived; intentional acts or apprehensions are also known
in the same way. We do not perceive our intentions, nor do
they appear to us as objects do, but, like sensations, they are
experienced.

This discussion of sense data and intentionality brings to a
close the series of definitions which are essential for treatment
of constitution in Husserl's philosophy. Despite the psychological flavor of some of them, they are the basis for concepts
which Husserl uses throughout his work. They provide the elements for Husserl's structural analysis of intentionality, and as
Fink remarks, "Intentional analysis first brings 'intentionality'
to light." [3] In our later studies, we will frequently refer to the
definitions we have now formulated, sometimes taking them just
as they are given here, sometimes modifying them in accordance
with Husserl's own evolution of thought, but always using them
as a fundamental point of departure.

Attention should be paid to the method Husserl uses to point

[1] "Ich sehe ein Ding, z.B. diese Schachtel, ich sehe nicht meine Empfindugen."
ibid., p. 360; 2nd ed., II, 1, p. 382.
[2] "Die Empfindungen und desgleichen die sie 'auffassenden' oder 'apperzipieren-
den' Akte werden hierbei erlebt, aber sie erscheinen nicht gegenständlich; sie werden
nicht gesehen, gehört, mit irgendeinem 'Sinn' wahrgenommen. Die Gegenstände
andererseits erscheinen, werden wahrgenommen, aber sie sind nicht erlebt." *ibid.*,
p. 363; 2nd ed., II, 1, p. 385.
[3] "Die intentionale Analyse bringt überhaupt erst 'Intentionalität' zum Vor-
schein." "Das Problem der Phänomenologie Edmund Husserls," *Revue internationale
de Philosophie*, 1 (1938-1939), p. 265.

out the various elements in intentionality. In separating meaning from acts of meaning, quality of acts from their material, and intentions from sensations, the method used is to see whether one aspect can change while another remains the same. If this can be done, Husserl feels justified in claiming that two irreducible aspects or elements are present and that they can be distinguished from one another.[1]

With these definitions as tools, Husserl approaches problems of constitution in the *Logical Investigations*, and tries to explain the origins of meanings and objects.

4. Constitution of meaning and constitution of objects

Meanings, whether associated with words or not, must be accepted as ideal, objective units, claims Husserl. The same meaning can appear in many different acts of meaning. If this is so, the question arises: where do meanings come from? There is something problematic about their existence; they are not given to us in the same way that things in the world are. Some sort of explanation is called for in order to clarify their strange manner of being.

Husserl uses the term "constitution" to state the way in which meanings come to be. A meaning is constituted in an act of meaning. "But it is certain that every utterance ... has its intending, and that the meaning is constituted in this intending...."[2] He speaks of "the acts, in which the meaning is constituted." [3] "We wish to consider whether this intuition itself is the act that constitutes the meaning...."[4] "[Perception] ... does not itself constitute meaning, not even a part of it." [5] He asks, "what this intending as such constitutes as regards its sense." [6]

We have seen how closely meaning and objects of reference are

---

[1] This procedure is a form of "free variation," and Husserl was quite aware of the method he was using. Cf. *Log. Unt.*, pp. 388-89; 2nd ed., II, 1, pp. 413-14.

[2] "Sicher aber ist, dass jede Aussage...ihre Meinung hat, und dass sich in dieser Meinung ... die Bedeutung konstituiert." *ibid.*, p. 45; 2nd ed., II, 1, p. 45.

[3] "den Akten, in denen sich die Bedeutung konstituiert." *ibid.*, p. 381; 2nd ed., II, 1, p. 406.

[4] "Wir wollen erwägen, ob diese Anschauung selbst der die Bedeutung konstituierende Akt ist...." *ibid.*, p. 485; 2nd ed., II, 2, p. 13.

[5] "Sie [die Wahrnehmung] konstituiert ... nicht selbst die Bedutung, auch nicht einem Teile nach." *ibid.*, p. 491; 2nd ed., II, 2, p. 19.

[6] "was dieses Meinen als solches, nach seinem Sinne konstituiert." *ibid.*, pp. 144-45; 2nd ed., II, 1, p. 146. In addition, cf. pp. 494-95; 2nd ed., II, 2, p. 22.

linked to one another. When a meaning is constituted, reference
to an object is also necessarily established. Husserl uses the
term "constitution" also to name the way in which an object is
so established, in which it becomes the object of reference for
a meaningful intentional act. Furthermore, the object is not
only constituted as given, but also as given with the meaning,
the sense, included in the intentional act which is referred to it.
"Where the meaningful intention is fulfilled on the basis of a
corresponding intuition, in other words, where the expression is
referred to a given object in actual naming, there the object is
constituted as 'given' in certain acts; and indeed it is given to
us... in the same way as the meaning intends it." [1] Husserl
speaks of "the act in which the perceived object is constituted
as such";[2] he even mentions the constitution of a thing.[3]

Thus every intentional act, or more accurately every objectivating act, operates a double constitution. It constitutes a
sense and a reference. In every objectivating act, a meaning is
constituted and an object is constituted as meant. This is true
of all objectivating acts, whether they are acts of perception
or only acts of empty intending, in which the intention is not
filled by the presence of its object. In the special case when an
act of meaning coincides with an act of perception, then the
object is constituted as given. It is not only constituted as referred to, as intended or meant, but also as really given to our
consciousness. Both cases of constitution are instances of the
general problem pervading the *Logical Investigations*, the problem
of how objectivity becomes present to subjectivity. Both
meanings and objects of reference are transcendent to subjectivity; how do they become manifest in it?

5. The "matter and form" schema used by Husserl for constitution
   In order to clarify the formation of meaning and reference,

---

[1] "Wo sich nämlich die Bedeutungsintention auf Grund korrespondierender Anschauung erfüllt, m.a.W. wo der Ausdruck in aktueller Nennung auf den gegebenen
Gegenstand bezogen ist, da konstituiert sich der Gegenstand als 'gegebener' in
gewissen Akten, und zwar ist er uns... in derselben Weise gegeben, in welcher ihn
die Bedeutung meint." *ibid.*, pp. 50-1; 2nd ed., II, 1, pp. 50-1.
[2] "der Akt, in dem sich der wahrgenommene Gegenstand als solcher konstituierte." *ibid.*, p. 75; 2nd ed., II, 1, p. 75.
[3] Cf. *ibid.*, p. 621; 2nd ed., II, 2, p. 149. Other statements of the constitution of
objects can be found on pp. 534, 606, 617, 625; 2nd ed., II, 2, pp. 52-3, 134, 145, 153.

Husserl uses a schema which was current in the psychological literature of his time. It is employed to make us see how the objectivity of sense and reference can be made to arise in the changing stream of our subjective experiences. Husserl says that during the flow of sensory experiences which occur in perception of a thing, I have a certain "consciousness of identity." I am aware of a single point of reference and a single sense which endures throughout my subjective changes, aware of an "objectivity" which transcends my own subjective experiences. "Now I ask, what lies at the base of such a consciousness? Should not this be the correct answer, that at both times different sensory contents are indeed given, but that they are interpreted (apprehended, apperceived) in 'the same sense,' and that the interpretation according to this 'sense' is an experience-characteristic that alone makes up the 'existence of the object for me'?" [1] Objectivity comes into my consciousness when sensory data are "apprehended" by intentionality.

This schematism of intentionality and sensory content, of sensory "matter" and intentional "form," is very important for Husserl's theory of constitution. It is the way in which he explains, in the *Logical Investigations*, the "relationship between the subjectivity of knowing and the objectivity of the content of knowledge," and it dominates his concept of constitution until it is gradually replaced by the schema of temporal constitution, a replacement which was entirely completed only in his theory of genetic constitution.

The schema presupposes two radically distinct elements, sense data and intentions. In themselves, sense data have no intentionality whatsoever. A creature that would have only sensations would not perceive things, houses, trees; its experiences would lack any "objectivating interpretation." [2] It is only the advent of intentionality that adds such objectivity to sensations,

---

[1] "Ich frage nun, was liegt diesem Bewusstsein zugrunde? Sollte da die Antwort nicht zutreffend sein, dass zwar beiderseits verschiedene Empfindungsinhalte gegeben, dass sie aber in 'demselben Sinne' gedeutet (aufgefasst, apperzipiert) sind, und dass die Deutung nach diesem 'Sinne' ein Erlebnischarakter ist, der allererst das 'Dasein des Gegenstandes für mich' ausmacht?" *ibid.*, p. 361; 2nd ed., II, 1, p. 383 (with slight changes; but one of the changes is significant. In the second edition, Husserl drops the word *Deutung*, "interpretation." He gradually abandoned this term in favor of the less ambiguous "apprehension"). Other quotations which express the same thing are cited above in this chapter, p. 50.

[2] "objektivierende Deutung." *ibid.*, p. 75; 2nd ed., II, 1, p. 75.

and consequently it is only the intentional moment that constitutes meaning and reference in our consciousness.

The words which Husserl uses to express the function of intentions are "interpretation" (*Deutung*), "apperception," and "apprehension" (*Auffassung*). The term *Auffassung* can also be translated "conception."[1] The sense of these terms is that intentionality "interprets" sensations, it carries out an operation on them, in such a way as to bring about objectivation. In saying that we interpret our sensations and thus constitute objectivity, however, Husserl does not mean that we first perceive sensations and then infer a reality from them. We do not, he insists, perceive sensations; they are experienced. The interpretation or apprehension involved here is the peculiar type which we have described in our definition of intentionality and sensory content: intentions animate sensations and are carried by them, and through them mean or intend objective reality.

Thus although meaning and reference come entirely from the intentional moment in the schema, intentionality is not entirely free in forming the sense and reference that arise, because it must operate on the specific sense data that are given to it in a particular case. In other words, although intentionality alone constitutes meaning and objects, sensations also have a role in determining their constitution, even though this role is a passive one, the role of a "raw material" out of which the objective is formed. However, Husserl does not succeed in explaining the function carried out by sensations, paradoxically, until he finally abandons the matter-form schema in his theory of genetic constitution. Until that time, they remain an unresolved knot in his phenomenology.

Husserl did not devise this schematism of sensations and intention himself. He gives credit to Brentano for discovering the concept of a specifically intentional moment in our experience, and although Bretano's concept had to be modified by Husserl, it is the basis for his distinction between intentional and non-intentional, sensory moments.[2] Furthermore, the schema

---

[1] Cf. Rudolf Boehm, "Deux points de vue: Husserl et Nietzsche," *Archivio di Filisofia*, 3 (1962), p. 174: "C'est ce phénomène d'"interpretation' d'un 'contenu sensible' dans et par une 'perception' qui forme le noeud du problème husserlien de la constitution d'objets."

[2] Cf. *Log. Unt.*, pp. 346-50; 2nd ed., II, 1, pp. 366-70.

was prevalent in psychological and philosophical writings of the period.[1]

Husserl sees a special relationship between the schema and the problem of language. When he attempts to give examples of the way intentionality objectivates by "apprehending" sensations, he says that the clearest case is that of language. "The best examples of all are given us by expressions. Let us suppose, for example, that certain figures or arabesques impressed us first in a purely esthetic way, and that suddenly there dawned on us the understanding that they might be symbols or word signs. Wherein lies the difference?" [2]

We recall that this same problem occupied Husserl in the article he wrote on logic in the year 1894, and in the *Logical Investigations* he makes reference to this article. The answer which he gives here is based on the schematism we have been discussing: "In these and in countless similar cases the modification lies in act-characteristics. All logical distinctions and, especially, all distinctions of categorical form lie in logical acts, in the sense of intentions." [3]

It is easy to see why the problem of language or symbolism provides the clearest paradigm for the schema. The material mark is an excellent example of a brute physical datum, completely devoid of any meaning or reference. The intentionality which informs it bestows an entirely new function upon it and brings to it a dimension which totally surpasses anything the mark has in itself. In this respect, the physical mark is like a

---

[1] An indication of how common this schema was is given by the following definition of *Wahrnehmung* in Rudolf Eisler's *Wörterbuch der philosophischen Begriffe und Ausdrücke* (Berlin: Mittler, 1899): "Die (Sinnes-)Wahrnehmung im engeren Sinne ist schon ein primitiver Denkakt, eine Deutung des Gegebenen als eines Gegenständliches." Cf. also Natorp, *Einleitung in die Psychologie nach kritischer Methode*, p. 63: "Die Deutung der Erscheinungen auf den darin erscheinende Gegenstand, die Objektivierung der Erscheinungen, das *ist* ihre Erklärung; eine andere gibt es nicht." For an extensive use of this schema, and for references to many others who use it, see Carl Stumpf, "Erscheinungen und psychische Funktionen," *Abhandlungen der königlich Preussischen Akademie der Wissenschaften*, 1906, pp. 1-40.

[2] "Die allergünstigsten Beispiele liefern aber die Ausdrücke. Denken wir uns z.B., es hätten gewisse Figuren oder Arabesken zunächst rein ästhetisch auf uns gewirkt, und nun leuchte plötzlich das Verständnis auf, dass es sich um Symbole oder Wortzeichen handeln dürfte. Worin liegt da der Unterschied"? *Log. Unt.*, p. 362; 2nd ed., II, p. 384.

[3] "In diesen und unzähligen ähnlichen Fällen liegt die Modifikation in den Aktcharakteren. Alle logische Unterschiede und zumal alle Unterschiede kategorialer Form liegt in den logischen Akten im Sinne von Intentionen." *ibid.*, p. 363; 2nd ed., II, 1, p. 384 (with slight changes).

brute sensation which in itself is likewise devoid of sense or reference until informed by intentional apprehension.

Husserl begins his *Logical Investigations* with an analysis of language, and he uses language as a way of defining what he means by sense and reference. Could his schematism of intention and sensation come from his reflection on the function of language? This is conceivable, but the fact that the schema is so prevalent in the psychological literature of this period would make us more inclined to put the source of Husserl's schema in this literature, and not specifically in his study of language.

6. *The explanation of the constitution of meaning*

When Husserl says that meaning is constituted by an act of meaning, that the intentional "form" brings meaning and reference to sensations, he thereby gives some indication of a solution to the problem of "the 'sources' out of which the basic concepts and the ideal laws of pure logic arise". [1] Meanings arise in the intentional moment of experience.

Can we clarify this any further, and show with greater precision where meanings arise? An act of meaning cannot be dissected into more basic acts, since it is itself a simple intentional act. It would be possible, however, to speak about the structure of such acts with the hope of finding there a deeper explanation of how meanings are constituted. This is what Husserl does, but without success.

The factors which enter into consideration are the quality and material of acts. Where do meanings fit in this structure? At first glance, it would seem most appropriate to equate them with the material of acts, since it is the component which determines the sense or aspect under which we consider an object. "Hence one might even be inclined (and I hesitated myself for a long time on this point) to define meaning precisely as this 'material'...." [2] Husserl rejects this possibility, however, since he feels that the act-quality also enters into the meaning constituted in an act: "But this would have the disadvantage that,

---

[1] "die 'Quellen,' aus denen die Grundbegriffe und die ideale Gesetze der reinen Logik 'entspringen'." *ibid.*, p. 4; 2nd ed., II, 1, p. 3.

[2] "Daher könnte man sogar geneigt sein (und ich selbst habe in diesem Punkte lange geschwankt), die Bedeutung geradezu als diese 'Materie' zu definieren...." *ibid.*, p. 559; 2nd ed., II, 2, p. 87.

in a statement of predication for example, the moment of actual assertion would be excluded from the meaning." [1] Thus it is not enough to place meaning in the act-material. The quality of acts also deposits a sense in the complete meaning, and to account for the full meaning, we must appeal to both material and quality.

In saying that meanings arise in both the quality and material of acts, Husserl has not really advanced his argument beyond what he already asserts through his schematism, where the meaning is said to arise when an intentional moment animates sensations. In objectivating acts, the quality and material taken together are equivalent to such an intentional moment. Meaningfulness resides in the intention alone and not in the sensations as such; Husserl's analysis says no more than this.

7. *Limitations in Husserl's explanation of the constitution of meaning*

Husserl's explanation for the constitution of meanings is severely limited. He declares that meanings arise when sensations are objectivated by an intention; this serves to locate meanings in the structure of intentionality, but it does nothing to explain how they arise in that structure. Meanings are simply there, but their origins are not explained. They are posited as ready-made in the intention.

Perception would be the logical place to look for a further explanation of the origins of meanings, but Husserl does not investigate it with this problem in mind. When he treats perception, it is only to show how meanings (which are already constituted in an intention) can be recognized or filled in a real object. He does not raise the question of how they can be discovered in perception.[2] Husserl's problematic demands an explanation of this, for he has set out to explain the origins of meanings, not simply to locate the element in intentionality where they can be found. His study of reason and reality in the *Ideas* will partially satisfy this need, but not until he introduces genetic

---

[1] "was aber die Unzuträglichkeit hätte, dass z.B. in der prädizierenden Aussage das Moment des aktuellen Behauptens von der Bedeutung ausgeschlossen wäre." *ibid.*

[2] Cf. *ibid.*, pp. 504-508; 2nd ed., II, 2, pp. 32-36.

constitution will he have a framework in which it can be satisfied more completely.

In addition, Husserl's analysis is purely formal. No attempt is made to show how one meaning can differ from another. His descriptions hold for meanings in general, and he does not explain in any way the contents proper to specific types of meanings. Such contents must be simply accepted as a given fact in subjectivity. Why they arise in this or that form, and how they can differ from one another (how the meaning of "animal" differs from that of "tree," how "color" differs from "extension" and "stone" or "house"), cannot be discovered from the analysis of intentional acts given in the *Logical Investigations*.

8. *Constitution of objects of reference*

Constitution of meaning always implies constitution of an object of reference. But such objects, claims Husserl, are not made present to us with no activity on our part. They depend on us in a certain way. We must actively carry out certain intentions if we are to become aware of them, just as we must perform intentional acts to allow meanings to arise. A subjective performance is required for them to become objects of our intention. "Objects that we are 'conscious' of are not simply there in our consciousness as though in a box, so that one could simply find them there and reach for them. Rather they are only constituted in various forms of objective intention, as that which they are and that which they signify for us." [1] It can be said that intentionality establishes its own objects of reference. By subjective activity, it constitutes an object.

The activity that brings such objective reference about is the objectivation of sense data by intentions. The dualistic schema functions for the constitution of objects of reference in the same way as it operates for the origin of meanings. Objectivation comes from the intentional moment, not from sensations.

In the specific case of perception of material things, however,

---

[1] "...[dass] Gegenstände, die uns 'bewusst' werden, nicht im Bewusstsein als wie in einer Schachtel einfach da sind, dass man die darin bloss vorfinden und nach ihnen greifen könnte; sondern dass sie sich in verschiedenen Formen gegenständlicher Intention als das, was sie uns sind und gelten, allererst konstituieren." *ibid.*, p. 164; 2nd ed., II, 1, p. 165.

Husserl gives something more to explain the constitution of objects. In these acts, the object is constituted not only as intended, but as given. How does this come about? To give a more accurate explanation, Husserl cannot break down the act of perception into more fundamental acts, because perception is a simple, uncomposed act.[1] However, the act is not simple in every respect; it is formed out of a series of what Husserl calls "partial intentions" which coalesce to form a simple act.[2] For instance, when I look at a box, my attention may wander from one side to another, from the shape to the color and back again, from one shade of color to the other, and so forth. All this takes a certain period of time, and involves a continuous change of the sensory contents, the representants, that carry my intentional act of perception. Throughout the whole period of time and throughout the continuous flux of such partial intentions, my attention is fixed on the same single object, this box. All the partial intentions combine into the synthesis of a single, temporally extended intentional act, and through this act the object is constituted as given. An act is the sum of a series of partial intentions. None of the partial intentions is an act by itself, but it is a more fundamental unit into which an act can be analyzed.

Furthermore, as a correlate to the flow of partial intentions, there is a continuum of aspects or profiles on the part of the object. Through the synthesis of these aspects, the object is constituted as really present to consciousness.

Husserl does not develop this inquiry any further, since his only reason for introducing it is to show how such perception differs from categorical constitution. Enough is said, however, to show that the constitution of perceived objects is a *process* carried out in intentionality, and some indication of what this process consists in (the synthesis of partial intentions) is given. Husserl's explanation of such constitution goes beyond simple structural analysis, therefore. Constitution is the result of an intentional process, and not simply the result of the presence of a structural element, apprehension, in intentionality.

---

[1] Cf. *ibid.*, p. 618; 2nd ed., II, 2, p. 146: "Sinnliche Gegenstände sind in der Wahrnemung in einer Aktstufe da...."
[2] Cf. *ibid.*, pp. 619-21; 2nd ed., II, 2, pp. 147-49.

9. *Sensory content and the constitution of meaning*

We have seen that Husserl gives sense data a central function in intentionality. Every concrete intentional act must have sensations as a component part. He even goes farther and says that sensations serve as the "raw materials" out of which the content, the meaning and object of reference, of acts is formed: "Phenomenological analysis also teaches that the content of sensations furnishes an analogous building material, so to speak, for the content of the object presented through it." [1] Sense data, "interpreted" or "apprehended" by intention, thus enter into the constitution of the meanings carried by acts. And yet, to what extent does the sensory content actually determine what is constituted? Does it modify the meaning and object constituted by the intentional act? Do changes in the sensory content imply changes in the meaning or object referred to?

Such questions arise because Husserl distinguishes so radically between sense data and the intentions that animate them. "I can find nothing more evident than the distinction appearing here between contents and acts; more exactly, between perception-contents in the sense of the representing sensations, and perception-acts in the sense of the apprehending intentions...." [2] The basis for this distinction lies in the fact that in a given act, the same meaning and referatum can be maintained while the sensory data change.[3] Husserl gives the familiar example of perceiving a material thing: the object may be in motion and present a continually changing series of sensory contents, but I perceive the same thing with the same sense throughout. Or inversely, the same unchanging sensory content can be the carrier for different types of intentional acts. On the basis of a given set of sensory data, for instance those associated with the perception of a brown house, I can "mean" this individual brown house, or this color brown, or even the species "house" or

---

[1] "Die phänomenologische Analyse lehrt auch, dass der Inhalt der Empfindung sozusagen ein analogisches Baumaterial abgibt für den Inhalt des durch sie vorgestellten Gegenstandes." *ibid.*, p. 75; 2nd ed., II, 1, p. 75.

[2] "Nichts kann ich evidenter finden, als den hierbei hervortretenden Unterschied zwischen Inhalten und Akten, spezieller, zwischen Wahrnehmungsinhalten im Sinne von präsentierenden Empfindungen und Wahrnehmungsakten im Sinn der auffassenden Intention...." *ibid.*, p. 362; 2nd ed., II, 1, p. 383.

[3] Cf. *ibid.*, p. 361; 2nd ed., II, 1, p. 382.

"brown." "In one case the appearance is the presentation-basis for an act of intending an individual. . . . In the other case it is the presentation-basis for an act of intending a species; . . . we do not intend this red moment inherent in the house, but redness." [1]

This distinction between sensory content and act does not present any serious difficulty in the case of symbolic intentional acts, because the sensory content is only used as a sign. It seems clear that the initiative in determining the meaning and the object meant lies on the side of the act. For such intentional acts, constitution is practically indifferent to what sensory contents function in them; what is constituted is determined primarily by the intentional essence.

But is the same true of acts of perception? Husserl's remarks about a meaning that stays the same while sensory data change (or vice versa: a changing meaning in permanent sense data) seem to imply a certain independence of meaning from sensory content. Wittgenstein expresses this same phenomenon very well: "And what does 'pointing to the shape,' 'pointing to the color' consist in? Point to a piece of paper. – And now point to its shape – now to its color – now to its number (that sounds queer). – How did you do it? – You will say that you 'meant' a different thing each time you pointed. And if I ask how that is done, you will say you concentrated your attention on the color, the shape, etc. But I ask again: how is *that* done?" [2] Husserl would agree, with Wittgenstein, that a given set of sensory data can be the basis of many different "perceptions," each carrying a different meaning.

Still, Husserl also says that in perception the meaning is not completely independent of sense data. "It is quite different in the case of purely intuitive representation. Here there is an internal, necessary connection between the material and the representant, a connection determined by the specific content of

[1] "Das eine Mal ist die Erscheinung die Vorstellungsgrundlage für einen Akt individuellen Meinens. . . . Das andere Mal ist sie Vorstellungsgrundlage für einen Akt spezialisierenden Meinens; . . . wir meinen nicht dieses Rotmoment am Hause, sondern das Rot." *ibid.*, p. 109; 2nd ed., II, 1, p. 109.

[2] *Philosophical Investigations*, trans. by G.E.M. Anscombe (Oxford: Blackwell, 1958), p. 16.

each." [1] Sensory data, in this passage, are said to determine the content of the meaning of perceptual acts.[2]

However, they do not determine it completely. Within certain limits, they permit determination to be carried out by the act. "In simple intuition, apprehension-sense (material) and representants were indeed internally united, they were related to one another and were not independent even in their variations. Still, they could undergo ample modifications towards one another." [3] On the basis of a given set of sensory data, only certain constitutions are possible, therefore, because the data determine the meanings to a certain degree.

Husserl does not develop this point any further in the *Investigations*. As it stands, his analysis of the role played by sense data in constitution is useful, because it indicates another factor to be considered in the constitution of meanings and outlines roughly the extent to which this factor operates. But it is far from exhaustive. It would be good to be told more precisely how far meanings are determined, respectively, by sense data and by intentional acts. Still more important would be an explanation of how sensations *can* determine meanings, which until this point had been considered the prerogative of the intentional essence of acts. The problem of sense data and constitution will reappear in the *Ideas* and will be treated somewhat more completely there, but the basic difficulty, how it is possible for sense

---

[1] "Ganz anders im Fall der rein intuitiven Repräsentation. Hier besteht ein innerer, notwendiger Zusammenhang zwischen der Materie und dem Repräsentanten, durch den spezifischen Gehalt der beiden bestimmt." *Log. Unt.*, p. 564; 2nd ed., II, 2, p. 92.

[2] Cf. Emmanuel Levinas, "Réflexions sur la technique phénoménologique," in *Husserl*, Cahiers de Royaumont, Philosophie III, p. 102: "La sensibilité n'est pas considérée comme simple matière brutalement donnée à laquelle s'applique une spontanéité de pensée soit pour l'informer, soit pour en dégager, par abstraction, des relations. Elle ne désigne pas la part de la réceptivité dans la spontanéité objectivante. Elle n'apparaît pas comme pensée balbutiante vouée à l'erreur et à l'illusion, ni comme tremplin de la connaissance rationelle.... La façon nouvelle de traiter la sensibilité consiste à lui conférer dans son obtusité même, et dans son épaisseur, une signification et une sagesse propres et une espèce d'intentionalité. Les sens ont un sens." What Levinas says can be applied without difficulty to the place of sensations in genetic constitution, but the matter is not so clear in Husserl's earlier doctrine. We have seen many passages where Husserl says precisely that sensations, in themselves, have no intentionality whatsoever, and that they serve as the brute matter to be informed by intentions.

[3] "Bei den schlichten Anschauungen waren zwar Auffassungssinn (Materie) und Repräsentant innig vereint, sie waren aufeinander bezogen und in ihren Variationen auch nicht ganz unabhängig; aber dabei konnten sie doch gegeneinander reichliche Verschiebungen erfahren." *Log. Unt.*, pp. 640-41; 2nd ed., II, 2, pp. 168-69.

data to function in the constitution ot meanings, will persist until Husserl looks at it under a new light in the context of genetic constitution. This occurs only in the period after *Ideas*.

10. *Categorical objects are constituted in categorical acts*

Husserl considers the first five of his *Logical Investigations* as preliminary studies for the sixth, in which the work reaches its apex. Within the sixth investigation itself, the second section is described as the main part; this is the section that describes categorical constitution.[1] The culmination of the *Investigations* at this point shows the importance that the constitution of categorical objects has for the problem this book was supposed to treat, the question of the basic components of pure logic and their sources.

What is a categorical object? It is possible to perceive a real, concrete object, such as an ordinary material thing. I can see the Matterhorn, or this tree. It is also possible, says Husserl, to perceive objects like a relationship; I can see that the Matterhorn is higher than Zermatt, or that this tree is next to that rock. Husserl calls the relationship, "The Matterhorn is higher than Zermatt," a categorical object. In general, a categorical object is what results from the union of a logical form with an ordinary object or objects. If real things or simple objects are said to be first-order objects, then categorical ones can be called second-order or, in general, higher-order objects.[2] "The Matterhorn" and "Zermatt" are names of first-order objects, while "The Matterhorn is southwest of Zermatt," is the name of a higher-order, categorical object, resulting from the union of a categorical form (relation) with first-order objects. Other categorical objects that Husserl discusses are conjunctions, disjunctions, universals, identity relationships, numbers, classes, states of affairs, and groups.[3] All are fashioned by first-order objects determined by a logical form.

Categorical objects are similar to what Husserl calls "concrete phenomena" in the *Philosophy of Arithmetic,* a term which he applies to groups, psychic relationships, the concept "something,"

---

[1] Husserl calls this section the *Hauptstock; ibid.*, p. 478; 2nd ed., II, 2, p. 6.
[2] Cf. *ibid.*, p. 619; 2nd ed., II, 2, p. 147.
[3] Cf. *ibid.*, pp. 615, 631, 633; 2nd ed., II, 2, pp. 143, 159, 161.

and so forth. Like concrete phenomena, categorical objects are not abstractions, nor are they simply logical forms. They are what results from concrete realization of such forms. A categorical object is an individual, concrete, complex object.

Like meanings, categorical objects have an ideal objectivity and identity. Once one is constituted, it can be repeated and perceived many times, but it remains identically the same object throughout all its repetitions. Categorical objects do not have the same ontic status as things in the world, but they do have an objectivity that we must recognize and account for.

Husserl accounts for categorical objects by the process of constitution. "When new acts of conjunction, disjunction, determined or undetermined conception of individuals (this – something), generalization, acts of simple knowledge, of relating and connecting knowledge appear, there arise then ... acts which... constitute new objectivities. There arise acts in which something appears as real and given in itself; and in such a way that what appears here was not given, and could not have been given, in the founding acts alone." [1] A new object, the categorical object, appears in categorical acts. It is constituted by them. The categorical object expressed by the words, "The Matterhorn is higher than Zermatt," comes into being when the act that compares the two is performed.

It is therefore misleading to say that a categorical object results from the *application* of a logical form to first-order objects, as though the form existed first and then was placed on them. Instead, all we have to begin with are the first-order objects. An operation is carried out on them which results in a new, higher-order object and, if we wish, we can abstract the logical form from this new object. The logical form is like the trace of the operation performed on first-order objects; it comes at the end of the process, not at the beginning. It arises in or is constituted by our intentional activity.

The problem of categorical constitution is much more ex-

---

[1] "Indem sich die neuen Akte der Konjunktion, der Disjunktion, der bestimmten und unbestimmten Einzelauffassung (das – etwas), der Generalisation, des schlichten, beziehenden und verknüpfenden Erkennens einstellen, erstehen damit...Akte, welche ...neue Objektivitäten konstituieren; es erstehen Akte, in denen etwas als wirklich und als selbst gegeben erscheint, derart dass dasselbe, als was es hier erscheint, in den fundierenden Akten allein noch nicht gegeben war und gegeben sein konnte." *ibid.*, p. 618; 2nd ed., II, 2, p. 146.

plicitly treated in the *Investigations* than is the constitution of meaning and reference. The term "constitution" itself appears frequently in this context, and Husserl gives a thorough analysis of how the constitution of categorical objects is achieved.[1]

11. Description of categorical constitution

Husserl's description of categorical constitution amounts to showing how categorical acts are built up on the basis of acts of simple perception, and how, consequently, categorical objects are built up on the basis of objects of simple perception.

Acts of simple perception are defined as those in which no logical form is present; they are "form-less" acts. Their prototype, says Husserl, are acts whose objects are expressed by a proper name, such as "Cologne" or "Rover." [2] In such acts, I mean and perceive the individual just as it is, without any qualifications. Categorical acts and their objects are built upon simple perceptions and their objects, and hence are called "founded"; simple perceptions and their objects are called, correlatively, "founding."

Husserl's description of categorical constitution begins by supposing an act of simple perception directed towards a thing.[3] We have already seen that such an act of simple perception is the synthesis of a continuum of partial intentions; my attention, although fixed on the same object, moves from one aspect of the thing to the other, from the color to the shape to the texture, etc.

Suppose that a categorical act now comes into play. Husserl describes the process in three stages, which we indicate by adding numerals to the following quotation:

(1) An act of perception grasps *A* as a whole, in one stroke and in a simple way. (2) A second act of perception focuses on *a*, the part or the dependent moment which belongs constitutively to *A*. These two acts however are not simply carried out, at the same time or in succession, after the manner of "unconnected" experiences, but rather (3) they tie themselves together into one act, in whose synthesis *A* first appears as having *a* in itself.[4]

---

[1] Cf. *ibid.*, pp. 622, 626, 628, 653; 2nd ed., II, 2, pp. 150, 154, 156, 161, 181, etc.

[2] Cf, *ibid.*. p. 602; 2nd ed., II, 2, p. 130.

[3] Cf. *ibid.*, pp. 619-21; 2nd ed., II, 2, pp. 147-49.

[4] "(1) Ein wahrnehmender Akt erfasst *A* als ein Ganzes, in einem Schlage und in schlichter Weise. (2) Ein zweiter Wahrnehmungsakt richtet sich auf das *a*, den Teil oder das unselbständige Moment, das dem *A* konstitutiv gehört. Diese zwei Akte vollziehen sich aber nicht bloss zugleich oder nacheinander in der Weise 'zusammen-

Thus we have three stages. First there is the simple sensory perception of a thing *A* (a box, for example). Secondly, one of the partial intentions in the original act (the partial intention directed at *a*) develops into an act of perception in its own right. It is no longer a partial intention in the original synthesis; it becomes a complete act itself. In our example, let us suppose the new perception focuses on the red color of the box. This new act does not break off entirely from the total act whence it originated; rather I realize, says Husserl, that the content of this new act of perception coincides with the content of the partial intention we started with.[1] Now the third step takes place. A third act is performed in which the two objects of perception are united, and the box is presented as being red. The third, synthesizing act is expressed in the statement, "This box is red." The categorical object, the state of affairs, is constituted in this synthesizing, categorical act.

In this way Husserl describes how categorical acts are performed, and how they are founded on lower-order sensory acts of perception. What is described here in the case of judgments can easily be transferred to the case of relationships and other categorical forms.[2] Although the description of categorical constitution given in the *Investigations* is sketchy, it gives the essentials of what always remained Husserl's way of explaining the process involved in categorical activity. His later analyses, although richer in detail and containing some elements neglected in the *Investigations*, such as the role of time and modalities, follow the pattern developed in the *Investigations* very closely.[3]

This description, furthermore, depicts a *process*. Categorical constitution is a process, just like the constitution effected in perception. Thus we now have two instances of constitution in the *Logical Investigations* where Husserl goes beyond mere structural analysis and appeals to a performance, an extended activity, carried out by consciousness.

---

hangsloser' Erlebnisse, vielmehr (3) knüpfen sie sich zu einem Akt zusammen, in dessen Synthesis das *A* erst als das *a* in sich habend erscheint." *ibid.*, p. 625; 2nd ed., II, 2, p. 153 (with slight changes).

[1] Husserl uses the expression *sich decken; ibid.*, p. 626; 2nd ed., II, 2, p. 154.

[2] Cf. *ibid.*, pp. 631-36; 2nd ed., II, 2, pp. 159-64.

[3] For example, see *Erfahrung und Urteil*, compiled and edited by L. Landgrebe (Hamburg: Claassen, 1954), pp. 242-55.

12. The intentional structure of categorical acts

The description of the process of categorical constitution has not made use of the dualistic schema of apprehension and sensation. No mention of it has been made. When Husserl begins to study the structure of categorical acts, however, he returns to his schematism and tries to impose it on such acts in order to explain the objectivity of categorical objects.

Husserl stresses their objectivity. Like real things in the world, they can be perceived. It makes sense for us to say not only that we perceive this paper or this house, but also that we perceive that this house is white, or that this paper is next to that book. The objects of our perception in the latter instances are states of affairs. They are the categorical objects expressed by the words, "This house is white," or "This paper is next to this book." [1] Thus categorical objects are, in this respect, similar to the groups and psychic relations described in the *Philosophy of Arithmetic*.

The acts in which categorical objects are constituted are also the acts in which they are perceived. Husserl speaks of them as objects "which are constituted directly only in founded acts of the type we have mentioned. That is, they can come 'themselves' to perception only in acts built up in this way." [2] In order to perceive a categorical object, we must perform the act that constitutes it. In order to see the relationship expressed by the terms, "This house is to the side of that tree," I must perform the act of relating that explicitly connects the object "this house" to the other object "that tree." Until I perform such a categorical act, I can perceive only this and that object, but I will not have explicitly and authentically perceived the relationship between them. [3]

Since categorical acts function as acts of perception, they belong to the class of intentional acts and must possess all the elements that Husserl says are found in such acts, namely

---

[1] Cf. *Log. Unt.*, p. 600; 2nd ed., II, 2, p. 128.

[2] "...die sich direkt nur in fundierten Akten der angedeuteten Art konstituieren, d.h. nur in so gebauten Akte 'selbst' zur Wahrnehmung kommen können." *ibid.*, p. 626; 2nd ed., II, 2, p. 154 (with slight changes).

[3] Cf. *ibid.*, p. 305; 2nd ed., II, 1, p. 314: "Wollen wir uns die Bedeutung des Wortes *und* klar machen, so müssen wir irgendeinen Kollektionsakt wirklich vollziehen und in dem so zu eigentlicher Vorstellung kommenden Inbegriff eine Bedeutung der Form *a und b* zur Erfüllung bringen." (Slight changes in 2nd ed.)

quality, material, and representants. Husserl has no difficulty in assigning quality and material to categorical acts; the only difference from their use in ordinary intentional acts is that the material in categorical acts is founded on the material of simple acts, just as the former acts themselves are founded on the latter.[1]

The question of representants or sensory content, however, is much more difficult. The problem is to find some sort of sense datum that will correspond to the categorical form. The categorical object expressed by the words, "This box is red," contains two distinct components: the categorical form, "*A* is *a*," and the first-order units "red" and "box," with which the form is united. The box and the color red have their own ordinary sensory contents, but what is to serve as the sense content, the representant, for the categorical form? What kind of sense datum can it be? It cannot be the same type as that associated with the simple perception of a thing, for if it were, the category would enjoy the same ontic status as things. We would perceive a form in the same way we perceive a material thing. Husserl's earlier analyses show this to be impossible; a categorical, higher-order object is not on the same level as a first-order, sensory object.

Husserl's solution is to place the representants in "the psychic bond which is experienced in actual identifying or collecting, etc."[2] A psychological experience is the sensory carrier of the intentional act directed towards a categorical object. This solution is consistent with Husserl's claim that in order to perceive a categorical object, we must perform the categorical act that constitutes it. The categorical act serves also to synthesize the acts on which it is founded; when actually performed, the synthesizing, constituting act is experienced on the psychic level. As such it can serve as the representant for the form constituted in it.

This answer did not satisfy Husserl, and in the second edition of the *Logical Investigations* he says that he has abandoned it, but he does not give any substitute.[3] For our purposes, the

---

[1] Cf. *ibid.*, p. 638; 2nd ed., II, 2, p. 166.

[2] "das psychische Band, das im aktuellen Identifizieren oder Kolligieren u. dgl. erlebt ist." *ibid.*, p. 645; 2nd ed., II, 2, p. 173.

[3] Cf. *ibid.*, 2nd ed., II, 2, p. v.

importance of his treatment of representants in the first edition is to show to what extent Husserl felt that his general theory of intentional structure was valid for all intentional acts, categorical ones included. It shows also to what extent Husserl felt that his schema of apprehension and sense content was absolutely necessary for the constitution of objectivity. In trying to find representants for categorical objects, Husserl is simply trying to force his schema on their constitution. He is so convinced that any objectivity we encounter can only be accounted for by the dualistic schema "apprehension-sensation," that he construes a way in which to fit this schema into our constitution of categorical objects.

The analysis which he gives for categorical constitution is the description of a process and as such it is essentially different from a static structural description. However, Husserl's concept of constitution is so intrinsically linked to his static schema that he feels that the process of constitution is not enough. The schema has to be introduced also in order to account for the objectivity of categorical objects. The schematism will be abandoned only gradually as Husserl expands his phenomenology, but only when he reaches genetic constitution will it be definitely disposed of. When this occurs, the concept of constitution as the result of a process will prevail, but in *Logical Investigations*, the idea of a process is entirely subordinated to his structural schema of apprehension and sense data.

13. Conclusion

In the *Logical Investigations*, the constitution of objectivity is always explained in function of a schematism: objectivity arises when sensations are apprehended (interpreted, animated) by intentions. Both objective meanings and objects of reference are constituted by the intentional, apprehending moment.

Constitution of categorical objects is also said to take place in intentional, categorical acts, but Husserl gives more of an explanation for them than he does for ordinary objectivating acts. In addition to the structural analysis, which holds even for categorical acts, he also describes the process which leads to the formation of such acts. He shows how they are founded on lower-order acts of simple perception. He shows how we are motivated, on the basis of what is given to us in simple acts, to form higher acts which in turn constitute complex, categorical objects. Since we are given an account of the process yielding categorical acts, we can "understand" more completely how categorical objects are constituted. In this sense, the constitution of categorical objects is more exhaustively explained than the constitution of meanings.

This is to be expected, since categorical acts are composite acts and lend themselves to an explanation that would show how they are formed out of more simple constituents. Since first-order acts are simple, there can be no possibility of explaining them in terms of more basic acts. However, there is a sense in which the "deeper" understanding we have of categorical constitution is illusory, for it is ultimately based on what we know about acts of simple constitution. Explanation of categorical constitution amounts to showing how categorical acts arise from simple intentional acts; hence whatever difficulties exist in our understanding of simple constitution remain as problems in categorical constitution. When the problem of categorical constitution is pushed to its ultimate elements, the same difficulties arise as exist in simple constitution.

Furthermore, the explanation of categorical objects by means of a process does not satisfy Husserl, for he tries to impose the schematism of apprehension and sense data on categorical acts. This is done to guarantee the objectivity of categorical objects. The constitution of objectivity, in the *Logical Investigations*, can be explained only by the use of the schema.

The schematism applies also to objects constituted in perception, but as in the case of categorical objects, this explanation is supplemented by description of a process, a synthesis of partial intentions. In neither instance, however, does Husserl replace his schematism with the concept of a constitutional process. The schema dominates his concept of constitution.

Husserl's structural explanation of meanings, which shows that they arise within the intentional essence of acts, suffices to locate meanings within acts, but it does not show how they arise, how they are constituted, within intentionality. Throughout his investigations, Husserl always supposes meanings as already given. In Husserl's later terminology, what the *Investigations* fail to provide is an account of the establishment (*Urstiftung*) of meaning, its original constitution.

A remedy for these difficulties might be found in showing how meanings arise from perception. However, Husserl's entire theory of perception is elaborated to show how meanings find their fulfillment in acts of perceiving. He always supposes that meanings are already constituted and shows how perception can, in various degrees of completeness, "fill" the meanings that are otherwise only intended. The argument always goes from meanings to their fulfillment in perception; a study in the opposite direction, from perception to the formation of meanings, would correct this weakness in the explanation of intentional constitution. Husserl's studies of reason and reality in the *Ideas* will partially satisfy this need.

Even in the *Investigations*, some elements towards a study of this sort are provided in what Husserl says about the function of sensory contents in the determination of meaning. Intentionality is not completely free in forming meanings in acts of perception. The sensory data it animates impose certain limits on which meanings can be constituted, and it seems that if we are to look for a more fundamental explanation of intentional constitution, it would be found in the sphere of sensibility. Sensory contents could be to simple constitution what simple intentionality is to categorical constitution: the more rudimentary level of experience where an explanation of constitution is to be found. Husserl's later works do investigate sensations with this in mind. The *Logical Investigations* do not probe very deeply into sensory experience as a foundation for intentional constitution, but the general indications given of its place in the structure of intentionality make such further inquiries possible.

CHAPTER III

THE CONSTITUTION PERFORMED
BY INNER TIME

1. The object of Husserl's lectures on time

The problem of time as a characteristic both of consciousness and of things known is only peripherally treated in the first two published works of Husserl.[1] Shortly after he wrote the *Logical Investigations*, however, he devoted an important part of his lectures for the winter semester of 1904-05 at Göttingen to the phenomenology of our consciousness of inner time. In these lectures, a transcription of which was published by Heidegger in 1928, he treats both the temporality of consciousness and our consciousness of time.[2]

To mark out the subject matter of his inquiry, Husserl makes some statements that foreshadow the phenomenological reduction of his later thought. He says, "We deal with reality only insofar as it is meant, presented, looked at, or conceptually thought of. Regarding the problem of time, this means: time experiences interest us." [3] Husserl will study time not as a reality, but as a phenomenon. His descriptions are concerned with how we experience time, how it is manifest in our consciousness. Time as an objective reality apart from us is not accessible to phenomenological study: "Just as the real thing, the real

---

[1] In the *Philosophy of Arithmetic*, temporality is considered as the basis for acts which form numbers and groups (supra, pp. 24-25). In the *Logical Investigations*, Husserl speaks of acts of perception that endure over a period of time and are composed of a series of partial intentions; in the second edition (II, 1, p. 259), he has an interesting passage describing the temporal extension of subjectivity, but it is not present in the first edition (pp. 252-53).

[2] *Vorlesungen zur Phänomenologie des inneren Zeitbewusstseins*, edited by M. Heidegger (Halle a. S.: Max Niemeyer, 1928). Textual problems concerning this edition are very great. Not only the appendices, but also the main text itself underwent modifications until the year 1917. Cf. Rudolf Boehm, "Deux points de vue: Husserl et Nietzsche," p. 174, n. 26.

[3] "Mit der Wirklichkeit haben wir es nur zu tun, sofern sie gemeinte, vorgestellte, angeschaute, begrifflich gedacht ist. Bezüglich des Zeitproblems heisst das: die Zeiterlebnisse interessieren uns." *Zeitbewusstsein*, pp. 373-74.

world, is not a phenomenological datum, so the world time, the
real time, the time of nature, is not one either. . . ." [1] But although
objective time is not reached by phenomenological reflection,
such reflection does attain the subjective experiences in which
time appears to us. "Time apprehensions, the experiences in which
the temporal in the objective sense appears, are phenomenological data." [2]

Although these statements comprise a sort of reduction, they
are an awkward expression of it in comparison to what Husserl
says later. The way he speaks here seems to imply that there
are two realities: the reality that is a phenomenon meant or intended by consciousness, and the reality that "really" exists.[3]
Such a distinction would not be made in the formulation of the
reduction found in *Ideas*, where the reality that is perceived in
intentionality is precisely the real world. But if we are aware of
this discrepancy and make an adjustment for it, the studies of
time found in Husserl's lectures can easily be accommodated
to fit the more definitive view of *Ideas*.[4]

After marking out the subject of his inquiry, what does Husserl propose to do with it? He intends to give a rigorous description of our experience of time as it becomes accessible to the
phenomenologist, and thus to provide us with an explanation of
the "essence" of time.[5] More fundamentally, he continues, such
a description will reveal to us the "sources" or "origins" of time.

---

[1] "So wie das wirkliche Ding, die wirkliche Welt kein phänomenologisches Datum
ist, so ist es auch nicht die Weltzeit, die reale Zeit, die Zeit der Natur..." *ibid.*, p. 369.
[2] "Phänomenologische Data sind die Zeitauffassungen, die Erlebnisse, in denen
Zeitliches im objektiven Sinne erscheint." *ibid.*, p. 370.
[3] The supposition of two realities is even more pronounced in the following text,
ibid., p. 369: "Es mag ferner eine interessante Untersuchung sein, festzustellen, wie
die Zeit, die in einem Zeitbewusstsein als objektive gesetzt ist, sich zur wirklichen
objektiven Zeit verhalte, ob die Schätzungen von Zeitintervallen den objektiv
wirklichen Zeitintervallen entsprechen, oder wie sie von ihnen abweichen. Aber das
sind keine Aufgaben der Phänomenologie."
[4] What saves Husserl's analyses in the lectures on time and makes them a-
daptable to his later studies is the fact that he considers only phenomenal time, even
though he seems to admit that another sort of time can exist. Later he will say that
only phenomenal time is real; the only effect this change has on the lectures is to
wipe away the possibility of real but non-phenomenal time. The investigations
themselves are not affected.
[5] Cf. *ibid.*, p. 373. "Die erkenntnistheoretische Frage nach der Möglichkeit der
Erfahrung (die zugleich die Frage nach dem Wesen der Erfahrung ist) erfordert den
Rückgang zu den phänomenologischen Daten, aus denen das Erfahrene phänomenologisch besteht."

"Accordingly, the question into the essence of time leads back to the question into the 'origin' of time."[1]

In formulating his aim in such terms, Husserl adheres to the methodology already followed in his *Logical Investigations* and *Philosophy of Arithmetic*, for in these works he sets out to determine the origins, respectively, of logical entities and arithmetical concepts. In the lectures, he gives us an explanation of what he means by a probe into the origins of time: "This question of origins is directed towards the primitive forms of time consciousness, in which the primitive differences of the temporal constitute themselves, intuitively and authentically, as the originary sources of all evidences related to time."[2] His inquiry into sources will thus try to determine and describe those fundamental states of consciousness in which the primitive distinctions involved in time first manifest themselves. Husserl will examine those elements of our experience where the most basic temporal distinctions are revealed to us, and where the primitive structure of time is first formed.[3] Our experience of time is composed of many varied aspects or elements which allow us to make many temporal distinctions. By showing such distinctions in their most fundamental, primitive occurrence, we clarify them phenomenologically. Our complex, evolved experience of time will thus be explained, promises Husserl, because we will know the basic and irreducible elements which go to make it up.

The problem of constitution in the lectures on time is best seen in the perspective of the search for the origins of time. The manner in which complex experience of time arises from the simple, basic temporal elements is to be considered the constitution of such complex experience. For example, the extended history of an individual subject is constituted in function of the

[1] "Demgemäss führt auch die Frage nach dem Wesen der Zeit zurück auf die Frage nach dem 'Ursprung' der Zeit." *ibid.*, p. 373.

[2] "Diese Ursprungsfrage ist aber auf die primitiven Gestaltungen des Zeitbewusstseins gerichtet, in denen die primitiven Differenzen des Zeitlichen sich intuitiv und eigentlich als die originären Quellen aller auf Zeit bezüglichen Evidenzen konstituieren." *ibid.*, p. 373.

[3] Cf. Ludwig Landgrebe, "Husserls Phänomenologie und die Motive zu ihrer Umbildung," p. 296: "In den Husserlschen Untersuchungen dagegen ist von vornherein eine ganz andere Frage gestellt, nämlich: wie kommen wir überhaupt dazu, etwas als zeitlich dauernd, zeitlich erstreckt zu empfinden, rein in sich selbst und nicht in bezug auf ein anderes? Irgendwo muss ja dieser Eindruck von Zeitdauer und von Verfliessen von Zeit ursprünglich entstehen, damit uns überhaupt solches gegeben werden kann, was auf seine Dauer hin messbar und vergleichbar ist...."

simple, primitive structure of the present moment taken together with its retention and protention. By showing how the complex history of a consciousness can be derived from the primitive elements of time, Husserl will explain how such a history can be temporally constituted. Likewise, the way in which temporal objects arise in our consciousness is described as the constitution of such objects out of primitive termporal elements and structures.

2. Time and objects in time. Various levels of temporality

Since time is always associated with objects that are "in" time, Husserl's studies must deal with our knowledge of temporal objects.[1] The objects in question will be both transcendent and immanent, both things "outside" subjectivity and sensations and intentional acts "within" it.[2] Each type of object will have its own sort of time associated with it. Transcendent things are in objective time, immanent objects are in inner time.

As the title of Husserl's lectures indicates, the main part of his investigations is directed towards the problem of inner time; consequently he is forced to treat extensively of immanent objects and their function in knowledge. As we shall see later in more detail, immanent objects are sensations and intentions. Their function in consciousness is a central theme in the lectures on time, so that Husserl's study of time becomes a decisive chapter in his theory of sensations and intentional acts.

The importance that these studies have for the problem of constitution as a whole is explicitly acknowledged in Husserl's *Ideas*. Immanent objects, noeses and sensations, are said to constitute objective, noematic reality. But the immanent objects themselves are constituted in inner time. Their temporal constitution is a type of constitution more basic than that which forms reality; it arises from what Husserl calls the "ultimate and true absolute."[3] Thus the ultimate source of all the achievements

---

[1] Cf. *Zeitbewusstsein*, p. 384: "So kann eine phänomenologische Zeitanalyse die Konstitution der Zeit nicht ohne Rücksicht auf die Konstitution der Zeitobjekte aufklären."

[2] "Immanence" is used in the lectures on time with the sense given it in the *Logical Investigations*. It refers to "real" elements in subjectivity as opposed to "transcendent" things in the world. Cf. Rudolf Boehm, "Les ambiguïtés des concepts husserliens d' immanence et de transcendance," *Revue philosophique de la France et de l'étranger*, 84 (1959), pp. 481-492.

[3] "letztes und wahrhaft Absolutes." *Ideen I*, p. 198. On the concept of the abso-

of subjectivity is found in the dimension of inner temporality, and hence the subject we wish to discuss is of fundamental importance for Husserl's entire theory of constitution.

Study of the constitution of immanent objects leads Husserl finally to the problem of the self-constituting stream of consciousness. Although real things are in objective time and immanent objects are in inner time, the self-constituting stream of consciousness itself is not in any sort of time. It is beyond temporality.

We can use Husserl's own words to summarize the three levels of objects and temporality studied in the lectures on time. He distinguishes:

> (1) The things of experience in objective time...
> (2) the constituting appearance-manifolds of various levels, the immanent units in pre-empirical time;
> (3) the absolute, time-constituting stream of consciousness.[1]

In section three, we shall begin with a brief study of how we encounter objective reality and objective time, and return to this subject in sections ten to thirteen. The intervening sections, four to nine, will discuss immanent objects and inner time. The problem of the self-constituting stream of consciousness will fit logically into section eight.

We wish to repeat the remark on terminology which we have made in the Introduction, concerning the distinction between "experience" and "encounter," a distinction which is important in Husserl's lectures on time. "Experience" (*Erlebnis*) refers exclusively to the awareness we have of immanent objects, "encounter" (*Erfahrung*) to our consciousness of external reality.[2]

---

lute, cf. Rudolf Boehm, "Zum Begriff des 'Absoluten' bei Husserl," *Zeitschrift für philosophische Forschung*, 13 (1959), pp. 214-242.

[1] "(1) Die Dinge der Erfahrung in der objektiven Zeit...

(2) die konstituierenden Erscheinungsmannigfaltigkeiten verschiedener Stufe, die immanenten Einheiten in der präempirischen Zeit;

(3) den absoluten zeitkonstituierenden Bewusstseinsfluss." *Zeitbewusstsein*, p. 428.

[2] Although Husserl adheres rigorously to the distinction between experience and perception throughout the body of the lectures, there are some places in the appendices where he confuses them and speaks of "inner perception" to express what he normally calls experiences. Appendix XII is especially faulty on this count. Husserl's slight inconsistency of terminology is noted in: Gunther Eigler, *Meta-physische Voraussetzungen in Husserls Zeitanalysen* (Meisenheim: Anton Hain, 1961), p. 78.

3. Objective time is manifest to consciousness through "time appearances"

The ordinary objects that we perceive in the world are on the first level of temporality. They are in objective time, the time which is measured by clocks and which seems to flow independently of our consciousness.

When we perceive an external object, it presents a series of aspects to us. There occurs, in a single act of perception, a stream of aspects or profiles. According to Husserl's schema for the structure of intentionality, such an aspect continuum has as its counterpart a stream of appearances, of animated sensations, in our act of perceiving. A sensation, animated by intentionality, is the subjective correlate for an objective aspect or profile. "The 'sensed' red is a phenomenological datum which, when animated by a certain apprehension-function, represents an objective quality...."[1] We have seen this in the *Logical Investigations*, where Husserl says that a thing is perceived through a series of "partial intentions," each of which makes possible the appearance of a profile by animating its correlative sensation.

Now just as an immanent "red" sensation can serve as the appearance of an objective red quality, so too can inner time function as an appearance for objective, noematic time, according to Husserl. As a thing appears colored by virtue of color appearances in our subjectivity, so it appears temporal by virtue of what we might call "time appearances." "Time apprehensions, the experiences in which the temporal in the objective sense appears, are phenomenological data."[2] There is something in our subjectivity, inner time, that serves to manifest objective time to us, and Husserl explicitly compares it to the space and color appearances that manifest objective color and space to us.

Time appearances thus have something in common with the ordinary appearances of objective qualities. But Husserl immediately adds that important differences exist. Although time appearances have a function similar to that of other appearances,

[1] "Das empfundene Rot ist ein phänomenologisches Datum, das von einer gewissen Auffassungsfunktion beseelt eine objektive Qualität darstellt...." *Zeitbewusstsein*, p. 371.

[2] "Phänomenologische Data sind die Zeitauffassungen, die Erlebnisse, in denen Zeitliches im objektiven Sinne erscheint." *ibid.*, p. 370. Husserl does not use the term "time appearances," but he does speak of *Temporaldaten, Temporalzeichen*, and an *empfundenes Zeitliches*. Cf. pp. 370-71.

their status is by no means the same. Inner time, the appearance for external time, is prior to all other appearances and makes it possible for us to experience them. Time appearances are not simply juxtaposed with other appearances; rather they make it possible for us to *have* color and texture appearances in our subjectivity. They make it possible for us to experience such appearances. Thus besides functioning to manifest objective time, inner temporality also serves as the structure basic to all inner experience.

We have discovered a strange phenomenological element, time appearances, which are radically different from all other appearances. They manifest objective time to us, but they also serve to make inner experience possible. How can they perform this double function? What can be said about their nature? Let us consider first how they make it possible for us to experience immanent objects.

4. Immanent objects are sensations and intentions

What does Husserl call immanent objects? In his own words, "These immanent contents are experiences, in the usual sense: sensory data, . . . like a red, a blue, etc.; in addition, they are appearances (a house-appearance, appearance of our surroundings, etc.). . . ." [1] We have two immanent objects mentioned in this passage, sense data and appearances. The difference between them is only one of complexity. A red datum and a blue datum are simple units, each correlative to a partial intention in a complete act of perception, whereas a "house-appearance" is complex, made up of many such primal data. The complex appearance is animated or apprehended by the complete, extended act of perception itself. The complete act unites many simple data into a complex whole. "In perception, a complex of sensation-contents, . . . which are themselves units constituted in the originary time flow, undergoes the unity of apprehension." [2]

Our problem centers on simple sense data, the primal sensory

---

[1] "Diese immanenten Inhalte sind die Erlebnisse im gewöhnlichen Sinne: die Empfindungsdaten, . . . etwa ein Rot, ein Blau, und dgl.; ferner die Erscheinungen (Hauserscheinung, Umgebungserscheinung, usw.) . . . ." *ibid.*, p. 437.

[2] "In der Wahrnehmung erfährt ein Komplex von Empfindungsdaten, . . . die selbst im ursprünglichen Zeitfluss konstituierte Einheiten sind, Einheit der Auffassung." *ibid.*, p. 444.

units constituted in the time flow. The first and most fundamental unification comes from the temporal flow, where such
simple sensations (*Urempfindungen*) are constituted. We can
safely disregard complex sensations in our discussion of inner
time, therefore, since they are only complicated formations of
simple sense data.

In his list of immanent objects, Husserl continues, "Then also
the 'acts' of utterance, desiring, willing, etc., and the reproductive modifications that belong to them...."[1] Intentional
acts are also immanent objects. Moreover, as we know from the
Logical Investigations, when we consider an intentional act under
its function of animating sensations, the act can be called an
"apprehension." Apprehensions then must also be constituted as
immanent objects. "As reflection teaches us, the perceptual
apprehension itself, in its own way, is something constituted by
immanent temporality...."[2] An intention, whether considered
as an act or as an apprehension, is an immanent object. Husserl
usually treats it from the point of view of apprehension, but
everything he says about the temporal constitution of apprehensions is applicable to intentional acts as well.

Basically, therefore, we have two immanent objects, sensations
and intentions. In the terminology of the *Ideas*, we would say
"hyletic data" and "noeses." We recognize the two immanent
objects as the two elements in the "matter-form" schema introduced by Husserl in the *Logical Investigations* to express objective
constitution; now Husserl will study how they are themselves
constituted in inner time.

It is important to note, however, that the constitution of acts
is not strictly parallel to constitution of sensations. Even the
most primitive form of sensation, even an indivisible sense datum,
is a constituted object; but only the full, extended intentional
act is so constituted. Its primitive elements, the partial intentions
that make it up, are *not* constituted immanent objects. To stress
this difference, consider the parallelism between acts and the

---

[1] "Sodann die 'Akte' des Aussagens, Wünschens, Wollens, usw. und die zuge-
hörigen reproduktiven Modifikationen...." *ibid.*, p. 437.
[2] "Die Wahrnehmungsauffassung in ihrem Modus ist, wie die Reflexion lehrt,
selbst etwas immanent-zeitlich Konstituiertes...." *ibid.*, p. 443. Cf. p. 473, Beilage
IX:"Ferner ist jeder Auffassungsakt selbst eine konstituierte immanente Dauer-
einheit."

sensations they animate. A full act animates a complex sensation, and both are constituted immanent objects. A partial intention animates a primal sense datum; the sense datum is still constituted as an immanent object, *but the partial intention is not.* What it is will be discussed later.

5. *First elements in an explanation for our experience of immanent objects*

Now that we have found what immanent objects are, what can we say about the way in which we experience them? The general principle is that we know them in a different way from the manner in which we perceive real things. "Immanent units are not known in their constitution in the same way as that which appears in transcendent appearance, or that which is perceived in transcendent perception." [1] We do not "see" our sensations or our acts.

Still, continues Husserl, there must be an analogy in the way both immanent and transcendent objects are known. "On the other hand, they still must have something in common."[2] The similarity consists in this, that immanent objects are constituted and experienced through a *manifold*, just as external objects are. In the case of external objects, it is a manifold of appearances, but in the case of immanent objects it is a manifold of temporal phases. "Immanent units ... constitute themselves in the flow of temporal profile-manifolds." [3] An immanent object is constituted in a series of temporal phases. In the experience of immanent objects, temporal profiles perform the function accomplished by appearances in our knowledge of external objects.

We shall discuss the nature of temporal phases in the next section. For the present let us examine Husserl's claim that the temporal constitution of immanent objects makes it possible for us to experience them.

If we are to be aware of immanent objects, claims Husserl, they must be spread out in a time flow. This is the necessary

[1] "Die immanente Einheiten sind in ihrer Konstitution nicht in derselben Weise bewusst wie in der transzendenten Erscheinung das Erscheinende, in der transzendenten Wahrnehmung das Wahrgenommene." *ibid.*, p. 444.

[2] "Andererseits müssen sie doch eine Gemeinsamkeit des Wesens haben." *ibid.*, p. 444.

[3] "Die immanente Einheiten... konstituieren sich im Fluss der temporalen Abschattungsmannigfaltigkeiten." *ibid.*, p. 444.

structural form that immanent objects must have if they are to be objects of experience, if we are to be conscious of them. "That this identification is possible, that an object is constituted here, depends on the structure of experiences: namely, that each phase of the stream turns into retention 'of,' and that this phase then turns again, etc. *Without this, a content [viz. a sensation] would be inconceivable as experience.* Otherwise an experience, in principle, would not and could not be given as a unit to the subject, and thus would be nothing."[1]

One of the reasons why immanent objects must be extended in time is that such extension gives them individuality and unity, which they must have in order to be experienced. An immanent object is individualized, it is made into a determined, distinct unit, only because it fills a certain section of the time flow, because it is constituted in certain temporal phases. "The [musical] tone point, in its absolute individuality, is held fast as regards its material content and its time location, and the latter first constitutes individuality." [2] Within the sphere of subjectivity, the only factor that identifies an object is its position on a certain section in the flow of inner time. In the sphere of immanent objects, the factors of space, color, texture, and so forth, do not operate to distinguish one object from another, nor to identify one object as a unit. The only relevant factor in immanent experience is time.[3]

These remarks already tell us something about the way inner

[1] "Dass diese Identifizierung möglich ist, dass hier ein Objekt konstituiert ist, das liegt an der Struktur der Erlebnisse: dass nämlich jede Phase des Stromes sich in Retention 'von' wandelt, diese wieder, usw. Ohne das wäre ein Inhalt als Erlebnis nicht denkbar. Erlebnis wäre sonst prinzipiell nicht dem Subjekt als Einheit gegeben und zu geben und wäre somit nichts." *ibid.*, p. 470, Beilage VIII; italics ours.

[2] "Der Tonpunkt in seiner absoluten Individualität wird festgehalten nach Materie und Zeitstelle, welche letztere erst Individualität konstituiert." *ibid.*, p. 422. Cf. also p. 439.

[3] The identification is phenomenological, not ontological. Husserl is not interested in finding an ontological principle of individuation.

It is true that an immanent object, whether act or sensation, can also be identified in relation to the external object it is associated with. We can speak of the act by which we know a certain event. But such identification is extrinsic to the immanent object itself. Within the structure of the immanent object, the only source of individuality is temporal location. Furthermore, even such identification by reference to an external object presupposes a temporal location; for it is not enough to identify an act or sensation by calling it the one associated with a given thing. A thing can be perceived in any number of different acts. Ultimately we identify which act or sensation we mean by stating the time when we perceived the object, and this puts us back in temporal location.

temporality makes experiences possible. Immanent objects must be spread out in time to be experienced, and one reason for this is the fact that only temporal location bestows individuality on immanent objects. To say this much, however, is not enough, for many structural problems remain. We can still ask, how *can* an immanent object be extended in time? And how does temporality account for the difference between perception and inner experience? These are important phenomenological questions, and Husserl tries to answer them. To discuss his answers we must investigate more closely the nature of temporal phases.

6. *Definition of temporal phases*

Immanent objects are constituted in a manifold of temporal profiles. What are these profiles? Concerning apprehension as an immanent object, Husserl says, "It is constituted through the manifold of now-phases and retentions." [1] A series of temporal phases is a series of "nows" and retentions.

Can we go a step farther and define the now-instant and its retentions, and also the protentions which accompany them? It is difficult to give an explicit definition of these concepts because they are basic in Husserl's phenomenology and are not strictly definable in terms of more fundamental elements. They can be described, however; Husserl tries to point them out in our consciousness and thus to give a sort of ostensive definition of them. "But strictly speaking, the now-point itself must be defined through original sensation. . . ." [2] All one can do to explain what a now-instant and its immediate retentions are is to indicate how we are aware of them. [3]

[1] "Es ist konstituiert durch die Mannigfaltigkeit von Jetztphasen und Retentionen." *ibid.*, p. 443.
[2] "Aber eigentlich ist der Jetztpunkt selbst durch die ursprüngliche Empfindung zu definieren. . . ." *ibid.*, p. 423.
[3] Cf. *ibid.*, p. 432: "Man kann da weiter nichts sagen als 'siehe': eine Urempfindung oder eine Gruppe von Urempfindungen, die ein immanentes Jetzt bewusst hat . . . wandelt sich stetig in Modi des Vorhinbewusstseins, in dem das immanente Objekt als vergangen bewusst ist . . . ."
Cf. Walter Bröcker, "Husserls Lehre von der Zeit," *Philosophia Naturalis*, 4 (1957), pp. 377-78: "Die Lehre von der Retention ist das Eigentümliche der Husserlschen Zeitlehre. Sie ist aber nichts anderes als ein Konstruktion, durch welche der Fehler, der durch die Lehre von der Punktualität der Gegenwart entstanden ist, wieder unschädlich gemacht werden soll." It does seem that the dialectic of Husserl's argument contributes to determination of the concepts he uses, so that what he claims to "see" in phenomenological reflection is, to a certain degree, what he *must* see in order to avoid falling into certain fallacies.

To explain how we experience time, Husserl says that the now-moment is not given as an unextended point in our consciousness dividing past from future; rather the present is given together with its horizons. It is given with retention of now-moments that have just elapsed and with protention into imminent "nows." [1] Our awareness of the present includes immediate, direct awareness of retentional and protentional phases. These are known as "just having occurred" and "just about to occur."

The phases of now-retention-protention are the phenomenological sources of time consciousness, for it is in them that we perceive, in their most fundamental and primitive states, the distinctions among present, past, and future. Retentions and protentions are given to consciousness in an original way together with the impression actually present to us in the now-instant. Husserl even goes so far as to say that in retention we perceive the past; the past is given to us "in person" in retention.[2]

The now-retention-protention structure is called the unchanging form of inner consciousness, the form which retains its structure permanently throughout the perpetually changing flow of experience it encompasses. But although the form remains the same, one now-point differs from every other one by its different position in the flow of consciousness.[3] One comes before the other; this is the only thing that differentiates them. When one is present, the other is already past. "The Now as actual Now is the present givenness of a time location. If the phenomenon slips into the past, the Now acquires the characteristic of a past Now, but it remains the same Now...."[4] For this reason, we

---

[1] Cf. Alwin Diemer, *Edmund Husserl* (Meisenheim: Anton Hain, 1956), p. 143: "Husserls spezifischer Ansatz wird dann darüber hinaus durch die Übernahme des Stern'schen Begriffs der 'Präsenzzeit' gekennzeichnet: sie fasst als originäre Gegenwart nicht nur, wie sonst üblich, das aktuelle Jetzt als Nullpunkt zwischen Vergangenheit und Zukunft, sondern umfasst zugleich als originäre Gegenwärtigung den aktuellen Horizont des Jetzt mit."

[2] "Die Vergangenheitsanschauung... ist ein originäres Bewusstsein." *Zeitbewusstsein*, p. 392. Cf. p. 401: "Nennen wir aber Wahrnehmung den Akt, in dem aller 'Ursprung' liegt, so ist die primäre Erinnerung Wahrnehmung. Denn nur in der primären Erinnerung sehen wir Vergangenes, nur in ihr konstituiert sich Vergangenheit, und zwar nicht repräsentativ, sondern präsentativ."

[3] Cf. *ibid.*, pp. 422-23.

[4] "Das Jetzt als aktuelles Jetzt ist die Gegenwartsgegebenheit der Zeitstelle. Rückt das Phänomen in die Vergangenheit, so erhält das Jetzt den Charakter des vergangen Jetzt, aber es bleibt dasselbe Jetzt...." *ibid.*, p. 422.

can speak of several phases, several now-points: the one actually present and those held in retention.

For our interests, the essential point to be retained from the discussion of temporal phases is Husserl's claim that elapsed moments of intentionality do not fall out of consciousness. Elapsed now-instants do not disappear as soon as they give way to a succeeding now-instant; rather, they are held in retention. They are still present to consciousness when they become retained phases. The importance of this point is that it allows us to say that a manifold of temporal phases can be present to our consciousness at one and the same instant, and that consequently an immanent object can be constituted for our experience in such a manifold. The manifold is composed of the actual now-instant together with the series of phases that have elapsed but are still held in retention.

7. Partial intentions are not constituted. They are identical with time phases

We now come to the heart of Husserl's study of inner time. In discussing immanent objects, we have seen that sensations, even in their most primitive form, are constituted. We have seen that full apprehensions and complete intentional acts are also constituted, but that primitive apprehensions, or partial intentions, are not. Let us examine why they are not constituted.

Husserl says, "Thus we must understand apprehension in a double sense: the one which is immanently constituted, and the one *which belongs to immanent constitution, to the phases of the original stream itself.* This is the primal apprehension (*Urauffassung*), *which is no longer constituted."* [1] Much is said in these statements. Husserl claims that there is a "primal apprehension" which is different from an ordinary apprehension in that (1) it belongs to the phases of the time flow, whereas ordinary apprehension is constituted by these phases. The primal apprehension is thus somehow identified with one of the points on the time continuum; (2) it is no longer a constituted unit.

Point two follows logically from point one. In the sphere of

---

[1] "Wir haben also Auffassung in doppeltem Sinne zu verstehen: diejenige, die immanent konstituiert ist, und diejenige, die zur immanenten Konstitution, zu den Phasen des ursprünglichen Flusses selbst gehört, die Urauffassung, die nicht mehr konstituiert ist." *ibid.*, p, 444; our italics.

immanent objects, the only manifold that constitutes units is the manifold of time phases, of points on the continuum of inner time. If primitive apprehension is identified with one of these points, it follows that it cannot be constituted. There is no further manifold to constitute it as a unit. It is given primitively as an indivisible unit, just as a now-point is.

Primal apprehension is the first element we have met in consciousness that is not constituted. Even primal sensations are constituted as units by temporal phases. In analyzing the structure of apprehensions, we come up against a final, primitive unit that is no longer constituted. Apprehension thus has the following structure: the complete, enduring apprehension that animates sensory content is an immanent object constituted as a unit by temporal phases. This extended apprehension can be broken down into primal apprehensions which are identical with *constituting* temporal phases. The primal apprehension, or temporal phase, is not constituted.[1]

How does Husserl describe this primal apprehension? He says, first of all, that it should not be called an act. "This primal consciousness, this primal apprehension, or whatever else one might call it, must not be misunderstood as an apprehending act." [2] Primal apprehensions are not acts; what are they? As indicated in the passage cited above, they are temporal phases, now-points either actually present, held in retention, or anticipated in protention. Husserl speaks of primal apprehension as something "that belong to the phases of the originary stream itself." [3]

Furthermore, a full apprehension is the same thing as an intentional act. We should expect therefore that the sections (partial intentions) that go to make up a full intentional act are also equated with temporal phases. Husserl fulfills our expectation. "We must also note that when we speak of an 'act of

[1] Cf. *ibid.*, p. 451, Beilage I: "Die Urimpression ist der absolute Anfang dieser Erzeugung, der Urquell, das, woraus alles andere stetig sich erzeugt. Sie selber aber wird nicht erzeugt, sie entsteht nicht als Erzeugtes.... Sie erwächst nicht (sie hat keinen Keim), sie ist Urschöpfung."

[2] "Man darf nur dieses Urbewusstsein, diese Urauffassung oder wie man es sonst nennen will, nicht als einen auffassenden Akt missverstehen." *ibid*, p. 473, Beilage IX. In one passage, Husserl considers the possibility of calling it an act, but decides against it; cf. p. 442, n. 1.

[3] "die zu den Phasen des ursprünglichen Flusses selbst gehört." *ibid.*, p. 444.

perception' and say that it is the point of authentic perceiving, to which there is attached a continuous sequence of 'retentions,' we have not thereby described any immanent temporal units, *but just moments of the stream.*" [1] When we consider only one point in an extended act of perception, the point of actual, authentic perception, we see that it is identified with a time phase. Similarly, Husserl speaks of "perceptual consciousness" and "retentional consciousness" as "that which constitutes time, as moments of the stream." [2] Intentional consciousness *is* a now-point on the time continuum, and retentional consciousness *is* a retention point on this continuum. Each of them is a temporal phase. Consciousness on this level is identified with temporality, according to Husserl.

Identification of primal consciousness with time phases is the pivot of Husserl's thought in his lectures on time. It is the basis for his doctrine on inner temporal constitution, and makes it possible for him to explain how, through a manifold of temporal phases, we are able to experience immanent objects. We are now in a position to complete the provisional study of inner experience we have undertaken in section five.

8. *Temporal phases, retention, and the complete explanation for our experience of immanent objects*

In section five, our description of experience showed that immanent objects have to be spread out in time in order to be objects of consciousness. With the more exact concepts we have elaborated in the last two sections, we can now go further in showing what makes immanent experience possible.

(A) *Experience of intentional acts and apprehensions*

We shall discuss this subject only from the point of view of acts, although what is said will be readily applicable to apprehensions.

[1] "Es ist noch zu bemerken, dass, wenn wir von 'Wahrnehmungsakt' sprechen und sagen, er sei der Punkt eigentlichen Wahrnehmens, dem eine kontinuierliche Folge von 'Retentionen' angeschlossen sei, wir damit keine zeitlichen immanenten Einheiten beschrieben haben, sondern gerade Momente des Flusses." *ibid.*, p. 430; our italics.

[2] Cf. ibid., p. 430: "...Die Hauserscheinung ist nicht das Wahrnehmungsbewusstsein und das retentionale Bewusstsein. Dieses kann nur verstanden werden als das zeitkonstituierende, als Momente des Flusses."

How can we express our problem? It is to give the structure of consciousness that makes inner experience possible. It is to show why we experience our own acts of thinking, seeing, or hearing in a manner different from the way we see stones, houses, or trees.

The difficulty we must overcome is a tendency to forget the distinction between inner experience and perception, and to talk as though we did "perceive" or "see" our own acts. Where would this tendency lead us, if we were to follow it? Since an object of perception is outside the consciousness that knows it, this misconception would force us to say that when we experience our immanent acts, we stand in a flow of consciousness different from the stream in which the acts themselves are formed. When experiencing our own stream of intentionality, we would be like another spectator who stands outside and observes it *ab extra*. This then leads to an infinite regress, for the second flow of consciousness, that of the "extra spectator," would require still another to account for the experience of its own acts, and so forth. This is the snare we must avoid in explaining inner experience.

In order to avoid it, we must show how experience of acts takes place in the *same* stream of consciousness in which the acts are formed. "The appearance of the stream to itself does not demand a second stream, but rather it constitutes itself as phenomenon within itself." [1] In explaining how this occurs, we shall show how inner experience differs from perception, for in the case of perception the object is, by definition, outside the stream of consciousness of the act which knows it. [2]

Both Husserl's doctrine of retention and his identification of partial intentions with time phases must be employed in his explanation. He describes the experience we have of our own acts in the following way. If we take the full, extended act of seeing a tree, we find that every partial intention in this act involves a double awareness. With my attention focused on the tree, each partial intention, as it occurs in a present now-instant, is orientated towards some aspect of the tree, towards one of

[1] "Die Selbsterscheinung des Flusses fordert nicht einen zweiten Fluss, sodern als Phänomen konstituiert er sich in sich selbst." *ibid.*, p. 436.

[2] Natorp conceives this problem in much the same terms. Cf. *Einleitung in die Psychologie nach kritischer Methode*, pp. 15-18.

its profiles. At the same now-instant, however, all the elapsed now-points are still retained in my consciousness, so that I am aware of them as retentional phases. In them, I am aware of the temporal phases that have elapsed from the present into retention, and I am conscious of inner duration. Hence there is a double awareness: perception of the tree, and experience of inner temporal extension.

The doctrine of retention is necessary here, because it allows Husserl to say that elapsed points of experience are still present to my consciousness. The doctrine of retention alone, however, is not enough. In addition, Husserl must identify temporal phases with partial intentions. This then allows him to say that the temporal phases which are held in retention are nothing but the elapsed partial intentions of my act. In retaining time phases, I retain my act in consciousness; in being still aware of elapsed time phases, I am aware of the act which I perform. Thus when I look at a tree, I have a double awareness. I perceive the tree, but at each instant of perception I am also aware of elapsed partial intentions which are held in retention. I experience my own act of perception as an immanent object extended in my inner time.

Thus to say that an act is constituted in a manifold of temporal phases means that elapsed partial intentions of the act are retained in my present consciousness and experienced. All this transpires in one flow of consciousness. The retained phases are merely prior sections of the stream of intentionality which are held fast in the present, actual phase of that stream. "What is retained is past consciousness in respect to its phase-sequence." [1] Husserl says, "The stream of immanent, time-constituting consciousness does not simply exist, but it is so remarkably and yet so understandably fashioned that necessarily a self-manifestation of the flow must take place within it. Hence the flow itself must necessarily be capable of being conceived in its flowing." [2]

---

[1] "Das Retinierte ist das vergangene Bewusstsein nach seiner Phasenreihe." *Zeitbewusstsein*, p. 436.

[2] "Der Fluss des immanenten zeitkonstituierenden Bewusstsein ist nicht nur, sondern so merkwürdig und doch verständlich geartet ist er, dass in ihm notwendig eine Selbsterscheinung des Flusses bestehen und daher der Fluss selbst notwendig im Fliessen erfassbar sein muss." *ibid.*, p. 436.

The process of retention and the identity of partial intentions with time phases are the structural elements that make experience possible. They enable us to experience our own acts by means of an awareness that occurs in the same stream of consciousness in which the acts are formed. This is the structural explanation of the difference between experience and perception or encounter.

In order to bring Husserl's argument into clearer light and to confirm the necessity of identifying temporal phases with partial intentions, let us see what would happen if we deny this identification and say that inner temporal phases are not the same thing as primitive intentions. Where would this supposition lead us? In such a case, when a series of temporal phases are held in retention, I would experience them as something over and against my present consciousness, as something *ex hypothesi* foreign and opposed to it. Consequently, the act constituted in these temporal phases would also be foreign to my present stream of consciousness and opposed to it. But this would imply that my present consciousness belongs to a stream different from that in which the act is formed, and we fall into the fallacy of the extra spectator. To avoid this, Husserl denies the distinction that leads to it. Temporal phases are not distinct from primitive, partial intentions. They are identified with them.

Once acts are thus constituted as immanent objects, it is possible for another act to thematize them. This is done in an act of reflection. "Precisely through this [viz. through retention] there are constituted duration units ... which are the objects of acts that look back at them.... It is thanks to retention, therefore, that consciousness can be made into an object." [1] However, an act of reflection is different from the inner experience, the immediate awareness of acts, that we have been describing. Immanent objects must already be constituted *before* reflection can turn upon them, but they are constituted as units *while* we experience them. Constitution of immanent objects and experience of these objects is the same process.

In describing the immanent constitution of intentions, Hus-

---

[1] "Eben dadurch [*viz.* durch Retention] konstituieren sich die Dauereinheiten,... die Objekte der rückschauenden Akte sind.... Der Retention verdanken wir es also, dass das Bewusstsein zum Objekt gemacht werden kann." *ibid.*, p. 472, Beilage IX.

serl does not try to make use of his schema of an intentional "form" versus sensory "matter." It is obvious that this distinction has no place here, since there is nothing that could conceivably serve as the sensation. Thus we are faced with a case of constitution where the schema does not apply. This fact has important implications, but we will draw them only after we have studied the inner constitution of sensations.

(B) *The self-constituting stream of consciousness*

With the principles we have explained, it is easy to see how Husserl can speak of the "time-constituting flow as absolute subjectivity."[1] If each primitive partial intention is identified with time phases, then the complete series of time phases, the time-constituting flow, is the same as subjectivity, the entire sum of partial intentions. His principles also explain how he can say that consciousness, the subjective time flow, constitutes itself as a phenomenal unit. As elapsed partial intentions can be retained in our awareness of the present instant, so the whole history of a stream of consciousness could, ideally, be retained and constituted as a phenomenon in the present moment of this flow.

In fact, there is less difficulty as regards the self-constitution of the entire subjective time flow than there is in regard to the constitution of acts as discrete units within this flow. The problem arises when we try to show how the entire time stream can be dissected, so to speak, into acts. From the principles that Husserl gives, there is no intrinsic reason to say that retention ever comes to an end. Speaking about the diagram he uses to illustrate the time continuum, he says, "In the diagram, no allowance is made for any boundaries on the time field. There, no end is foreseen for retention, and ideally a consciousness is quite possible in which everything remains held in retention."[2] Husserl does claim, it is true, that retention comes to an end and that time phases ultimately fall into oblivion, from which they can be recalled by acts of remembering. Factually, this is what happens and Husserl must state it. But in his principles governing

---

[1] "Der zeitkonstituierende Fluss als absolute Subjektivität." *ibid.*, p. 429.

[2] "Auf die Begreztheit des Zeitfeldes ist im Diagramm keine Rücksicht genommen. Dort ist kein Ende der Retention vorgesehen, und idealiter ist wohl auch ein Bewusstsein möglich, in dem alles retentional erhalten bleibt," *ibid.*, p. 391, n. 1.

the flow of time, there is nothing that intrinsically demands such limitation. His principles, left to themselves, would lead to one long intentional act, enduring through the whole history of a time-constituting consciousness. What becomes problematic, given the principles Husserl uses as explanation, is not the constitution of absolute subjectivity, but the constitution of distinct acts within subjectivity.

The reason the problem arises in this way is that Husserl's doctrine on time has no effect on the *quality* of acts which are constituted in inner time, except for acts of remembering, anticipating, and reflecting, which by nature derive their quality from temporal factors. What he says about time has nothing to do, for instance, with whether an act is an act of desire or dislike, an act of perception or imagination. Purely from temporal principles we have no way of indicating when an act of simple perception gives way to an act of desire. We have no way of breaking up the homogeneous flow into distinct acts. Acts do succeed one another and the time flow is broken up into distinct units, but this must be explained by non-temporal factors, such as the quality of acts or the material content of sensations. It is not explained by the laws governing time consciousness.

This limitation on the effectiveness of Husserl's principles for time consciousness do not mean that they are incorrect. It simply means that they are not enough, in themselves, to give a full description of the structure and activity of intentionality. They must be supplemented by other analyses, such as those begun in the *Logical Investigations* and more fully developed in the *Ideas*.

(C) *Experience of sensations. A false solution*

It seems easy to understand how primitive consciousness can constitute full intentional acts; this process appears to be no more than building a whole out of its parts. An act is the sum of its partial intentions assembled in retention. The case of the constitution of simple sensations, however, seems more difficult to accept. How can we say that our consciousness constitutes sensations, that it constitutes our sensations of color, sound, or pain? Sensations, says Husserl, are constituted by temporal phases; but temporal phases are identified with primal intentions.

Are we to conclude that our intentions (or apprehensions) constitute sensations? Furthermore, sensations possess temporal phases intrinsically, as something inherent in them; are we to say that sensations also possess consciousness as something intrinsic to themselves?

There is an easy solution to our difficulty, but it is a false one. Perhaps Husserl held it himself at one time; some texts in the lectures on time seem to indicate that he did, but the many revisions that the lectures underwent make it difficult to pass definite judgment on the matter. The solution is based on applying the schematism of intentional "form" and sensory "matter" to the case of sensations, and on distinguishing between a temporal, intentional element and a non-temporal, material element in them.[1]

If we allow this distinction, we would say that temporal phases (primal consciousness) constitute sensory data as temporal units, but that they do not constitute the non-temporal element in sensations. The material elements, as opposed to the temporal form, do not come from consciousness and its temporal phases; they come from "outside." The operation carried out by consciousness merely constitutes sensations qua temporal; it gives them inner temporality, but it supposes a separate, component element that comes into subjectivity and is informed by consciousness.[2] Thus perception would involve a certain passive reception that takes in something new and foreign to consciousness, something not produced by the activity of consciousness. This foreign element is the non-temporal, material moment of

---

[1] The difficulty in determining Husserl's thought on this point stems from the textual problems we mention above, p. 74, n. 2. Passages where Husserl seems to speak of a distinction such as we mention in our text can be found on pp. 419-21.

[2] Cf. *ibid.*, p. 451, Beilage I: "Die Eigentümlichkeit dieser Bewusstseinssponta-neität aber ist, dass sie nur Urgezeugtes zum Wachstum, zur Entfaltung bringt, aber nichts 'Neues' schafft." To underscore the distinction between temporal form and sensory matter, Husserl uses the term "spontaneity" to describe the process achieved by temporal phases. "Spontaneity" is to be taken in a loose sense, however. It is chiefly used to oppose the creative stream of consciousness to what consciousness receives from outside. In later works, Husserl refers to the time constituting flow as something passive. Cf. Rudolf Boehm, "Zijn en tijd in de filosofie van Husserl," *Tijdschrift voor Philosophie*, 21 (1959), p. 273. See also Eigler, *Metaphysische Voraussetzungen*, p. 88: "Überhaupt sind zur Kennzeichnung dieses Geschehens die starren traditionellen Begriffe der Rezeptivität und Spontaneität nur andeutungsweise brauchbar."

primitive sensation. It is the "matter" that is "informed" by temporal intentionality.[1]

This solution is attractive, but it leads to contradictions. It supposes a real distinction between the temporal and non-temporal moments of sensations; such a distinction is impossible. For, in the first place, it leaves us with the same problem one step removed; how do the non-temporal moments in their turn become temporalized? We have to make another distinction within them, and so on *ad infinitum*.

There is still another difficulty. Temporal phases are consciousness; but if this is so, we must say that the non-temporal moments are not conscious, and we are left with an unconscious element in primal sense data, a conclusion that contradicts Husserl's quite comprehensible principle that everything in consciousness is conscious. There is no way out except to renounce the distinction between two irreducible elements in sense data and to say, purely and simply, that time phases or primal consciousness constitute our primitive sense data. In other words, we must discard the schematism of matter and form; we have found another case of constitution where it does not apply. Husserl became aware of the unsuitability of this schema shortly after he actually delivered the lectures on time, and in a footnote which has been dated as written in approximately 1907-08, he was forced to admit that the schema cannot be used in all cases of constitution. In discussing the constitution of sensations, he says, "Not every constitution has the schema: apprehension content – apprehension." [2]

(D) *The meaning of Husserl's final explanation of the constitution of sensations*

We are thus left with the conclusion that consciousness, by virtue of its temporal flowing, constitutes sensations as immanent objects. There still seems to be something uncomfortable

---

[1] Cf. *Zeitbewusstsein*, p. 451, Beilage I: "Die Erzeugung des Bewusstseins aber geht von a zu a', von xa' zu x'a''; dagegen das a, x, y ist nichts Bewusstseins-Erzeugtes, es ist das Urgezeugte, das 'Neue,' das Bewusstseinsfremd Gewordene, Empfangene, gegenüber dem durch eigene Bewusstseinsspontaneität Erzeugten."

[2] "Nicht jede Konstitution hat das Schema Auffassungsinhalt – Auffassung." *ibid.*, p. 371, n. 1. On the date of this passage, see Rudolf Boehm, "Deux points de vue: Husserl et Nietzsche," p. 174, n. 28.

about this; how can it be said that consciousness constitutes sensations of color, pain, sound, etc.?

The difficulty comes from a false understanding of sensations. If we examine our experience more carefully, we shall see that sensations are really not radically distinct from our states of consciousness. Husserl has already said, in the *Logical Investigations*, "That which the ego or consciousness experiences is precisely its own experience. Between the experienced, conscious content and the experience itself, there is no distinction. What is sensed, for example, is no different from the [act of] sensing." [1] My experiencing is what I experience; specifically, my sensing is my sensation. Husserl denies the duality between sensation as an object and sensation as awareness.

To illustrate this, let us analyze the experience of pain. If we apply the statements just made to the case of pain, the result is, "My experience of pain is pain." Another way of saying this would be the truism that pain, to exist, must be conscious pain. A pain we are unaware of does not exist, and similarly a sensation of color or sound that is not impregnated with consciousness does not exist either. As Husserl says, "For in this case, 'being' and 'being-innerly-conscious' coincide." [2] Sensations must carry consciousness in themselves.

To bring this out still further, Husserl's argument can be rephrased in two ways. (1) There is not an X, an object of some sort, behind my sensations which is revealed to me through them and which I call a "pain." My sensations themselves are the pain. (2) There is no consciousness outside the sensations which is directed towards them and acknowledges them as pain. All there is in consciousness is the row of successive instants during which I am in pain. Everything transpires within the same flow of consciousness, and within this flow there is only a sensation-state which we call pain. The sensation thus bears consciousness within itself; pain, to exist, must be conscious pain. [3]

---

[1] "...Das, was das Ich oder das Bewusstsein erlebt, [ist] eben sein Erlebnis. Zwischen dem erlebten und dem bewussten Inhalt und dem Erlebnis selbst ist kein Unterschied. Das Empfundene z.B. ist nichts anderes als die Empfindung." *Log. Unt.*, p. 330; 2nd ed., II, 1, p. 352.

[2] "Denn hier fällt ja Sein und Innerlich-bewusst-sein zusammen." *Zeitbewusstsein*, p. 471, Beilage VIII.

[3] If we were to deny either of the two statements numbered above, we would fall

What is true of pain is likewise true of other sensations. If I have a "red" sensation, a "soft" sensation, or a "loud" sensation, they must all be conscious if they are to exist as immanent objects in my subjectivity. Thus the implications of Husserl's description of the temporal constitution of sensations are quite acceptable. They appear paradoxical at first only because of a tendency to treat sensations like external objects and to imagine that in our experience of them, we stand over and against them. Husserl's analysis shows us rather that consciousness permeates sensations, and that there is no difficulty in saying that consciousness constitutes sensations as immanent objects. Primal apprehension, therefore, is what constitutes sensations as immanent objects. By its animating function, it bestows inner temporality on them and makes it possible for us to experience them.

Husserl's temporal analysis, furthermore, gives us an explanation of how sensations are experienced. Instead of being left with the brute fact that sensations incorporate consciousness, we are told the temporal structure that makes it possible for this to occur. The phases of a primal sensation that have elapsed from the present are retained in the actual present, and we are thereby aware of the sensation. The structure making experience possible is the same here as in the case of our experience of acts as immanent objects.

(E) *Implications of Husserl's analysis of sensory constitution*

We wish to mention two implications of Husserl's doctrine that primal consciousness constitutes sense data. The first of these is a lacuna in what Husserl's explanation achieves. We have already rejected, with Husserl, the real distinction between temporal and non-temporal moments in sensations, but now we must admit that there is at least an aspect of sensations that Husserl's constitution does not explain; it does not show why or how one sensation is "green," another "red," still another "loud," and so on. Just as temporal constitution of acts does not explain the quality of acts (it does not explain why one act is desire and another perception), so the temporal constitution of sensations does not account for their qualitative element. There is a certain

again into the fallacy of the extra spectator. Our sensations would be formed in a stream of consciousness different from the one in which we experience them.

formalism in Husserl's theory of the temporal constitution of immanent objects.

How can this be resolved? Must we go back to the distinction we have rejected, between temporal and non-temporal parts in sensations? Husserl does not do this, and consequently he simply leaves his theory of constitution with a hollow spot, an unexplained factor. This is not surprising; the same lacuna can be found in regard to the content of meanings and objects in the *Logical Investigations*, and we have discovered it in regard to the quality (and hence content) of acts in both the *Investigations* and the lectures on time. As long as Husserl keeps to structural analysis of subjectivity, he is incapable of saying anything about contents. The theory of genetic constitution will help fill this void, but even there a certain unexplained element, a certain facticity, is present.

The second point we wish to mention concerns Husserl's schema of intentional "form" animating sensory "matter." We have seen that it does not apply to the constitution of sensations, and we have also discovered that the constitution of intentions does not require it either; both cases of immanent constitution do without it, and we are led to conclude that the schema does not apply to immanent constitution.

But there is still a deeper implication. Both sensations and intentions are now said to arise from the same source; they are both constituted by primal consciousness, both formed out of the same "raw material." Now what basis do we have for making any distinction at all between intentions and sensations, between noeses and hyletic data? When we look at them from the point of view of temporality, which is the ultimate and decisive point of view for phenomenology, sensations and intentions fall together; there are no longer two immanent objects, but only one. The distinction which Husserl makes in the *Logical Investigations*, the distinction which served there as the base of his concept of constitution, collapses when we study inner temporality, and in all logical rigor Husserl should conclude that no constitution at all has the schema "intentions-sensations." He does draw this conclusion, but only after he has found a new way of explaining objective constitution through genetic analysis.

9. The meaning of the term "constitution" in the formation of immanent objects

Throughout our study of Husserl's lectures on time, we have made use of the word "constitution." Let us now focus our attention on the meaning attributed to this term in connection with the formation of immanent objects.

Immanent objects are constituted in a manifold of temporal phases. In the case of both primitive sensations and intentional acts, it is incorrect to picture the immanent object as a single unit "behind" the manifold of phases. It would be better to say that the object is simply the sum of its phases. Allowance must constantly be made, of course, for the peculiar way in which elapsed phases or partial intentions are assembled in retention to form such a sum of phases. Given this qualification, constitution has the sense of building up a whole by the injection of parts. The correct image to be used is that of a flow or stream; one part pushes its predecessor and in turn is pushed back by its successor, and so on. An immanent object is constituted by accumulation of a series of component phases or partial intentions.

Constitution is thus a *process* again, a process which is simply accumulative. As a process it is a subjective activity, one which Husserl calls the spontaneity of consciousness. Constitution of immanent objects is achieved by a performance of subjectivity; not in the sense of a distinct act which constitutes them, but in the sense of a constant, creative stream of partial intentions or phases that are added together, one upon the other in retention, until a complete object arises. This spontaneity of consciousness is automatic and necessary.

The process of immanent constitution replaces Husserl's dualistic schema of the *Logical Investigations*, which uses the distinction between intentional and material moments. This duality does not exist in the sphere of immanent time; constitution here has what could be called a monistic structure.

Explanation of the constitution of immanent objects is not just an account of what they are made of and how they are put together. It is also an explanation of how they are experienced in consciousness. Within inner experience, explanation of how an object comes to be is necessarily also the explanation of how it is experienced for, as Husserl says, "in this case, 'being' and 'being-innerly-conscious' coincide." [1] Immanent objects are transparent to inner consciousness, and Husserl's explanation of the constitution of such objects shows why this is so. The immanent object is only the sum of elapsed phases of consciousness itself, held in retention. Constitution of immanent objects explains both their being and their knowability.

Although inner consciousness explains how immanent objects arise and are experienced, it does not explain everything in them. There is a foreign element in them about which temporal constitution has nothing to say. In regard to acts, this element is the quality of the acts in question, and in regard to sensations it is the material aspect in sense data. Still more important, the process of temporal constitution has nothing to say about the constitution of meaning which arises in acts. In his *Formal and Transcendental Logic*, Husserl admits this limitation himself: "For not all [conscious experiences] have this ability [to bestow sense]. Experiences of original passivity, operative associations, the experiences of consciousness in which the original time consciousness, the constitution of immanent temporality, takes place, etc., – all these are incapable of it." [2] The constitution achieved in inner temporal consciousness is formal. It represents a sphere of consciousness and performance that is presupposed by all further constitution, but does not interfere with the content of such subsequent constitution. Thus the question raised during our treatment of the *Logical Investigations* about the source of meanings does not find any reply in the lectures on time.

The process which Husserl describes, however, does show the sources of time. It reveals those experiences where time is presented in its most primitive form: retention, where the past is immediately given, and protention, where the future is directly given, all within the experience of the present moment.

---

[1] *Supra*, p. 96, n. 2.

[2] "Denn nicht alle [Bewusstseinserlebnisse] haben diese Fähigkeit [sinngebend zu sein]. Erlebnisse ursprünglicher Passivität, fungierende Assoziation, die Bewusstseinserlebnisse, in denen sich das ursprüngliche Zeitbewusstsein, die Konstitution der immanenten Zeitlichkeit abspielt und dgl. sind dazu unfähig." p. 22. See also Alfred Schütz, *Der sinnhafte Aufbau der sozialen Welt* (Vienna: Springer, 1960), p. 49: "Nur das Erlebte ist sinnvoll, nicht aber das Erleben." Schütz says we must reflect on our experience before it acquires meaning.

These basic distinctions in temporality are explained as the achievement of subjective, spontaneous activity.[1]

Valuable as they are, these conclusions are not the ultimate aim of Husserl's time lectures. The analyses of inner time that we have been discussing are carried out with a further end in view: to explain how objective, real time can arise from inner experience and be known through it.

10. Formulation of the problem of objective constitution and first elements in a solution through structural analysis

At the beginning of our discussion of time, we introduced our subject by speaking of "time appearances." There is something in our subjectivity that both manifests objective time and serves as the basis for inner experience. Until now we have been occupied with inner experience and have seen that temporal phases, which are identical with partial intentions of consciousness, are what make it possible. Let us now return to the problem of objective time and see how the same temporal phases serve as "time appearances" to manifest objective time to us.

The problem of how objective time can be constituted in our awareness of inner time dominates Husserl's introduction to the lectures. His ultimate goal is to show "how temporal objectivity, and thus individual objectivity in general, can constitute itself in subjective time consciousness." [2] The same problem which was at the root of Husserl's *Logical Investigations*, that of the "relationship between the subjectivity of knowing and the objectivity of the content of knowledge,"[3] is transferred to a new domain, our consciousness of time.

How does Husserl state his problem? He says he will not discuss objective time as such, but only so far as it is known or presented to us. "On the other hand, we are interested in the fact that in these experiences [*viz.* the inner experiences of time] 'objectively temporal' data are meant. Precisely this description,

---

[1] Cf. Gunther Eigler, *Metaphysische Voraussetzungen*, p. 99: "Die Zeit ist das Werk der Subjektivität, zwar kein willkürliches Werk der Subjektivität, sondern das ursprünglichste, weil sich in der ständigen Konstitution des 'jetzt' als des Horizontes ihres Seins die Subjektivität erst für sich konstituiert als ein für sich selbst Seiendes."

[2] "Wie sich zeitliche Objektivität, also individuelle Objektivität überhaupt, im subjektiven Zeitbewusstsein konstituieren kann." *Zeitbewusstsein*, p. 368.

[3] Cf. *supra*, p. 39.

that the relevant acts mean this or that 'objectivity,' belongs to
the range of phenomenology...."[1] The question is, how is it
possible that our consciousness can "mean" anything objective
through the experiences present in inner awareness? How is it
possible that objectivity can be present in subjectivity?

Husserl's problem arises because objectivity seems, at first sight,
to be entirely foreign to subjectivity. Through the continuous flow
of changing experiences which makes up our subjective consciousness, there appears something which is considered, by this very
same consciousness, as objective, permanent, and independent
of subjective change. How is this paradoxical appearance
possible? "In the flow of time, in the constant sinking away into
the past, there is constituted a non-flowing, absolutely fixed,
identical, objective time. That is the problem." [2] Husserl gives
the following example.[3] Suppose that I look at a piece of chalk.
I look at it awhile, then close my eyes, then open them and look
at it again. I have two perceptions, but in both I see the same
chalk. I have two temporally separated complex sensations, and
in my inner time I have two separated experiences, but there is
no separation or interruption on the part of the chalk. I encounter and recognize it as the "same" objective thing. Somehow
objectivity and permanence have entered my continually changing
experience. How does this occur?

Husserl's first approach to this problem follows exactly the
same procedure as we have found in the *Logical Investigations;*
he tries to install his matter-form schema for the constitution of
objective time, just as he used it to explain objective constitution
in general. To do this, he has to posit a "temporal sense datum" to
serve as the matter for an "apprehending" form. The temporal
sense datum will be perfectly analogous to ordinary sense data,
such as color, texture, or space sensations, and it will function
just as these do. "A second side of objectivation arises from

[1] "Dagegen interessiert uns, dass in diesen Erlebnissen 'objektiv zeitliche' Daten
gemeint sind. Es gehört zum Bereich der Phänomenologie eben diese Beschreibung,
dass die betreffenden Akte dieses oder jenes 'Objektive' meinen...." *Zeitbewusstsein,*
p. 374.
[2] "Im Zeitfluss, im stetigen Herabsinken in die Vergangenheit konstituiert sich
eine nicht fliessende, absolut feste, identische, objektive Zeit. Das ist das Problem."
ibid., p. 420.
[3] Cf. *ibid.,* p. 372.

apprehension of the representants for time locations." [1] Still
more clearly, he says: "The 'sensed' temporal data are not only
sensed; they are also charged with apprehension-characters...."[2]
According to this schema, therefore, we must experience some
sort of temporal datum which, just like any other sense datum,
undergoes an objectivating apprehension; as a result, objective
time is constituted.

We shall show that such a matter-form duality is impossible
for the constitution of objective time, and that Husserl himself
abandoned it shortly afterwards. Let us leave this criticism aside
for the moment and continue with Husserl's present explanation.

Just as apprehensions objectivate all the material appearances
of an object, such as its color, size, etc., they serve also to objectivate the real time of the object. How does this happen?

At each now-instant of consciousness, the immanent time
phase is objectivated and thus constitutes a correlative, objective now-point in real time. We are not only aware of the
now-instant as a characteristic of inner experience; we are also
aware of an objective "now." This is explained, as all objectivation is explained, by the function of apprehension. Then,
immanent now-points elapse continually into retention. When this
happens, the time phases still retain their objective reference.
Husserl speaks of "maintaining the objective intention in retentional transformation." [3] He adds, "But while it [viz. the
elapsed Now] has lost its character as Now, it keeps itself absolutely unchanged in its objective intention; it is intention towards
an individual objectivity, and moreover, it is still an intuiting
intention." [4]

As a result, the *objective* time point correlated to each inner
time phase is also kept in retention. It keeps its identity and
objectivity while its way of being given changes; it is no longer
present, but is now perceived as elapsed. The accumulation of

---

[1] "Eine zweite Seite der Objektivation entspringt der Auffassung der Zeitstellen-
repräsentanten." *ibid.*, p. 422.

[2] "Die 'empfundene' Temporaldaten sind nicht bloss empfunden, sie sind auch
mit Auffassungscharakteren behaftet...." *ibid.*, pp. 371-72.

[3] "Erhaltung der gegenständlichen Intention in der retentionalen Abwandlung."
ibid., p. 418.

[4] "Aber während es [viz. das eben herabsinkende Jetzt] seine Charakter des Jetzt
verloren hat, hält es sich in seiner gegenständlichen Intention absolut unverändert,
es ist Intention auf eine individuelle Objektivität, und zwar anschauende Intention."
ibid., p. 419.

immanent temporal phases in inner retention thus constitutes a
correlative, objective accumulation of points in "real" time.[1]
Correlative to the stream of now-instants and retentions in our
subjectivity, there is constituted a stream of now-points and
past moments in objective, transcendent time. The row of
elapsing points in inner time constitutes, by virtue of its objectivating character, an objective row of time points, so that we
perceive objective time as an independent reality throughout
its flow. "Real" time is constituted for subjectivity.

In this way, Husserl explains the constitution of objective
time by means of a combination of two factors: the process of
retention, which takes place in immanent time, and objectivation, which is achieved through apprehension and continues
to function even in elapsed temporal phases, and thus builds up
a stream of objective time.[2]

*11. Criticism of this explanation. Rejection of the matter-form
schema in constitution of objective time*

This explanation of objective time constitution rests on the
assumption of a special sense datum which is informed or objectively interpreted by intentionality. Here again Husserl tries
at first to use his dualistic schema. We have already seen that
this schematism crumbled when Husserl tried to apply it to
immanent constitution, and now we shall see that it again fails
when he attempts to use it for objective constitution; for a
temporal sense datum, distinct from the intentionality that animates it, cannot exist, according to Husserl's principles concerning
inner temporality.

The difficulty can be expressed as follows. Immanent temporality is equivalent to the flow of time phases; these phases are

---

[1] Cf. *ibid.*, p. 475, Beilage X: "Jede verschiedene Zeitstelle im präempirischen
Bildfluss stellt eine verschiedene objektive Zeitstelle dar. Sonst erschiene ja nicht ein
Ding, das als solches seine Dauer hat, eine erfüllte objektive Zeitreihe."

[2] Cf. Yvonne Picard, "Le temps chez Husserl et chez Heidegger," *Deucalion*, 1
(1946), pp. 121-22: "Or l'objectivation se fait, nous l'avons vu, par la confrontation
des divers contenus de la conscience des phénomènes subjectifs (Erscheinungen) de
la chose.... Maintenant, pour dire que la durée de la chose elle-même soit objective,
il faut que les contenus ne soient pas considerés uniquement de ce point de vue, comme
les porteurs d'un lien intentionnel, mais qu'ils soient objectivés tels qu'ils sont en
eux-mêmes, dans toute leur 'largeur,' que chaque point du contenu représente donc
un point différent de la durée de la chose, et qu'ainsi il soit identifié, du point de vue
du temps, non aux points correspondants des autres contenus, mais à tous les points
différents du contenu dont il fait partie."

identical with primal intentions. Thus *all* inner temporality must be identified with inner consciousness. But Husserl now demands another immanent time unit, his temporal sense data. Where is this other element supposed to come from? It must be distinct from intentions, because it has to be informed by them; but how is it supposed to arise in the first place as something distinct from them, if they are themselves the unique source of all immanent time?

It is obvious therefore that Husserl cannot assert the existence of time sensations as independent of intentionality. Once again his attempt to use the dual schema of matter and form is a failure, and once again he must renounce duality and turn to a monism to account for temporal constitution. He was aware of this difficulty himself; in a later note, which we have discussed above, he asks himself whether his "time sensations" are really formed in the same way as ordinary sensations.[1] He dismisses this question with the statement, "Not every constitution has the schema: apprehension content – apprehension." His conclusion therefore is that in the constitution of objective time, the matter-form schema does not apply. There is no such thing as a temporal sense datum independent of intentions, and once again he is forced to abandon the schema which was so fundamental for his theory of constitution in the *Logical Investigations*.

Thus we can no longer look for a "sense datum" that will represent objective time in the way that red sense data represent the color red. The subjective correlate for objective time is not an animated sensation; it is *only* the apprehension. The constitution of objective time does not take place under the schema of apprehension animating sense data; it takes place in the apprehension alone.

12. *Acts of remembering and the full constitution of objective time*

So far, our explanation has shown how a series of distinct, individual time points can be constituted in objectivity. In itself, says Husserl, this explanation is not sufficient. "With mainte-

[1] Cf. *Zeitbewusstsein*, p. 371, n. 1: "Empfunden wäre dann also Anzeige eines Relationsbegriffes, der in sich nichts darüber besagen würde, ob das Empfundene sensuell, ja ob es überhaupt immanent ist im Sinne von Sensuellem, m.a.W. es bliebe offen, ob das Empfundene [Zeitliches] selbst schon konstituiert ist, und vielleicht ganz anders als das Sensuelle." On the date of this passage, see *supra*, p. 95, n. 2.

nance of the individuality of time points as they sink back into the past, we still do not have consciousness of a unitary, homogeneous, objective time. For the coming-to-be of such a consciousness, reproductive remembering ... plays an important part."[1] We must also take into account the role of remembering in constitution of objective time.

What occurs in remembering? Husserl says that memory does not only recall to consciousness an object previously known, but that it also reproduces consciousness of the time horizon, the flow of temporal phases, that accompanied the object when it was first perceived.[2] An object is identified basically by its position on the time continuum. Because of the reproduction of a given time interval with the object contained in it, it is possible for us to affirm the identity of a given object we have once encountered.

Possibility of such re-identification is a necessary element for the constitution of objective time. "The possibility of remembering belongs to the constituting of time; I can ... grasp the same thing again and again; the same duration with the same content, the same object."[3] Only when I am aware of the possibility of returning as often as desired to the same object I have once perceived, in the same temporal horizon in which I then perceived it, can I say that the complete objectivity of time is present to my consciousness, for only then do the concepts of an objective "before" and "after" arise. My possibility of returning to a past object enables me to compare it temporally with other objects and to say that it comes before or after them. When I can do this, I am conscious of objective time as an ordered sequence of points in which every real object has its place, a sequence of

---

[1] "Mit der Erhaltung der Individualität der Zeitpunkte beim Zurücksinken in die Vergangenheit haben wir aber noch nicht das Bewusstsein einer einheitlichen, homogenen, objektiven Zeit. Für das Zustandekommens dieses Bewusstseins spielt die reproduktive Erinnerung ... eine wichtige Rolle." *Zeitbewusstsein*, p. 425.

[2] Cf. *ibid.*, p. 460, Beilage IV: "Wiedererinnerung ist nicht nur Wiederbewusstsein für Objekt, sondern wie die Wahrnehmung eines Zeitobjektes seinen Zeithorizont mit sich führt, so wiederholt die Wiedererinnerung auch das Bewusstsein dieses Horizontes."

[3] "Zur Konstituierung der Zeit gehört die Möglichkeit der Identifizierung; ich kann immer wieder ... dasselbe erfassen: dieselbe Dauer mit demselben Inhalte, dasselbe Objekt." *ibid.*, p. 461, Beilage IV.

points which is distinct from subjective temporality. "And thus does objective time first constitute itself ...." [1]

The principle of explanation Husserl uses here is the correlation between an objective sense and subjective structure. For the full constitution of objective time, things we encounter in time have to be "rememberable." The ultimate basis for this sense of "memorability" in real objects is something in our subjectivity; it is the capacity we have to perform acts of remembering and to return to an object with the same temporal horizon in which we once perceived it. [2] Husserl does not explain objective time in itself; he explains it by correlating it to subjectivity. In terms of the *Ideas*, the structure of noematic time is explained by means of its correlation to the structure of noetic time. The basis of his explanation of objective constitution is in subjectivity.

With treatment of the role of remembering, Husserl's study of objective time comes to an end. His explanation has shown how it is possible for objective, real time to be constituted in the perpetual flux of subjective temporality. It has shown how we can constitute a flow of time that is independent of and transcendent to our own immanent, subjective time, and that contains all real objects and events. Husserl's explanation revolves around the doctrine of retention and the principle that apprehensions constitute objectivity for us. With these concepts, he is able to show how our subjective time flow builds up a correlative stream of objective time. Then he uses the possibility of remembering to complete the objectivity of time, to establish the relationship of objective before and after, and the permanent identifiability of objects in real time.

13. The concept of objective constitution in the case of time

In order to explain how objectivity comes into our consciousness, Husserl focuses his attention on elements in subjectivity, on the intentional factor called "apprehension." [3] Thus he finds his explanation for objectivity in an analysis of subjectivity:

---

[1] "Und so konstituiert sich erst die objektive Zeit...." *ibid.*, p. 461, Beilage IV.

[2] "Ich habe ein ursprüngliches Schema: einen Fluss mit seinem Inhalt; aber dazu eine ursprüngliche Mannigfaltigkeit des 'ich kann': ich kann mich an jede Stelle des Flusses zurückversetzen und ihn 'nochmals' erzeugen." *ibid.*, p. 461, Beilage IV.

[3] Cf. *ibid.*, pp. 372-73: "... Objektivität konstituiert sich ... in den Auffassungscharakteren und in den zu dem Wesen dieser Charaktere gehörigen Gesetzmässigkeiten."

the constitution of objective time is explained by showing the
factors in subjectivity which bring it about and by examining
the laws which govern these factors. "We seek to bring the apriori
of time into the clear when we examine time consciousness, and
bring its essential constitution to light...." [1]

The presupposition underlying this method is that there is a
correlation between objectivity and subjectivity. Objective reality is not totally independent of our consciousness. Furthermore, there must not only be correlation between the two, but
consciousness must, in some way, be the basis of objective time
as it appears to us. Subjectivity explains reality; this means that
reality does not have an ultimate explanation in itself, but that
it must somehow depend, phenomenologically, on consciousness.
Husserl expresses this dependence by saying that consciousness
"constitutes" phenomenal objectivity. In terms used in the
Ideas, noematic reality is constituted by noeses. It is grounded
in them.

Why does Husserl try to explain objectivity by subjectivity?
He does not treat this question explicitly in his lectures on time,
but he does make incidental remarks which show that he chooses
to use subjectivity as the basis of explanation because it is a
region in which there can be no doubt or error. Thus he claims
that he does not wish to treat "real" time as such, because this
would imply the assumption that real time exists. Instead, he
will treat only "the time that appears, the duration that appears,
as such. But these are absolutely given, and to doubt them
would have no sense." [2] Although he has to disregard "real"
time, however, Husserl can accept immanent, subjective time
as existent: "Thus, it is true, we do also presuppose an existent
time, but it is not the time of the world of encounter. It is the
immanent time of the passage of consciousness." [3] Within this
sphere of time, "we have an evidence that makes any doubt or

<hr/>

[1] "Das Apriori der Zeit suchen wir zur Klarheit zu bringen, indem wir das Zeitbewusstsein durchforschen, seine wesentliche Konstitution zutage fördern...." *ibid.*,
p. 374.
[2] "erscheinende Zeit, erscheinende Dauer als solche. Das aber sind absolute Gegebenheiten, deren Bezweifelung sinnlos wäre." *ibid.*, p. 369.
[3] "Sodann nehmen wir allerdings auch eine seiende Zeit an, das ist aber nicht die
Zeit der Erfahrungswelt, sonder die immanente Zeit des Bewusstseinsverlaufes."
ibid., p. 369.

denial appear devoid of sense." [1] The desire to operate in a field
of experience where doubt and error are impossible is what motivates Husserl to look into subjectivity for his philosophical explanations. This subject will be extensively treated when we discuss
Husserl's transcendental reduction in the *Ideas*.

The idea that the structure of real time can be clarified by
analysis of the structure of subjectivity is similar to the conviction that has been operative in both the *Philosophy of
Arithmetic* and the *Logical Investigations*, where Husserl explains
categorical objects by means of the structure of categorical acts.
There are important differences, however, between what is said
in the lectures on time and what is found in the earlier works.
In the lectures on time, it is not an act which constitutes the
structure of objective time, but the pre-act structure of intentionality itself. We have to dig deeper into intentionality to find the
laws and structures correlative to the structure of objective time.
We must go beyond acts and into the primitive elements which
form them, the time phases or partial intentions. The implication of this procedure is that even the deepest layers of intentionality influence the structure of objectivity as it is known
to consciousness.

Another difference is that the scope of the constitution treated
in the lectures on time is much broader. Whereas both of Husserl's earlier works explain specific logical entities as the work
of subjective acts, the lectures describe the entire objective time
stream as constituted by subjectivity. They present the complete
background of all our external encounter as something constituted by intentionality.[2]

This brings us to the main lacuna in temporal constitution.
It is purely formal. It explains the temporal background for all
we encounter in the world, but it has nothing to say about the
material content of the things that fit into this background. It
explains the constitution of temporality, but nothing more. It
does not explain how one object in time is constituted as a man,

---

[1] "haben wir eine Evidenz, die jeden Zweifel und jede Leugnung sinnlos erscheinen
lässt." *ibid.*, p. 369.
[2] Husserl also discusses constitution of categorial objects in his lectures on time,
pp. 448-49, 486-90. What is peculiar to them is the fact that once they are constituted, they escape the constant change of the flow of consciousness; they become
atemporal. Concrete individual objects, such as material things, are confined to
definite places on the time continuum, but logical entities are not.

another as a stone, and a third as a painting. We still find a
certain formalism that has been present in all of Husserl's studies
so far.

14. Excursus. Difficulties concerning Husserl's theory of sensations

In the *Logical Investigations*, Husserl raises the problem
whether non-intentional sensations are possible. Can we experience a sensation (a pain, an auditory disturbance, a visual image)
which does not refer to a transcendent object? The question is
left undecided in the *Investigations*, and in the *Ideas* as well.[1]

In one of the appendices to the lectures on time, Husserl seems
to make a decision regarding this problem. He says that all
sensations are intentional and that consequently non-intentional
sensations are impossible. "Primary contents are everywhere
bearers of rays of apprehension and do not emerge without them,
no matter how vague the apprehensions might be."[2] Furthermore,
the principles he develops concerning sensations seem to imply
that all sensations are intentional. Every sensation is constituted
by virtue of its temporality; but the temporal phases, which
effect this, are identical with primitive apprehensions. Since apprehensions have an objectivating, intentional function, every
sensation must be given intentionality, objective reference, by
means of its apprehension.

In another appendix, however, Husserl says precisely the
opposite: "The apprehension is 'animation' of a sense datum.
However it remains to be asked whether the apprehension
commences together with the sense datum, or whether the latter
...must be constituted before the animating apprehension can
set in. It seems that the latter case is true." [3] The sensation
must be constituted as an immanent temporal unit *before* it can
be incorporated into an act of perception, before it can be animated by apprehension. The reason for this claim is that a part
of the sensation must already be held in retentional phases before

---

[1] Cf. *supra*, p. 49.

[2] "Die primäre Inhalte sind überall Träger von Auffassungsstrahlen, und ohne
solche treten sie nicht auf, mögen diese auch noch so unbestimmt sein." *Zeitbewusstsein*, p. 456, Beilage III.

[3] "Die Auffassung ist 'Beseelung' des Empfindungsdatums. Zu fragen bleibt je-
doch, ob sie zugleich mit dem Empfindungsdatum anhebt oder ob dieses nicht...
konstituiert sein muss, ehe die beseelende Auffassung einsetzen kann. Es scheint,
dass dies letzteres zutrifft." *ibid.*, p. 462, Beilage V.

it can be animated. "For in the moment that the apprehension sets in, a part of the sense datum has already elapsed and is still held only in retention." [1]

Thus the coordination between inner constitution and objective constitution seems to be broken. Throughout the lectures on time, Husserl holds that immanent objects, sensations and acts, are constituted simultaneously with the constitution of objective things, because temporal phases, identical with apprehension, effect both constitutions. Now this reciprocity is denied. Immanent constitution must precede objective constitution.

Let us consider the immanent constitution that is said to take place before objectivation. It seems to be a psychic or even physical organization of sense data.[2] Even though it precedes objectivation, however, it is still something of which we are conscious. We experience it, even though we have not yet perceived an objective reality through it. "For it is an absurdity to speak of an 'unconscious' content which only subsequently becomes conscious. Consciousness is necessarily consciousness in each of its phases." [3] "If it were not present, then no retention would be conceivable either; retention of an unconscious content is impossible." [4] Even on this primitive level of constitution, we are aware of what is being constituted. An unconscious sensation, like an unconscious pain, is a contradiction in terms. Therefore the sensation must be constituted as an immanent object, which we experience, before it is given objectivation through apprehension.

How are we to account for this new concept? It seems to contradict the rest of Husserl's doctrine in the lectures on time and certainly differs from his doctrine in the *Logical Investigations* and *Ideas I*. For our solution, we turn to *Ideas II*, where we find a similar concept. Husserl says. "By analysis we are led farther and farther back, and come finally to sensory objects

[1] "Dann ist in dem Moment, in dem die Auffassung einsetzt, ein Teil des Empfindungsdatums schon abgelaufen und nur noch retentional erhalten." *ibid.*, p. 462, Beilage V.

[2] Husserl compares it to a psychic state that psychologists might study. Cf. *ibid.*, pp. 461-62.

[3] "Es ist eben ein Unding, von einem 'unbewussten' Inhalt zu sprechen, der erst nachträglich bewusst würde. Bewusstsein ist notwendig Bewusstsein in jeder seiner Phasen." *ibid.*, p. 472, Beilage IX.

[4] "Ware es nicht vorhanden, so wäre auch keine Retention denkbar; Retention eines unbewussten Inhalts ist unmöglich." *ibid.*, p. 473, Beilage IX.

in another sense. These objects are the basis (*sc.* constitutively understood) of all spatial objects and likewise of all thing-objects in material reality. In turn, they lead us back to certain ultimate syntheses; *but to syntheses, that come before any thesis.*" [1] Husserl thus speaks of a type of constitution that takes place in sensibility before any objectivation, any "thesis" takes place.

He makes his point in still clearer terms in a series of other passages: "It must be understood that such a tone datum could be constituted without the performance of any spatial apprehension whatsoever. . . ." [2] "With the pure sense datum, we come up against a prior givenness that lies even before the constitution of an object as object." [3] He refers to "a state of sensation that, admittedly, functions as a stimulus in reference to the ego, but does not possess the property of an object-consciousness. . . ." [4] And finally he mentions "the case of a state of sensation which is not yet objective apprehension." [5]

The solution of our difficulty seems to lie in a change in Husserl's thought. The *Logical Investigations* and *Ideas I* do not decide whether or not there can be non-intentional sensations. The lectures on time seem to claim that such sensations are impossible. Appendix V, however, claims that they are possible, and *Ideas II* concur in this opinion. The passages from *Ideas II* were written sometime before 1916, and Appendix V of the lectures on time could have been composed at any time between 1905 and 1917. [6] Since *Ideas I*, published in 1913, still leave the question undecided, it seems that Husserl accepted the possibility of non-intentional sensations sometime between 1913 and

---

[1] "Wir werden analytisch immer weiter zurückgeführt und kommen schliesslich auf Sinnengegenstände in einem anderen Sinn, die allen Raumgegenständen und somit auch allen Dinggegenständen von materieller Realität zu Grunde liegen (sc. konstitutiv verstanden) und die uns wieder auf gewisse letzte Synthesen zurückführen; aber auf Synthesen, die vor aller Thesis liegen." *Ideen II* (The Hague: Martinus Nijhoff, 1952), p. 22; italics ours.

[2] "Es ist einzusehen, dass solch ein Tondatum konstituiert sein könnte, ohne dass eine räumliche Auffassung überhaupt vollzogen wäre. . . ." *ibid.*, p. 22.

[3] "Wir stossen hier bei dem puren Empfindungsdatum auf eine Vorgegebenheit die noch vor der Konstitution des Gegenstandes als Gegenstandes liegt." *ibid.*, pp. 22-3.

[4] "einen Empfindungszustand, der zwar in Bezug auf das Ich als Reiz fungiert, aber nicht die Eigenheit eines Gegenstandsbewusstseins besitzt. . . ." *ibid.*, p. 23.

[5] "der Fall einer Empfindungszuständlichkeit, die noch nicht gegenständliche Auffassung ist." *ibid.*, p. 23.

[6] Cf. Marly Biemel's introduction, *Ideen II*, p. xvi. For the dates concerning the time lectures, see *supra*, p. 74, n. 2.

1916. When he wrote the main text of the lectures on time, sometime before 1905, he seems to have been inclined to deny such a possibility.

The possibility of non-intentional sensations that precede objectivation is important for the concept of constitution. In these sensations, we arrive at the most primitive of all constitutions that take place in consciousness. "From such objects we are led ultimately to sense data, which are constituted in the most primitive way, constituted as units in the originary time consciousness." [1] It is a constitution achieved by temporality.

Then there arises the task of tracing the constitution of objects, of the various regions we encounter, from these primitive sensations. This is constitutional analysis carried to its ultimate extreme. It is the authentic phenomenological problem which, says Husserl, Hume saw, but which he could not appreciate in its proper sense because of his materialistic presuppositions.[2] It is, however, a question which belongs properly to genetic constitution, and we must leave it aside until a later chapter.

15. Conclusion

The identification of inner time phases with partial intentions is the center of Husserl's argument in the lectures on time. It is the principle that allows him to explain the constitution both of immanent objects and external, transcendent time.

As regards immanent objects, sensations and acts, the mechanism Husserl uses to explain their constitution is retention. Elapsed time phases, or partial intentions, are retained in my present consciousness, so that even while I focus my direct attention on a transcendent thing, I am still aware of the act in which I perceive the thing. I experience the act as an immanent object. Sensations are the same; each now-moment of a state of sensation retains a series of elapsed phases, so that my sensation too is held in consciousness as an immanent object, even though my explicit, thematic interest is focused on a real thing.

Constitution in this immanent sense means bringing an immanent object to consciousness, but it also means bringing it

---

[1] "Von solchen Gegenständen werden wir aber schliesslich geführt auf die in der primitivsten Weise konstituierten Empfindungsdaten, die sich als Einheiten konstituieren im ursprünglichen Zeitbewusstsein." *Ideen II*, p. 24.

[2] Cf. *Erste Philosophie I* (The Hague: Martinus Nijhoff, 1956), pp 173-74.

into existence. To constitute a sensation as an object of experience is to constitute it as existing. Such constitution is achieved
by temporal phases, the continual flow of time points (partial
intentions) succeeding one another in inner temporality. The
process of constitution is correctly pictured as a flow, a stream,
an accumulation of parts into a whole. In explaining immanent
temporal constitution, Husserl is forced to abandon his matter-
form schema of intentionality informing sense data. In its place,
he uses the image of a stream.

Furthermore, the matter-form schema cannot be applied to
the constitution of objective time either; it is impossible to posit
such a thing as a "temporal sense datum," because all inner
temporality comes from intentions. A temporal sense datum
distinct from intentionality and only subsequently informed by
it is inconceivable. There is no duality in the sphere of inner time.
In addition, Husserl's studies throw doubt on the possibility of
using the schema even in the higher sphere of intentionality;
they throw doubt on the very distinction between sensations and
intentions. Both of them are constituted out of the same stuff,
out of primal consciousness; what right do we have to make a
distinction between them?

Temporal phases also explain how objective time is constituted in our consciousness. They act as "appearances" for real
time, and by virtue of their inherent objectivation, when
supplemented with the activity of remembering, they explain
the transcendent time that appears to our consciousness. The
significant point in Husserl's explanation of objective time is
that he clarifies it by means of subjectivity. The structure of
real time is explained, philosophically, by the structure of subjective time. This presupposes that real time, as far as it appears
to us, depends philosophically on inner time. This dependence
is implicitly expressed in the very terms Husserl uses: real time
is "constituted" in inner time. What this dependence means and
how it is justified are questions not treated in the lectures on
time. They will occupy us in the *Ideas*.

We have stressed that Husserl's temporal analyses are formal.
They explain the temporality of subjectivity and the time in
which all transcendent objects are located, but they do not explain the material content of objects in time. This is true of both

immanent and transcendent objects. Temporality does not explain how the quality of one act differs from another, nor how one
sensation differs materially from another; it does not explain
why one act is perception and another is phantasy, why one
sensation is green and another loud. Similarly, temporal analysis does not explain how constitution of a tree differs from
constitution of a statue in real time. It explains a framework
that encompasses all our experience and encounter, but it does
not explain the origins or composition of the contents present in
this framework.

Finally, through the doctrine of temporal phases, Husserl
achieves his aim of showing the ultimate "sources" of time. All
time, both subjective and objective, arises from the now-retention-protention structure. Every now-instant is surrounded by
its horizon of retentional and protentional phases, and in them
we directly experience the structure of temporality in its most
primitive form. Even the present-past-future form of objective
time has its basis here. It is built up from inner time through
objective constitution.

CONSTITUTION AND HUSSERL'S
QUEST FOR A RIGOROUS SCIENCE

1. The "Ideas" and philosophy as a rigorous science

Husserl composed the first volume of his *Ideas* [1] in order to realize the project marked out in his article of 1910, "Philosophy as a Rigorous Science." [2] The main preoccupation of Husserl in this volume is to elaborate philosophy, or more specifically phenomenology, as a rigorous science; not as an equal among other sciences, but as something that will provide a foundation for, and an explanation of, other sciences and even all human experience. Phenomenology is to be established as the first philosophy, the ultimate field of inquiry to which all knowledge must appeal to acquire final rationalization.

Husserl's concept of what sort of science philosophy should become is already outlined in his *Logos* article. He is not simply interested in giving it systematic form. This is to be done also, but the chief aim he has is to establish philosophy as the radical clarification of knowledge. He wants to remove presuppositions and assumptions. As long as these are still present, we do not have true science or knowledge, and the darkness covering the foundations of empirical science is an indication that even they are not fully rationalized. We do not really know what we are

---

[1] *Ideen zu einer reinen Phänomenologie und phänomenologischen Philosophie. Erstes Buch: Allgemeine Einführung in die reine Phänomenologie.* Edited by Walter Biemel (The Hague: Martinus Nijhoff, 1950). The text of Biemel's edition incorporates notes, changes, and additions made by Husserl in his own copies of *Ideas.* Since we are interested in Husserl's thought as it had developed until 1913, we will remove all changes from Biemel's text in our citations and refer to the *Ideas* as composed for the first edition.
There is an English translation of this work by W.R. Boyce Gibson: *Ideas. General Introduction to Pure Phenomenology* (London: George Allen and Unwin, 1931). We have used it as an aid in translating the German text in some passages, but since it requires revision in many places, we did not wish to use it as the standard English text. Most of the translations, therefore, are our own, and in places where Gibson's text was used, reference is made to his work.
[2] "Philosophie als strenge Wissenschaft," *Logos,* I (1910-1911), pp. 289-341.

doing when we carry out mathematics or physics; we do not,
he claims, understand the foundations of these sciences. Phenomenology is to correct this defect, this "spiritual distress of
our time." [1] But to do so it must not bear the same defect within
itself. It must be aware of and understand its own presuppositions, it must be the science of absolute assertions which have
no area of unclarity within themselves. "But philosophy is, according to its essence, science of true beginnings, of origins, of
the ῥιζώματα πάντων. Science of the radical must also be radical
in its procedure, and this in every respect. Above all it cannot
rest until it has won absolutely clear beginnings, i.e. absolutely
clear problems, the methods predelineated in the authentic sense
of these problems, and the most profound sphere of research
where its data (Sachen) are given in absolute clarity." [2] Thus
philosophy as a rigorous science means more for Husserl than
a logically rigorous system. It must be a presuppositionless
science, a science which bears its justification within itself.

The first volume of Ideas is dedicated to establishing phenomenology as such a presuppositionless science. The primary
difficulty which this involves is to discover an entrance into
phenomenology, to determine the attitude to be taken in order
to see the field explored by this science. [3] This is the problem of
the transfer from the natural attitude to that proper to phenomenology, the problem of phenomenological reduction. In
addition, the first volume of Ideas has the purpose of giving a
general idea of the structure of pure consciousness (the field of
phenomenological inquiry) and a description of the problems
and methods of inquiry proper to the science investigating it. [4]
Thus Ideas I is chiefly geared to showing that phenomenology

---

[1] Cf. ibid., p. 336.

[2] "Philosophie ist aber ihrem Wesen nach Wissenschaft von den wahren Anfängen,
von den Ursprüngen, von den ῥιζώματα πάντων. Die Wissenschaft vom Radikalen
muss auch in ihrem Verfahren radikal sein und das in jeder Hinsicht. Vor allem darf
sie nicht ruhen, bis sie ihre absolut klaren Anfänge, d.i. ihre absolut klaren Probleme,
die im eigenen Sinn dieser Probleme vorgezeichneten Methoden und das unterste
Arbeitsfeld absolut klar gegebener Sachen gewonnen hat." ibid., pp. 340-41.

[3] Cf. Ideen I, p. 5: "Es wird die vornehmste Aufgabe dieses ersten Buches sein,
Wege zu suchen, auf welchen die übergrossen Schwierigkeiten des Eindringens in
diese neue Welt sozusagen stückweise überwunden werden können."

[4] Cf. ibid., p. 7: "... Wir wollen auch versuchen, bestimmte Vorstellungen von
der allgemeinsten Struktur dieses reinen Bewusstseins zu gewinnen und, dadurch
vermittelt, von den allgemeinsten Problemgruppen, Untersuchungsrichtungen und
Methoden, die der neuen Wissenschaft zugehören."

is a science, to describing what sort of science it is, and to
marking out its subject matter and methodology.

2. *Verbal analysis of the place of the term "constitution" in the structure of "Ideas I"*

Husserl develops his argument in *Ideas* in a systematic fashion,
first opening the field of phenomenological inquiry and then
going on to structural analyses and more specific problems raised
in this inquiry. There is a clear logical pattern discernible in this
work. It will be useful, at the beginning of our study, to describe
how the term "constitution" fits into this pattern, in order to
see the contexts into which the concept is introduced. This preliminary analysis is only verbal; it limits itself to showing where
the word "constitution" appears. Nevertheless, it also provides
us a clue to the place assigned to the concept of constitution in
the overall system of phenomenology as a rigorous science.

The book is divided into four sections. In the first, the term
"constitution" does not appear with the technical, intentional
sense given it by Husserl except for one incidental remark
concerning categorical constitution.[1] This section contains only
preparatory logical considerations and criticism of naturalistic
misinterpretations of philosophy.

Section two is of great importance in the argument of *Ideas*,
for it marks the transition from the natural attitude to the
philosophical or phenomenological. This section is entitled, "The
Phenomenological Fundamental Meditation"; it describes the
point of view taken by phenomenology as a science, and tries
to communicate and justify this point of view. The questions
dealt with in this section concern the very basis of phenomenology as a scientific and philosophical discipline.

Let us look more closely into this section. In chapter one,
Husserl explains the concept of the natural attitude and its
suspension. This chapter presents the idea of phenomenological
reduction. Chapter two distinguishes two regions of our experience, consciousness and natural reality, and in doing so shows
why the phenomenological reduction is possible. It is possible,

---

[1] Cf. *ibid.*, p. 29. There are many uses of the term in a non-technical sense, that is,
to denote the constitutive parts or characteristics of things, with no reference to
intentionality.

argues Husserl, because one of the regions we experience
(consciousness itself) can be conceived without the other (existent reality). However, throughout these first two chapters, in
which the concept of phenomenological reduction and the possibility of performing it are exposed, the term "constitution" does
not appear at all in its technical sense.[1]

However, once Husserl does perform the transcendental epoche
in chapter three of this section, he says that we have not really
lost reality by turning our attention upon subjectivity, but that
we retain it all as "constituted." [2] This statement is made in
§ 50; furthermore, in § 48 and § 49 the term is also used in its
technical sense.[3] Thus throughout his argument to explain and
justify the transcendental reduction, "constitution" is not found,
and yet in the actual performance of the epoche (and also just
before the actual performance of it), the term suddenly acquires
a central position. Is Husserl justified in using this term in such
an apparently unwarranted and sporadic way? Examination of
this question will be one of the main problems of our study of
constitution in *Ideas*. The importance of this question comes
from the fact that in these passages Husserl is trying to establish
the foundations of his phenomenology.

From this point on, "constitution" appears frequently in
section two; it arises in reference to the constitution of nature,
of things, of units we encounter in the world, of the natural
world itself, and so on.[4] All these references simply elaborate
and specify what is contained in the statement that reality still
remains as constituted in the phenomenological residuum.
Finally, the few instances of "constitution" in chapter four do
not add anything to what we have found in chapter three.

We move now to section three, to discussion of methodology
and to the problems found in pure consciousness. In this section,
the term "constitution" arises in three principal contexts. After
a first chapter discussing methodology in which constitution
does not appear with its technical meaning, Husserl goes on to
describe, in chapter two, the general structure of pure conscious-

---

[1] On p. 69 of Biemel's edition, the term is used in its technical sense, but this is
not found in the 1913 edition. It is an addition made later by Husserl.

[2] Cf. *ibid.*, p. 119.

[3] Cf. *ibid.*, pp. 114-15,

[4] Cf. *ibid.*, pp. 121-22, 128-30, 133-35.

ness. In this chapter, temporal constitution is treated schematically, but Husserl feels it is better to leave treatment of time
out of consideration in this volume.[1] He then examines the
problem of sense data and their animation by intentionality,
and this gives him the opportunity to introduce constitution as
a problem on the level of sense experience. [2] Once again we find
him using the matter-form schema to express the relationship
between noeses and sensations. Then there follows a chapter
introducing the concepts of noesis and noema. "Constitution"
is not used technically in this chapter, but it does arise again in
chapter four when Husserl discusses the reciprocal interaction
of noesis and noema. The noema is presented as a unit constituted in a noetic manifold, and variations in noeses are described
as constituting new levels of meaning in the noema.[3] The noesis-
noema correlation is especially examined in regard to founded
acts, such as moral evaluations or esthetic acts, syntactical or
categorical acts, and polythetic ones. Thus in section three, the
term "constitution" is employed at three different stages in
Husserl's description of the structure of pure consciousness: in
connection with time, in connection with the animation of
sensory data, and in connection with the correlation between
noesis and noema.

The fourth section of *Ideas* is entitled "Reason and Reality."
After having exposed the structure of pure consciousness, Husserl now approaches the problem of the correct use of consciousness. What makes experience and encounter reasonable? How
can we describe its function of revealing reality, as opposed to
its function of merely intending, of imagining, etc.? Such are
the questions raised by his studies in this section. In chapter one,
Husserl sets up the framework in which he will formulate and
handle such problems. He describes the relationship between
meaning and objects of reference, and the term "constitution"
appears frequently only in the last paragraph, with no new
change in sense. Chapter two is a discussion of what "reason"
means; it is especially an analysis of evidence. Constitution appears only in the last paragraph, where Husserl begins to speak

[1] Cf. *ibid.*, pp. 196-203.
[2] Cf. *ibid.*, pp. 212-15.
[3] Cf. *ibid.*, pp. 247-49, 285-95.

of evidence as something belonging to the constitution of certain noemas.[1] In chapter three, which passes in review various levels of the problem of reason and evidence, the term arises more abundantly than anywhere else in *Ideas I*. Husserl sketches briefly how phenomenological studies of reason can be carried out for various ontological regions, each implying a methodology and problematic of constitution proper to itself.

To summarize our results, we find that the term "constitution" does not appear uniformly throughout *Ideas I;* it is present very frequently in certain contexts and entirely absent in others. It arises especially in the following five critical places: in connection with the phenomenological reduction, during the brief treatment of temporality, in connection with sense data and their animating noeses, during treatment of noetic-noematic correlations, and during analysis of problems of reason, reality, and evidence.

A verbal investigation such as we have carried out is not sufficient or conclusive in itself, but it does indicate at least which contexts evoke the problem, and thus shows in a general way how constitution fits into Husserl's conception of phenomenology as a science. We shall use the five contexts listed above as the main sections in our analysis of *Ideas*. The greatest part of our study will be concerned with the first context, the problem of constitution and the transcendental reduction.

3. Husserl's proof of the possibility of transcendental reduction

Section two of *Ideas I* is dedicated to establishing the point of view taken by phenomenology. In § 46, Husserl makes the following statement: "Our meditation has hereby grown to its culminating point. We have won the knowledge we need. In the essential interconnections which have been disclosed to us, there already lay the chief premises for the conclusions we wish to draw concerning the separability, in principle, of the entire natural world from the domain of consciousness, the existence-sphere of experiences...."[2] He has arrived at the culminating

---

[1] Cf. *ibid.*, p. 353.

[2] "Unsere Betrachtung ist damit zu einem Höhepunkt gediehen. Wir haben die Erkenntnisse gewonnen, deren wir bedürfen. In den Wesenszusammenhängen, die sich uns erschlossen haben, liegen schon die wichtigsten Prämissen beschlossen für die Folgerungen, die wir auf die prinzipielle Ablösbarkeit der gesamten natürlichen

point of his fundamental phenomenological meditation and found
the experiences which show the possibility of carrying out the
phenomenological reduction, of considering subjectivity as a
field of inquiry that can be isolated from factual reality. Thus
Husserl has solved the problem he stated at the beginning of
§ 33 with the words, "We have learned to understand the sense
of phenomenological epoche, but by no means the possibility of
performing it." [1] The investigations carried out between these
two statements, those extending from § 33 to § 46, are supposed
to cause us to understand the possibility of carrying out the
phenomenological epoche.

What factors does Husserl present in these investigations to
justify the phenomenological reduction? The studies in question
are those which describe the difference between our knowledge
of inner experience and our knowledge of external reality. Inner
experience and outer reality are the two main regions of being:
"Therein is manifest the distinction, in principle, of modes of
being, the most pivotal there is, the one between consciousness
and reality." [2] Each of these regions, furthermore, has its own
manner of being given to our consciousness: "To this opposition
between immanence and transcendence there belongs a distinction in principle of the ways of being given...." [3] Husserl
exploits this distinction between reality and consciousness in
order to find a foundation for his phenomenology. We shall
follow his argument through the "fundamental meditation"; in
order to clarify what he says, we must distinguish two themes
present in his thought.

Welt von der Domäne des Bewusstseins, der Seinssphäre der Erlebnisse, ziehen
wollen...." *ibid.*, pp. 109-10.

[1] "Den Sinn der phänomenologischen Epoche haben wir verstehen gelernt, keines-
wegs aber ihre mögliche Leistung." *ibid.*, p. 69. This statement is misinterpreted
in the translation of Paul Ricoeur, who makes it read: "Nous avons appris à entendre
ce que signifie l'époché phénoménologique, mais non les services qu'elle peut rendre."
Idées directrices pour une phénoménologie (Paris: Gallimard, 1950), p. 105. The same
misinterpretation is found in Gibson's English translation, p. 112.

[2] "Darin bekundet sich eben die prinzipielle Unterschiedenheit der Seinsweisen,
die kardinalste, die es überhaupt gibt, die zwischen Bewusstsein und Realität."
Ideen I, p. 96.

[3] "Zu diesem Gegensatz zwischen Immanenz und Transzendenz gehört ... ein
prizipieller Unterschied der Gegebenheitsart." *ibid.*, p. 96.

(A) The first theme: the quest for a sphere of apodictic, adequate givenness

The first problem is to find a region where a rigorous science is possible, a region where a science without presuppositions can be erected. To this end, Husserl makes the following observations. Material things, he says, are always given to us in a continuum of profiles: "We perceive the thing through the fact that it 'presents profiles' for all the determinations 'really' there in a given case and strictly 'falling' within the perception." [1] Inner experience, on the contrary, does not involve such a profile continuum. "An experience does not present profiles in this way." [2] The reason Husserl gives for the different manner of awareness is that objects of inner experience are not spatial, and where there is no spatial extension, it makes no sense to speak of perceiving things only under certain profiles.[3] This limitation inherent in the perception of transcendent things is not present in our experiences of immanent objects, which are non-spatial and hence totally and exhaustively given to consciousness.

The profile continuum in things and its absence in inner objects is a fact, a simple description of what we are conscious of. What implications does Husserl draw from it? He concludes that because of these profiles, a thing is never apodictically or adequately given to us. Although we may think that we perceive such and such a thing, the subsequent profiles may turn in such a way that we find that we have been mistaken. Such a possibility of doubt or even total negation is inherent in things and our encounter of them; it is "in principle" a characteristic of their manner of being known. Therefore, says Husserl, we cannot base an apodictic, presuppositionless science, a rigorous science, on real things, because the possibility of doubt or error can never be excluded from them. "This holds by an essential law: the existence of things is never demanded by virtue of their givenness, but in a certain way it is always contingent. This means: it can

---

[1] "Das Ding nehmen wir dadurch wahr, dass es sich 'abschattet' nach allen gegebenfalls 'wirklich' und eigentlich in die Wahrnehmung 'fallenden' Bestimmtheiten." *ibid.*, pp. 96-7.

[2] "Ein Erlebnis schattet sich in dieser Art nicht ab." *ibid.*, p. 97.

[3] Cf. *ibid.*, p. 97: "Wo kein räumliches Sein, da hat eben die Rede von einem Sehen von verschiedenen Standpunkten aus, in einer wechselnden Orientierung, nach verschiedenen, sich dabei darbietenden Seiten, nach verschiedenen Perspektiven, Erscheinungen und Abschattungen keinen Sinn."

always happen that the further course of encounter will compel
us to abandon what we once justly posited on the basis of encounter. It was, so we say later, mere illusion, hallucination,
merely a coherent dream, and the like." [1]

However, because inner experience does not present profiles,
this defect is not present in our consciousness of immanent
objects. We never have to fear that subsequent profiles will
make us revise our estimate of what immanent objects are, because there are no profiles here. At each moment, immanent
objects are given apodictically and adequately. "In this absolute sphere, conflict, appearance, being otherwise, have no place.
It is a sphere of absolute position." [2] Thus the region of subjectivity becomes a candidate for Husserl's rigorous science;
such a science can, perhaps, be founded on our absolute experience of subjectivity.

Husserl makes another observation concerning the difference
between our awareness of reality and consciousness. Inner experience is directed towards objects which belong to the same stream
of consciousness as the act which knows them, whereas perception
of reality is directed to objects outside this stream. [3] This is an
observation that Husserl uses frequently in his lectures on time.
What lesson does he draw from it? From this fact, he concludes
that an act of inner perception forms an indivisible whole with
the inner object it knows. The essence of such an act *demands*
the existence of its object; it cannot be studied or described apart
from its object. To separate an act of inner perception and to
treat it in isolation from its object is to falsify it: "Here, perception encloses its object in itself so that it can be detached from
this object only abstractively, only as something essentially

---

[1] "Wesensgesetzlich gilt: Dingliche Existenz ist nie eine durch die Gegebenheit
als notwendig geforderte, sondern in gewisser Art immer zufällige. Das meint: Immer
kann es sein, dass der weitere Verlauf der Erfahrung das schon mit erfahrungs-
mässigem Recht Gesetzte preiszugeben nötigt. Es was, heisst es nachher, blosse
Illusion, Halluzination, blosser zusammenhängender Traum u. dgl ." *ibid.*, p. 108;
translation adapted from Gibson, pp. 144-45.

[2] "In dieser absoluten Sphäre hat Widerstreit, Schein, Anderssein keinen Raum.
Es ist eine Sphäre absoluter Position." *ibid.*, p. 108.

[3] Cf. *ibid.*, p. 85: "... Unter immanent bezogenen intentionalen Erlebnissen verstehen wir solche, zu deren Wesen es gehört, dass ihre intentionalen Gegenstände,
wenn sie überhaupt existieren, zu demselben Erlebnisstrom gehören, wie sie selbst...
Transzendent gerichtet sind intentionale Erlebnisse, für die das nicht statthat...."

dependent." [1] The essence of inner perception implies the real existence of its object as something actually present to it. For example, if we experience a pain, we cannot be mistaken about it; the experience itself guarantees the existence of the pain we feel. As Husserl has already said in the lectures on time, "being" and "being an object of awareness" coincide in the sphere of immanent experience.

This consideration serves to reinforce Husserl's claim that a rigorous science must concern itself with subjectivity. Through the argument from profiles, and through the argument from immanent experience, he concludes that in subjectivity we have indeed a region of experience where a presuppositionless science can be grounded. The existence of immanent experience is guaranteed by the very fact that it is experienced: "Each thing that is given 'in person' (*leibhaft*) can also not exist; no experience given 'in person' can be nonexistent...." [2] Furthermore, the essence and structure of immanent objects are also indubitably given to us, just as their existence is. "But my empathy and my consciousness in general are given originally and absolutely, not only according to essence, but also according to existence." [3] Thus when we fashion a science of subjectivity, we are not presuming anything, neither the existence nor the nature of the things we wish to study. They are guaranteed by the apodictic, adequate manner in which they are given to us.

Reality, on the other hand, does not qualify for a rigorous science, because of the presumptiveness of its existence. We are never freed from the possibility of doubt or negation in our awareness of reality, and so we must always make an assumption

---

[1] "Das Wahrnehmen birgt sein Objekt hier so in sich, dass es von diesem nur abstraktiv, nur als wesentlich Unselbständiges abzusondern ist." *ibid.*, p. 86. In saying that an act of inner perception can be considered only *abstraktiv* when it is separated from its object, Husserl uses the terminology of "part-whole" which he has developed in the third of his *Logical Investigations*. There he speaks of a part-whole relationship in which the sense of a given part demands to be related to the whole; it cannot properly be understood apart from its whole. If we do speak of it apart from the whole, then we do so "abstractedly." This is the case, he claims, for inner perception and its objects. Together they build a whole whose parts can be separated only "abstractedly." This recalls in turn his doctrine of "primary relationships" in the *Philosophy of Arithmetic*.

[2] "Alles leibhaft gegebene Dingliche kann auch nicht sein, kein leibhaft gegebenes Erlebnis kann auch nicht sein...." *Ideen I*, p. 109.

[3] "Aber mein Einfühlen und mein Bewusstsein überhaupt ist originär und absolut gegeben, nicht nur nach Essenz, sondern nach Existenz." *ibid.*, p. 107.

that it really exists as it is given to us. This permanent assumption, inherent in principle in reality, vitiates any science
built upon it. No "rigorous science" of reality is possible.

This argument is the first step to show the possibility of
reduction and phenomenology as a rigorous science. It reveals
a sphere of experience that can be characterized as apodictic and
adequate; in this experience we are given subjectivity as
something "absolute." "It belongs to the essence of immanent
givenness precisely to give an absolute, one that cannot present
itself in aspects and profiles." [1]

Let us reflect for a moment on Husserl's use of the term "absolute" in this context. As far as we have gone, the term simply
means "adequate" or "apodictic." Its contrary, in the context
we have studied, is simply "presumptive"; consciousness is absolute because it is given indubitably and adequately, while reality
is non-absolute because it is given only in profiles. From the
theme we have discussed so far, the absoluteness of subjectivity
means this and no more. It does not yet mean that reality depends
in any way on consciousness; it will acquire such a meaning when
we go further, but at the present it has only the limited sense of
something which is given apodictically and adequately, a region
of experience where the rigorous science called for in the *Logos*
article can be realized, because absolute affirmations can be made
about it.

(B) *The second theme: reality as relative to consciousness and
constituted by it*

From the argument we have discussed so far, the first impression given is that Husserl is preparing the ground for a
science that will consist in exploring subjectivity as a closed,
isolated region. Reality, it would appear, has no place in his
phenomenology because of the doubtfulness inherent in our encounter of it.

Such a science is not what Husserl wants. When he actually
performs the epoche in § 50, when he extinguishes belief in real
existence and turns to transcendental subjectivity, he says,
"We have strictly lost nothing, but have won the entire absolute

---

[1] "...[Es] gehört zum Wesen der immanenten Gegebenheit, eben ein Absolutes
zu geben, das sich gar nicht in Seiten darstellen und abschatten kann." *ibid.*, p. 102.

being which, *when correctly understood*, encloses all worldly tran-
scendences in itself, 'constitutes' them in itself." [1] Transcendent
reality is retained in subjectivity after the reduction, but retained as "constituted." In order that this be seen, says Husserl,
absolute being, subjectivity, has to be correctly understood.
What is correct understanding here? Does Husserl give any
explanation or foundation for it? To answer these questions, we
must investigate a second train of reasoning which is present in
the fundamental phenomenological meditation, and which must
be carefully distinguished from the one we have discussed in
our previous section.

We turn our attention first to § 47–§ 49 of Husserl's *Ideas*, to
the paragraphs immediately preceding the epoche of § 50. We
recall that Husserl has already revealed that subjectivity is a
region of adequate experience, capable of supporting a rigorous
science. In § 46, he has made this point, and claims that he
already has the necessary premises to perform the reduction;
yet he does not perform it right away. There follows the argument
of § 47–§ 49, which he says is to be added to the conclusion
already reached in § 46.[2] Why do these pages have to be added
before the reduction is carried out? What is the burden of their
argument?

They hover around the following statement: consciousness can
be conceived apart from reality, but reality cannot be conceived
apart from consciousness. This is the theme that is developed
here.

First, consciousness can be conceived apart from reality. The
clearest statement of this comes in § 49, where Husserl says that
if we imagine that the whole real world, as we know it, were
annihilated, consciousness would still survive. This is a thought
experiment which he performs to show that the nature of transcendental consciousness is such that it is totally independent
of the real world. Reality and consciousness are two entirely
different types of beings, and annihilation of reality would leave
consciousness still existent, still intact as regards its nature.

---

[1] "Wir haben eigentlich nichts verloren, aber das gesamte absolute Sein gewonnen,
das, recht verstanden, alle weltliche Transzendenzen in sich birgt, in sich 'konstituiert'." *ibid.*, p. 119; italics ours.
[2] Cf. *ibid.*, p. 110: "In Anknüpfung an die Ergebnisse des letzten Kapitels stellen
wir folgende Überlegung an."

"Immanent being, doubtlessly, is thus absolute being in the sense that, in principle, *nulla 're' indiget ad existendum.*" [1] We experience consciousness in such a way that if all our awareness of reality were to fall asunder, so that we could say that there is no "real world" any longer, we would still experience consciousness as we did before; it would present the same nature to us. To put it another way, consciousness does not have any foundation in reality; it exists by itself, and as such it is separable from reality.

The case of reality is quite different. Reality, claims Husserl, is thoroughly relative to consciousness. He states this in strong terms: "On the other hand, the world of transcendent 'res' is entirely related to consciousness; and not to a logically conceived consciousness, but to an actual one." [2] He says further, "On the other hand, the entire spatio-temporal world is . . . according to its sense, simply intentional being, and consequently a being that has only the secondary, relative sense of a being for consciousness." [3] "The being that is the first for us is, *in se*, the second; i.e. it is what it is only in 'relation' to the first. . . . Reality, the reality of things taken individually as well as the reality of the whole world, essentially (in our strict sense) lacks independence . . . . It has the essence of something that in principle is only intentional, only something we are conscious of, something presented, something appearing."[4]

What does this relativity mean? Are there any indications to give us a clue to its sense? Where he is speaking of the relativity of the real world, Husserl says, "We must always bear this in mind: what things are, . . . they are as things of encounter. It is encounter alone that prescribes their sense for them. . . ."[5]

---

[1] "Das immanente Sein ist also zweifellos in dem Sinne absolutes Sein, dass es prinzipiell nulla 're' indiget ad existendum." *ibid.*, p. 115.

[2] "Andererseits ist die Welt der transzendenten 'res' durchaus auf Bewusstsein, und zwar nicht auf ein logisch erdachtes, sondern aktuelles angewiesen." *ibid.*, pp. 115–16.

[3] "Andererseits ist die ganze räumlich-zeitliche Welt . . . ihrem Sinne nach blosses intentionales Sein." *ibid.*, p. 117; trans. adapted from Gibson, p. 153.

[4] "Das Sein, das für uns das Erste ist, ist an sich das Zweite, d.h. es ist, was es ist, nur in 'Beziehung' zum Ersten. . . . Realität, sowohl Reaität des einzeln genommen Dinges als auch Realität der ganzen Welt, entbehrt wesensmässig (in unserem strengen Sinne) der Selbstständigkeit. . . . Es hat die Wesenheit von etwas, das prinzipiell nur Intentionales, nur Bewusstes, Vorstelliges, Erscheinendes ist." *ibid.*, p. 118.

[5] "Es ist hier immer zu beachten: Was die Dinge sind, . . . das sind sie als Dinge der Erfahrung. Sie allein ist es, die ihnen ihren Sinn vorschreibt. . . ." *ibid.*, p. 111.

Also, in the paragraph that recapitulates and closes this chapter, Husserl says again, "In a certain way and with some caution in our use of words, we can also say: all real units are 'unities of sense.' Unities of sense presuppose . . . consciousness which gives sense, consciousness which is itself absolute and does not itself exist through a giving of sense." [1] Reality is relative to subjectivity because it depends on subjectivity for its sense. Subjectivity is what gives sense or meaning, it is the source of sense, and because reality bears a meaning, it is dependent on and relative to consciousness.

This argument, which is already mentioned earlier in *Ideas* but not as clearly as in § 47–§ 49, is a second stage in the fundamental phenomenological meditation. Reality is not independent of consciousness; by the nature of things, we are forced to conceive "the natural world as the correlate to consciousness." [2] Although we can conceive of consciousness apart from the world, we cannot conceive of the world apart from consciousness. What world is it that is thus relative to subjectivity? The world which is meant, thought of, intended; the phenomenal, intentional world, the world that carries a "sense." ". . . The world itself has its entire being as a certain 'sense,' which presupposes absolute consciousness as the field in which sense is given. . . ." [3]

The term "absolute" appears again in this theme, and with a different sense from that which it had in the first theme. There it was a question of apodicticity and adequateness in the way reality and consciousness were experienced. The absolute was contrasted to and opposed to the presumptive, the inadequately given. In this second theme, it is a question of dependence. The sense of reality is dependent on subjectivity because only subjectivity is capable of giving sense; consciousness, on the other hand, is not dependent on something outside of itself that gives it its sense. It has its sense in itself, it is absolute. Here, the absolute is contrasted to the relative, to that which depends on

---

[1] "In gewisser Art und mit einiger Vorsicht im Wortgebrauche kann man auch sagen: Alle realen Einheiten sind 'Einheiten des Sinnes.' Sinneseinheiten setzen . . . sinngebendes Bewusstsein voraus, das seinerseits absolut und nicht selbst wieder durch Sinngebung ist." *ibid.*, p. 134.

[2] "Die natürliche Welt als Bewusstseinskorrelat." *ibid.*, p. 110.

[3] ". . . die Welt selbst ihr ganzes Sein als einen gewissen 'Sinn' hat, der absolutes Bewusstsein, als Feld der Sinngebung, voraussetzt. . . ." *ibid.*, p. 135.

something else for its sense. It is important to keep these two uses of the term "absolute" distinct.

In following this argument, we have not strayed from our original interest, which was to show how reality can appear as constituted in subjectivity. In § 48, while claiming that reality acquires its sense from subjectivity, Husserl makes the following statement: "If there are worlds and real things at all, the encounter-motivations that constitute them must be able to reach into my encounter and that of every ego...." [1] Even before he performs the reduction in § 50, Husserl already calls reality the result of constitution. In § 49, the term is again used twice.[2] Thus Husserl slips from calling reality "phenomenal" and "relative" into calling it "constituted." The means by which reality acquires its relativity, the process by which it acquires the sense that it has, is called constitution. Constitution of the world is synonymous with the relativity of the world that has been stated throughout § 47–§ 49 of the *Ideas*. Thus this second theme, the one declaring the absoluteness of subjectivity and the relativity of real things, is simply another way of stating the fact that reality, with all the sense that it has, is constituted by subjectivity. It is in connection with this second theme that Husserl brings the concept of constitution into his phenomenology. To say that reality cannot be conceived apart from consciousness is to say that it is constituted by consciousness.

When Husserl makes his epoche in § 50, therefore, he is quite justified in saying that reality can still be retained in subjectivity as constituted. The meaning of this statement is that if we consider reality as the correlate of consciousness, as something intentional, as a "sense" which arises from the source of all sense, subjectivity, then it can be maintained in the sphere of absolute subjectivity. We have to reduce reality to a pure phe-

---

[1] "Gibt es überhaupt Welten, reale Dinge, so müssen die sie konstituierenden Erfahrungsmotivationen in meine und in eines jeden Ich Erfahrung hineinreichen können...." *ibid.*, p. 114, trans. adapted from Gibson, p. 150.

[2] Cf. *ibid.*, p. 115: "Es mag dabei sein, dass doch in einigem Umfange rohe Einheitsbildungen zur Konstitution kämen, vorübergehende Haltepunkte für die Anschauungen, die blosse Analoga von Dinganschauungen wären, weil gänzlich unfähig, konservative 'Realitäten,' Dauereinheiten, die 'an sich existieren, ob sie wahrgenommen sind oder nicht,' zu konstituieren."

nomenon, to something entirely "constituted." [1] When we do so, it can fit into the region to be studied by phenomenology, the rigorous science.

In this way, the reality we lose in performing the reduction is found again, and takes its place within the sphere of absolute being and absolute experience. The world itself is not made absolute, and it does not become given to us authentically and apodictically in itself, but its correlation to perception is given absolutely. If we can clarify this correlation, this "constitution," through phenomenological research, we will be giving an absolute, apodictic explanation of the sense of reality, and will thus carry out philosophy as a rigorous science. It will be a self-justifying science, unmarred by the possibility of error or doubt because, Husserl claims, we are no longer operating in the field in which error and doubt are possible. We profit from the a-podicticity of subjective experience to build up an apodictic science, says Husserl, and since reality has a place in subjectivity as its correlate, our science will have things to say about reality as well. It will be able to explain, in its own fashion, minerals, houses, civil laws, triangles, animals, the family, and so on, all as "constituted" by subjectivity. It will provide a clarification and rigorous explanation of all the knowledge which the sciences give us. [2]

(C) Interdependence of the two themes

The two themes we have distinguished, each with its own specific sense of "absolute," are both necessary factors in the process leading to reduction. They complement one another; the

[1] For the phenomenologist, reality must be looked at purely as phenomenon, in the sense described by H.L. Van Breda in "Het 'zuivere Phaenomeen' volgens Edmund Husserl," *Tijdschrift voor Philosophie*, 3 (1941), pp. 472-73: "Husserl wil echter het phaenomeen bereiken, niet in zoo ver het verwijst naar een ontische werkelijkheid, maar juist het phaenomeen als phaenomeen ... Husserl gaat bewust uit naar een nieuw phaenomeen-begrijp; een begrijp meet een – eenigszins althans – volstrekt nieuwen inhoud: het phaenomeen als volstrekt subjektief bewustzijnsgegeven, het zuivere phaenomeen. Enkel daarop kan de eigenlijke phaenomenologie bouwen, als theoretische wetenschap van het volstrekt subjectieve domein." Cf. also Roman Ingarden, "Le problème de la constitution," *Husserl*, Cahiers de Royaumont, Philosophie III, p. 245: "... Celui qui met hors circuit [la thèse générale du monde] effectue le passage des objectivités du monde réel... à des simples phénomènes d'objet ou à des simples sens d'objet."
[2] Cf. *Ideen I.*, p. 148: "Als angewandte Phänomenologie leistet sie also an jeder prinzipiell eigenartigen Wissenschaft die letztauswertende Kritik und damit insbesondere die letzte prinzipielle Klärung ihrer Methodik. So begreift es sich, dass die

first tries to reveal a domain of apodictic, adequate experience, where a rigorous science can be built, and the second gives us something to do with this apodictic field. It provides material to be studied. It shows that subjectivity is to be described insofar as it constitutes various types of things in reality.

When Husserl develops his thought further in connection with the transcendental reduction, he will distinguish several "ways to reduction." A "way to reduction" is a consideration which is supposed to motivate us to turn to subjectivity and to see in it the source of constitution. In other words, it is an argument that is supposed to prompt or even force us to make the transcendental reduction, to adopt the phenomenological attitude. The two chief ways to reduction are the Cartesian and the ontological ways, and they are an outgrowth of the two themes we have just studied. [1]

The Cartesian way is the search for a region where doubt is excluded. It starts with the desire to find scientific rigor and apodicticity, and it leads to subjectivity as the only place where this can be found. This procedure is what we have described in our first theme.

The ontological way proceeds by asserting that reality is not autonomous and independent in itself. By its very nature, reality is correlated to subjectivity, and if we are to explain reality completely, we must take this correlation into account. We must turn our attention to subjectivity and investigate it through phenomenology.[2] This pattern of thought is the same as that which we have described under our second theme. By virtue

Phänomenologie gleichsam die geheime Sehnsucht der ganzen neuzeitlichen Philosophie ist."
  [1] Cf. Iso Kern, "Die drei Wege zur transzendental-phänomenologischen Reduktion in der Philosophie Edmund Husserls," *Tijdschrift voor Philosophie*, 24 (1962), pp. 303-49. Husserl speaks of three ways at least, but the two we have mentioned are the most important. For a condensed study of these two ways, see Husserl's short essay included in *Erste Philosophie II* (The Hague: Martinus Nijhoff, 1959), pp. 219-28.
  [2] Cf. Iso Kern, *ibid.*, pp. 327-38: "An allem positiven oder objektiven ontologischen Apriori ist eine letzte Unklarheit fühlbar, die zum Anlass von verkehrten Sinnunterschiebungen und Fehlintenterpretationen wird. Diese Unklarheit hat ihre Quelle im 'abstrakten' Charakter der positiven ontologischen Erkenntnis, die von der Bezogenheit alles objektiven Apriori zur Subjektivität absieht.... Aus der sich stellenden Aufgabe, das ontologische Apriori zu klären, ... ergibt sich die Forderung einer radikalen Reflexion, die die Einseitigkeit (Abstraktheit) der positiv-ontologischen Erkenntnis überwindet und das ontologische Apriori in seiner Korrelation zur Subjektivität betrachtet."

of this second theme, reality as constituted can be given a place within the apodictic, adequate and absolute region discovered through the first theme, through the Cartesian procedure. [1]

It is important to note, however, that in the second theme (the forerunner of the ontological way to reduction) Husserl does not set out to prove that reality is constituted. Just as in the *Logical Investigations*, Husserl does not set before himself the task of showing the relativity of reality; this is not a thesis he tries to justify. He assumes, as something plainly given, that reality receives its sense from subjectivity, and that it is therefore relative to consciousness and constituted by it. If we were to analyze his argument logically, we would have to say that the relative, constituted nature of reality is an axiom, and not the conclusion of any argument.[2] It is simply a statement of the fact that consciousness is what gives sense, even to reality.

4. The transcendence of things itself is constituted by subjectivity

There is a way in which Husserl's statements about reality as constituted could easily be misunderstood. One might be inclined to say that consciousness constitutes the reality that exists "for us," but that the reality "in itself" remains independent of subjectivity. Such a misconception would amount to a Kantian dichotomy between the thing in itself, which remains beyond the reach of subjectivity, and appearances, which are fashioned and formed by subjectivity and are accessible to it. Husserl is aware of this possible misunderstanding: "The 'true being' would then be entirely and in principle determined in a different way from that which is given in perception as reality 'in person'...." [3]

Husserl treats this misunderstanding in a chapter entitled

---

[1] Kern finds the ontological way present in the *Ideas*, but only mentions § 26 as a passage in which it is found. Cf, *ibid.*, pp. 335-36. We feel that it is present also within Husserl's "fundamental meditation" itself.

[2] It is still another question to justify this statement as an axiom. Heidegger's remarks, given in an appendix to the Louvain edition of Husserl's *Phänomenologische Psychologie* (The Hague: Martinus Nijhoff, 1962), p. 602, express this difficulty: "Das erste in der Darstellung des transzendentalen Problems ist die Klärung dessen, was 'Unverständlichkeit' des Seienden besagt. In welcher Hinsicht ist Seiendes unverständlich? d.h. welcher höhere Anspruch von Verständlichkeit ist möglich und notwendig. Im Rückgang worauf dieses Verständnis gewonnen?"

[3] "Das 'wahre Sein' wäre also durchaus und prinzipiell ein anders Bestimmtes als das in der Wahrnemung als leibhafte Wirklichkeit gegebene...." *Ideen I*, p. 90.

"Clarification of an Error of Principle." [1] He says that the difficulty stems from the tendency to treat sensations or appearances as signs or symbols of real things which are not directly accessible in themselves. This conception, he says, is wrong; we do not see appearances and then infer reality from them, but we perceive reality directly through appearances and sensations. "In directly intuitive acts we intuit something 'in itself'...."[2] The world that we perceive, the world that we "constitute," is the real world. The world of phenomena is not a veil between us and reality; it is reality itself.

These remarks are important for the doctrine of constitution. They enable Husserl to say that when he describes the constitution of this or that object, he is explaining the constitution of a reality, and not just a concept or appearance.[3] It is the constitution of a transcendent reality, and thus the phenomenological explanation of it. Husserl's claim is an answer to the project posed in § 41 when he says, "We must now be concerned with gaining deeper insights into the way that the transcendent stands to a consciousness that knows it, and to see how this reciprocal relationship, which has its own enigmas, is to be understood." [4] It is an attempt to state the enigma, the riddle, of how transcendent reality is related to consciousness.

Husserl does not claim to solve or dissolve the enigma of transcendence. Even after he has said that reality is directly constituted by subjectivity, that it receives its sense from subjectivity, he has not caused the riddle to evaporate. It still remains a paradox that reality, something which is transcendent to consciousness, is accessible to consciousness in its very tran-

---

[1] "Aufklärung eines prinzipiellen Irrtums." *ibid.*, p. 98.
[2] "In den unmittelbar anschauenden Akten schauen wir ein 'Selbst' an...." *ibid.*, p. 99.
[3] Emmanuel Levinas stresses the importance of this step for Husserl's phenomenology in *La théorie de l'intuition dans la phénoménologie de Husserl* (Paris: Alcan, 1930), p. 59: "Le pas en avant effectué par Husserl sur Descartes consiste à ne pas séparer la connaissance de l'objet – plus généralement, le mode d'apparaître de l'objet dans notre vie – de son être; à voir dans son mode de connaissance l'expression et la caractéristique de son mode d'être. C'est pourquoi, dans sa philosophie, il y a pour la première fois possibilité de passer de la théorie de la connaissance, et à travers la théorie de la connaissance, à la théorie de l'être."
[4] "Es gilt jetzt tiefere Einblicke zu gewinnen in die Art, wie das Transzendente zum Bewusstsein steht, dem es bewusst ist, wie diese Aufeinanderbeziehung, die ihre Rätsel hat, zu verstehen ist." *Ideen I*, p. 92.

scendence. [1] What reality is in itself can be reached by consciousness even though it must remain, in principle, radically distinct
from and transcendent to consciousness. This is the mystery of
intentionality, the mystery of consciousness.[2] The doctrine of
intentional constitution is not presented to dissolve the enigma;
it is only carried out to see what can be said about it. The
doctrine of constitution is an attempt to think about the enigma
of intentionality. Unlike Hegel, who identifies reality and
consciousness, Husserl maintains both terms in the paradox:
consciousness on one hand, and transcendent reality on the
other. Both are kept as irreducible to one another: "Between
consciousness and reality there yawns a true abyss of sense." [3]
And yet, by intentionality, reality is related to consciousness in
knowledge, in constitution.

Husserl expresses the same conviction in another passage.
"We should not let ourselves be misled by talk about the transcendence of a thing towards consciousness, or about its 'being
in itself'." We must not be tricked by such terms, he says, into
thinking that the real thing can be reached only by somehow
surpassing our human encounter; rather, says Husserl, "The
genuine concept of the transcendence of the thing ... can be
drawn only from the essential content proper to perception, or
from those definitely ordered interconnections which we call
warranting encounter. The idea of this transcendence is thus the
eidetic correlate to the pure idea of such warranting encounter." [4]

---

[1] Cf. Levinas, *La théorie de l'intuition*, p. 139: "La corrélation avec la conscience,
qui fait l'être même du monde, ne signifie pas que le monde est une pure construction du subjet, suivant les règles d'une logique (analytique ou synthétique), et où
la réalité, ou l'irréalité, dépendrait de la correspondance ou de la non-correspon-
dance à ces règles. La transcendance de l'objet, par rapport à la conscience, – cette
transcendance en tant que telle – est quelque chose d'irréductible à une construction
au moyen des catégories, elle ne se résout pas en relations."

[2] In his lectures published as *Die Idee der Phänomenologie* (The Hague: Martinus
Nijhoff, 1958), pp. 10-11, Husserl also speaks of the "mystery" of intentionality:
"Die Sache wird aber weniger gemütlich, wenn wir uns die Gegebenheiten näher
ansehen. Zunächst: die cogitationes, die wir als schlichte Gegebenheiten für so gar
nicht Mysteriöses halten, bergen allerlei Transzendenzen." On p. 55, he speaks of
"die Rätsel, die Mysterien, die Probleme um den letzten Sinn der Gegenständlichkeit der Erkenntnis."

[3] "Zwischen Bewusstsein und Realität gähnt ein wahrer Abgrund des Sinnes."
Ideen I, p. 117.

[4] "Man darf sich also durch die Rede von der Transzendenz des Dinges gegenüber
dem Bewusstsein oder von seinem 'An-sich-sein' nicht täuschen lassen. Der echte
Begriff der Transzendenz des Dinglichen... ist doch selbst nirgendwoher zu schöpfen,
es sei denn aus dem eigenen Wesensgehalte der Wahrnehmung bzw. der bestimmt

The real concept of transcendence is to be found simply in our acts of perceiving reality, and if we are to talk about this transcendence, we have only to look to our conscious life. The transcendent is the correlate to our perception. If we are to clarify it, all we can do is describe how the transcendent is correlated to subjectivity, how it is constituted by it.

In discussing this point we have, as Husserl himself states, touched upon the enigma of intentionality and constituted reality. An enigma involves the retention of two apparently contradictory characters, and in this case it is retention of the transcendence, the independent, objective existence of reality, together with the relative existence of reality "for us." Reality acquires its sense of transcendence precisely by being constituted by subjectivity, by being an object for us. Thus Husserl does not reduce reality to consciousness, nor does he dissolve consciousness into the objective world. Each of these procedures would upset the enigma of transcendence. He keeps both elements precisely in their paradoxical correlation and attempts, by the doctrine of constitution, to say something about them and their relationship to one another. We have already met this problem in the *Logical Investigations*, where Husserl states that the structure of intentionality is such that it must constitute an object and, paradoxically, this object has to be constituted as objective and transcendent.

5. *The doctrine of constitution is not an idealism of sense*

In this way, Husserl prevents us from making a "Kantian" misconception of his phenomenology. However, there is still another misconception we must guard against, one which is easy to commit because of Husserl's own terminology. If the whole sense of reality is dependent on and relative to subjectivity, must we not conclude that subjectivity is the *source* of all meaning and sense? When Husserl says that subjectivity "constitutes" the world, does he mean that it forms the entire meaning and content which the world has? Does he claim that the distinctions and contents in meaning that are found in the world

gearteten Zusammenhänge, die wir ausweisende Erfahrung nennen. Die Idee dieser Transzendenz ist also das eidetische Korrelat der reinen Idee dieser ausweisenden Erfahrung." *ibid.*, p. III.

are all caused by our consciousness? This would be a form of idealism. To find out if this is his intention, let us examine more closely the "relativity" which the world is supposed to have towards subjectivity. In doing this, we operate within the second theme we have distinguished above, the theme that states that reality cannot be conceived apart from consciousness.

If reality cannot be conceived apart from correlation to the mind, this implies at least that consciousness is a condition *sine qua non* for the real. Consciousness is a fundament for the world in the sense that the world cannot become "real" (*verum*) unless there is a consciousness. To use a metaphor, subjectivity is a fundament for the world as real in the same way that the keel of a boat is a necessary condition for the boat itself. Without the keel, no boat can be formed; and yet, the keel itself is not the boat, nor can it alone "cause" the boat. It is simply a condition that is necessary for the coming-to-be of the vessel.[1]

There is nothing surprising about this assertion, nor is there anything idealistic about it. Real things, since they are units of sense, presuppose subjectivity as their necessary correlate, because sense can only arise in connection with intentional subjectivity.

Is it possible that Husserl means more than this? Can he mean that subjectivity is not only a *sine qua non*, a necessary condition for the world as real, but also its sufficient cause? If this were so, then subjectivity would actually "make" or "create" the sense of phenomenal reality when it constitutes it. The senses or meanings such as "tree," "animal," "chairs," "values," "numbers," and all the other meanings in the world, would be caused by subjectivity. All such distinctions and definitions would be made by consciousness acting spontaneously and crea-

---

[1] The concept of subjectivity as a necessary condition for reality as such, as expressed in a metaphor such as we use here, is from Rudolf Boehm. Cf. his "Zum Begriff des 'Absoluten' bei Husserl," p. 237: "Das zwischen Bewusstsein und Realität bestehende Grund-Verhältnis selbst ist nun mit zwei Worten zu charakterisieren: als ein *fundamentales* und *transzendentales*. Das Grund-Verhältnis zwischen dem absoluten Sein, das das Bewusstsein ist, und dem realen Sein als einem bloss darauf relativen ist insofern ein Fundamental-Verhältnis, als ein *Fundament* eine notwendige Grundlage oder eine unumgängliche, unentbehrliche 'Bedingung der Möglichkeit' für das Sein eines Seienden, nicht aber damit auch schon ein 'zureichender Grund' oder eine 'bewirkende Ursache' des Seins dieses Seienden ist." Italics original. Both concepts of "foundation" and "transcendence" have to be retained to give Husserl's doctrine of constitution the balance and the originality, the philosophical value, which it has.

tively on a mute reality, which has no sense or meaning in itself. Is this strong interpretation of relativity and constitution the one that Husserl intends to use?

Within the fundamental phenomenological meditation in *Ideas*, we already have some reason to choose the first alternative, and to say that consciousness is only a necessary condition for reality to appear. Our choice is based on the profound distinction Husserl makes between consciousness and reality; between the two there stretches an "abyss" of sense. They are fundamentally, irreducibly different. They have a different ontic status. But if we were to say that subjectivity causes the sense and meaning found in reality, then this radical distinction would vanish. The senses and meanings in reality would have the same generic status as subjectivity has, because they would simply be effects or emanations from consciousness. In other words, the enigma of transcendence would be destroyed. The transcendence and objectivity of real sense would be dissolved into a projection of subjectivity. To avoid this, to maintain the proper nature of transcendent subjectivity, we must choose the first possibility. If subjectivity is only a condition for the emergence of sense, then the objective transcendence of sense can be maintained.[1]

In addition, we will come across further reasons later in the *Ideas* to choose the first alternative. We shall see that Husserl's analyses of constitution remain formal. They do not explain the origin of the content of what is constituted. The objects and senses which are given as intentionally constituted are simply accepted as given; their origins or sources are not explained totally by subjectivity. There is a certain givenness or facticity in them which is not entirely the work of consciousness. If this is the case, it must be so because the contents of meanings or objects cannot be accounted for by means of subjectivity. Consciousness does not "create" them; it *allows* them to emerge as real, but does not make them. In other words, it is a necessary

---

[1] Boehm maintains the transcendence of reality towards consciousness on the basis of what Husserl says about the "heterogeneity in principle" between consciousness and reality. Cf. *ibid.*, p. 233: "Doch müssen wir überrascht feststellen, dass Husserl gerade diese Bildung eines Ganzen absoluten Seins aus Bewusstsein und Realität verneint – und somit weiterhin jede 'Wesensgemeinschaft' zwischen Bewusstsein und Realität."

condition for them, but not an all-pervading, sufficient cause.[1] We will have more to say about this when we examine constitution as it is concretely described later in the *Ideas*. For the present, let us conclude that the relativity which Husserl says characterizes the sense of the world is not idealistic in the sense of affirming that all meanings arise from subjectivity. Consciousness is the necessary condition for the emergence of meaning and objects, but it does not create them.

Through his fundamental meditation, Husserl has opened the field of study where his rigorous science is to operate. He will examine transcendental subjectivity, and will study it insofar as it constitutes various types of objects. He observes that the *Logical Investigations* already contained such a study of subjectivity, but that they carried it out successfully only in regard to a few objects, especially categorical ones. This is not enough; "We must gain this insight not only regarding the essences and essential relationships of formal logic or ontology (thus for essences like 'assertion,' 'inference,' etc., and also 'number,' 'arrangement,' 'manifold,' etc.) but also as regards the essences taken from the sphere of the real world (as 'thing,' 'corporeal form,' 'man,' 'person,' etc.)." [2] The entire world must be analyzed in the way it is constituted by subjectivity. The study of subjectivity with this aim in mind will comprise phenomenology as a rigorous science.

6. *Constitution under its hyletic and noetic aspects. Husserl's matter-form schema*

After he has opened the field of pure subjectivity to philosophical study, Husserl begins to carry out his newly founded science. Chapter one of section three discusses methodology and

---

[1] Gaston Berger, in *Le cogito dans la philosophie de Husserl* (Paris: Aubier, 1941), seems at first to attribute an "idealism of meaning" to Husserl's concept of constitution. Cf. p. 94: "Saisir la constitution du monde par l'Ego consistera donc à voir comment le Je donne un sens à tout ce qui s'offre à nous dans le monde, comment, en particulier, il donne à certains aspects de ce monde un sens existentiel, une valeur d'être." Likewise, p. 97: "Ainsi la constitution n'est pas seulement 'informante.' Elle est vraiment créatrice." However, he modifies these statements later and restores the balance of realism and idealism in Husserl: "Il faut apprendre à unir des concepts que nous sommes habitués à opposer: la phénoménologie est une philosophie de l'intuition créatrice." *ibid.*, p. 100.

[2] "Man muss nicht nur hinsichtlich der formallogischen, bzw. ontologischen Wesen und Wesensverhalte (also für Wesen wie 'Satz,' 'Schluss,' u.dgl., aber auch 'Zahl,' 'Ordnung,' 'Mannigfaltigkeit,' usw.) diese Einsicht gewinnen, sondern auch hin-

problems, and in chapter two he begins the description of the
general structure of consciousness. He discusses reflection first,
and then brings in the problem of temporal constitution. He says
that this form of constitution, although of extreme importance
for phenomenology, makes up a closed region which can be safely
set aside in view of his aims in the *Ideas*. We will discuss this
question later, disregarding it at present in order to follow the
development of Husserl's thought more logically. The next point
we meet is the introduction of sensations and noeses.

Phenomenology has been introduced as the science of pure
subjectivity. In his structural analysis of subjectivity, the first
elements Husserl describes are sensations and noeses. These are
the "real" components of intentional experience, they are the
components we find when we simply reflect on our acts.[1] Husserl
describes them as he does in the *Logical Investigations*, but now
uses new terminology. "Sensory" content is now called "hyletic
data," "material data," or simply "hyle," while the intentional
moment is now called "noesis." Noeses animate the hyletic data
by apprehension. Thus the stream of pure consciousness has
a noetic and a hyletic level.

The distinction between hyletic matter and noetic form is
simply the introduction of the schema which Husserl used
throughout the *Logical Investigations*. However, as soon as he
introduces it, he makes a reservation. We can distinguish between
intentional form and sensory matter, he says, only because we
restrict ourselves "to the level of observation to which we are
limited until further notice, which prevents us from descending
into the obscure depths of the ultimate consciousness that
constitutes all the temporality of experience." [2] Husserl is aware
of the conclusions we have found in his lectures on time; if he
were to descend into the deeper levels of intentionality, he
would have no right to distinguish between the two elements

sichtlich der Wesen, die entnommen sind der Sphäre der natürlichen Welt (wie 'Ding,'
'körperliche Gestalt,' 'Mensch,' 'Person,' usw.)." *Ideen I*, pp. 146-47.
   [1] Cf. *ibid.*, p. 218: "Auf der einen Seite haben wir also die Teile und Momente zu
unterscheiden, die wir durch eine reelle Analyse des Erlebnisses finden, wobei wir
das Erlebnis als Gegenstand behandeln wie irgendeinen anderen, nach seinen Stücken
oder unselbständigen, ihn reell aufbauenden Momenten fragend."
   [2] "Auf der Betrachtungsstufe, an die wir bis auf weiteres gebunden sind, die es
unterlässt, in die dunklen Tiefen des letzten, alle Erlebniszeitlichkeit konstituierenden Bewusstseins hinabzusteigen . . . ." *ibid.*, p. 208.

of noeses and sense data. He makes the distinction only because he limits himself to the higher, superficial level of intentionality.

Furthermore, as soon as he has brought in the concepts of noeses and sense data, he immediately puts them to the same use they had in the *Investigations*. They are to express and explain how objectivity can come into our consciousness: "Yet the greatest problems of all are the functional problems, or those of the 'constitution of objectivities of consciousness'." [1] Husserl goes on to explain how he conceives this constitution of objects and the problems concerned with it. Sense data must be arranged into a certain pattern, and the noeses themselves, which animate and assemble the sensations, must interweave with one another in a definite pattern, so that a certain object can be constituted as their correlate.[2]

The task of phenomenology then becomes to describe what noetic and hyletic patterns are prescribed for different types of objects. "We must therefore investigate, in the most comprehensive and universal way, how objective unities of each region and category are 'consciously constituted.' We must show systematically how all the interconnections of real and possible consciousness of them ... are prefigured in their essence...." [3] In describing these elements in subjectivity, we will be giving the subjective conditions which are required for the constitution of a given type of object. We will be giving the conditions necessary for the emergence of a given sense.

There are two sides to such a description, the noetic and the hyletic. A certain pattern of sensations is a necessary subjective correlate for the constitution of a specific sense; the complex of sensations provides a sort of raw material for in-

---

[1] "Doch die allergrösste Probleme sind die funktionelle Probleme, bwz. die der 'Konstitution der Bewusstseinsgegenständlichkeiten'." *ibid.*, p. 212.

[2] Cf. *ibid.*, p. 212: "Sie betreffen die Art, wie z.B. hinsichtlich der Natur, Noesen, das Stoffliche beseelend und sich zu mannigfaltig-einheitlichen Kontinuen und Synthesen verflechtend, Bewusstsein von Etwas so zustande bringen, dass objektive Einheit der Gegenständlichkeit sich darin einstimmig 'bekunden,' 'ausweisen,' und 'vernünftig' bestimmen kann."

[3] "In umfassender Allgemeinheit gilt es also zu erforschen, wie sich objektive Einheiten jeder Region und Kategorie 'bewusstseinsmässig konstituieren.' Es gilt systematisch zu zeigen, wie durch ihr Wesen all die Zusammenhänge wirklichen und möglichen Bewusstseins von ihnen ... vorgezeichnet sind...." *ibid.*, p. 214; trans. adapted from Gibson, p. 253.

tentional formations.[1] Nevertheless, he adds, this hyletic study
is of very secondary importance in phenomenology. "The in-
comparably more important and richer analyses lie on the side
of the noetic."[2] In noetic analysis, we see what has to occur in
the pattern of noeses in order that a certain object be constituted. Noetic analysis will describe the types of acts, their
relationships to one another, their sequence, pattern, and evolution, as the manifold which is necessary for the constitution of
a given object.

The general structure of sensations and animating noeses
which Husserl describes is similar to that of the *Logical Investigations*. In both works, the intentional component is given the
predominant role in determining constitution of the object and
its sense. The hyletic element is given only a secondary, passive
role.

It is strange that Husserl uses the schema of noetic form and
hyletic matter in this way in the *Ideas*. As soon as he introduces
it, he says that it is only provisional, that if we were to descend
into the sphere of temporality, we would see that the distinction between noesis and hyle does not hold. But the temporal
sphere is the "final and true absolute" for phenomenology; thus
the point of view taken from inner temporality is the final and
true viewpoint, and therefore there should "really" be no distinction between noesis and sensations. Strictly speaking, Husserl admits that this distinction is false. Why then does he use
it?

Husserl uses this schema because he has no other way of expressing the objectivity which is constituted by intentionality.
It is the means he has used until now to state how objectivity
comes into our consciousness, and he still has not found any
substitute for it, even though he knows from his analysis of inner
time that it is unwarranted phenomenologically. Thus there is a
contradiction in the *Ideas* between the higher level of intentional-

---

[1] Cf. *ibid.*, p. 243: "Wir gewinnen sogar, im Vollzuge der phänomenologischen
Reduktion, die generelle Wesenseinsicht, das der Gegenstand Baum in einer Wahrnehmung überhaupt als objektiv so bestimmter, wie er in ihr erscheint, nur dann
erscheinen kann, wenn die hyletischen Momente (oder falls er eine kontinuierliche
Wahrnehmungsreihe ist – wenn die kontinuierlichen hyletischen Wandlungen) gerade
die sind und keine anderen."

[2] "Die unvergleichlich wichtigeren und reicheren Analysen liegen auf seiten des
Noetischen." *ibid.*, p. 212.

ity and the deeper, temporal level, a contradiction which Husserl
does not have the means to solve. When he introduces his theory
of genetic constitution, he will be able to resolve the difficulty.
Then the temporal nature of consciousness will reach even into
the higher regions of intentionality and as a result, Husserl will
finally drop the distinction between noeses and sensations, even
on this higher level. In the *Ideas*, there is still no genetic constitution. The higher level analyses are all static, and their static
nature makes it impossible for Husserl to reconcile the mobile
temporality of inner subjectivity with them. These points will
become clearer when we go further in our study of the *Ideas*, and
will reach their culmination in our study of genetic constitution
in Husserl's later works.

7. *The noema*

Intentional consciousness has two real components, sensations
and noeses. It also has what Husserl calls an "intentional"
component, the noema. He introduces this element by appealing
first to the fact that each intentional act must carry a meaning,
a sense. "Every intentional experience is, thanks to its noetic
moment, precisely noetic; it is its essence to conceal something
like a 'sense,' or even perhaps a multiple sense, in itself...." [1]
This "sense" which all intentional acts must have is what Husserl calls the noema: "the noematic correlate that here ... is
called 'sense'." [2] The noema is the ideal component of acts, and
is correlative to the noesis. We note in passing that once again,
as in the *Logical Investigations*, the "sense" is conceived as
arising strictly in the noetic element of subjectivity, not in the
hyletic. [3]

As to the structure of the noema itself, Husserl makes one

[1] "Jedes intentionales Erlebnis ist, dank seiner noetischen Momente, eben noe-
tisches; es ist sein Wesen, so etwas wie einen 'Sinn' und ev. mehrfältigen Sinn in
sich zu bergen...." *ibid.*, pp. 218-19.
[2] "das noematische Korrelat, das hier ... 'Sinn' heisst." *ibid.*, p. 219
[3] Husserl also makes use of the transcendental reduction to explain what he means
by noema. After we suspend belief in real existence, we can no longer speak about
things as they are in reality, but we find that reality is still retained within subjectivity as noema. "Die 'transzendentale' Reduktion übt epoche hinsichtlich der
Wirklichkeit; aber zu dem, was sie von dieser übrig behält, gehören die Noemen...."
ibid., p. 245. Reality as an independent existence is put into brackets by reduction,
but reality as meant, as intended, is still retained in subjectivity. It is now ideal,
not "real." Cf. *ibid.*, p. 222.

fundamental distinction. "We note here that we must distinguish, within the full noema, ... essentially distinct layers
that are grouped around a central 'nucleus,' around the pure
'objective sense'...."[1] This nucleus or objective sense is the
element in the noema in which the object of reference is meant,
as distinct from the various senses or predicates which are meant
as belonging to this object of reference. This nucleus performs
the role which was carried out by the objectivating act in the
Investigations. By virtue of it, an intention is referred to a
definite object. The importance of this distinction between nucleus and layers of sense will make itself felt when we discuss the
final and culminating point of Husserl's constitutional analyses,
the treatment of reason and reality.

From what has been said in our preceding section, it is easy
to see what form Husserl's investigations in intentional constitution will take from now on. He has established the correlation
between noesis and noema, and has already shown that certain
noetic patterns are necessary for the constitution of various
types of objects. It simply remains for him to carry out the
implications of this program, by showing specifically what sort
of correlations do occur between noesis and noema, and by
showing which noetic manifold must be present in order to constitute a given noematic unit. "There is indeed a parallelism between
noesis and noema, but in such a way that the formations must
be described on both sides and in their essential reciprocity. The
noematic is the field of units, the noetic that of the 'constituting' manifolds." [2] The noesis found in a given type of act will
deposit a corresponding noematic sense in its object, and constitutional analysis consists in showing how this takes place. For
example, acts of imagination deposit a sense of "imaginary" in
their noematic correlation, acts of remembering a sense of
"past," and so forth.

We will sketch briefly the pattern of Husserl's analyses and

---

[1] "Wir merken hierdurch, dass wir innerhalb des vollen Noema ... wesentlich
verschiedene Schichten sondern müssen, die sich um einen zentralen 'Kern,' um den
puren 'gegenständlichen Sinn' gruppieren...." *ibid.*, p. 227. The noema serves much
the same purpose as the act-material did in the *Logical Investigations*.

[2] "Ein Parallelismus zwischen Noesis und Noema ist zwar vorhanden, aber so,
dass die Gestaltungen beiderseits und in ihrem wesensmässigen Sich-entsprechen
beschrieben werden müssen. Das Noematische sei das Feld der Einheiten, das Noetische das der 'konstituierenden' Mannigfaltigkeiten." *ibid.*, p. 248.

the different noetic variations which he describes. His descriptions are grouped into several classes, each of which follows a particular theme, a particular manner in which noeses can vary. Thus the first is a study of how intentionality can present or represent its object in different ways; the second is a study of modal variations in noeses; the third is a general study of noeses that are built upon one another. The interest each of these studies presents is not so much in the noetic variation itself, but in the noematic sense which is constituted by it.

8. Studies in noetic-noematic correlations

If we consider noeses insofar as they present an object in consciousness, we find that the basic, unmodified form is that of perception, in which an object bears the sense of being actually present. Modifications of perception are noeses of remembering, imagining, anticipating, picturing, symbolizing, and so on. In each of them, the object is not present but only re-presented, and it bears a sense correlative to the noeses which bring this about. Another series of investigations is possible when we consider the modal aspects of intentional acts. Here the fundamental form is one of belief, of position; we normally affirm the reality of what we have presented to consciousness. The noematic correlate is a thetic, posited, "doxic" character in the object. "In the series we are now concerned with, the certainty of belief clearly plays the part of the unmodified or ... the 'unmodalized' primal form of the manner of belief. Corresponding to this in its correlate: the being-character pure and simple (the noematic 'being certain' or 'being real') functions as the primal form of all modalities of being." [1] Modifications in this case would be characteristics of possibility, impossibility, doubt, probability, negation, and so on, in the noema, each correlated to corresponding noetic characters. Here, as in the case of presentation and its modifications, various noetic combinations are possible and result in complex noematic senses. For example, I can imagine a non-

---

[1] "In der jetzigen Reihe spielt offenbar die Glaubensgewissheit die Rolle der unmodifizierten, oder ... die 'unmodalisierten' Urform der Glaubensweise. Dementsprechend im Korrelat: der Seinscharakter schlechthin (das noematische 'gewiss' oder 'wirklich' seiend) fungiert als die Urform aller Seinsmodalitäten." *ibid.*, pp. 257-58; trans. adapted from Gibson, p. 298.

probable state of affairs or, in the case of presentation, I can remember the symbolic presentation of an object.

A special case of modal modification is what Husserl calls "neutralizing." An act thus qualified is deprived of all modal character. The object is not posited nor doubted nor negated, it is simply contemplated as an object. As Husserl observes, the whole problem of "reasonableness" disappears in the case of neutralized acts. I can be reasonable or unreasonable when I affirm or doubt something, call it possible, impossible, probable, or improbable, or negate it, but if I only contemplate it neutrally, the question of my reasonableness cannot be raised. "For neutralized [noeses], the question of reason or unreason has no sense...."[1]

The correlations of noesis-noema discussed so far have all been based on modifications of acts. Other series of correlations are possible when we consider founded noeses and their noemas. On the basis of a perception noesis, I can carry out an act of evaluation or desire and thus deposit a new sense in the noema, which then becomes "valuable," "worthless," or "desirable."

Still another field of inquiry in founded acts is opened by the possibility of composite acts. They yield the noemas which, in the *Logical Investigations*, are referred to as "categorical objects." The noetic process carried out here involves various forms of relationships between simple acts and results in judgments, collections, comparisons, and other types of noematic relations. Such combinations give rise to what Husserl calls "formal-ontological" categories.[2] They express the various relationships an object can enter into simply by virtue of being an object of consciousness.

All such noetic-noematic descriptions are what Husserl means when he speaks of studies in noetic constitution. This type of classification and description is, in his view, much more important and fruitful than the hyletic analyses we mentioned in the previous section.[3]

---

[1] "... Für die neutralisierten [Noesen gibt] die Frage nach Vernunft und Unvernunft keinen Sinn...." *ibid.*, p. 266.

[2] Cf. *ibid.*, p. 293.

[3] Concerning these examples of the use of phenomenological method, Husserl notes: "Nur ein Bruchstück ist wirklich gegeben." *ibid.*, p. 7, n. 1.

9. The noesis objectivates the noematic sense which it constitutes

In correlation to each noetic characteristic, there is constituted a noematic character. This noematic aspect, furthermore, is
objectivated. As Husserl says, we spontaneously believe in its
objectivity. The noematic character is deposited in the object as
a sense which the object "really" possesses. We find the noematic
character in the object itself. "Every emergence of new noetic
characteristics, or every modification of old ones, constitutes
not only new noematic characters, but there are also constituted
eo ipso new ontic objects for consciousness. To noematic characters
there correspond predicable characters inherent in the object
containing sense; and indeed they are present as real predicables,
and not merely noematically modified ones." [1] For example,
noeses of esthetic appreciation deposit an objective, real sense
of "beautiful" in the object of perception. I can say that this
object *is* really beautiful, or that this event *is* desirable. Such
predicates are not simply expressions of my subjective dispositions; they are the expression of real attributes, objective
senses, which the objects in question possess.

It is obvious that objectivation of esthetic noematic characteristics is different from the objectivation carried out in simple
perception. The sense constituted in each case belongs to a
different type. It is precisely the task of phenomenology to
analyze the various senses that arise in such different ways and
to show the distinctions and relationships that exist among them.

Such objectivation occurs by reason of the very nature of
intentionality. Noetic characteristics necessarily have noematic,
objective counterparts; they are "consciousness of" something.
Furthermore, just as simple intentionality constitutes the sense
of "an object in general" and thus provides the basis for formal
ontology, so all the modifications and additions which intentionality undergoes constitute corresponding objects or object levels,
which then give rise to ontologies proper to themselves. "All
acts whatsoever – even acts of feeling and will – are objectiva-

---

[1] "Jedes Hinzutreten neuer noetischen Charaktere, bzw. jede Modifikation alter,
konstituiert nicht nur neue noematische Charaktere, sondern es konstituieren sich
damit eo ipso für das Bewusstsein neue Seinsobjekte; den noematischen Charak-
teren entsprechen prädikable Charaktere an dem Sinnesobjekt, als wirkliche und
nicht bloss noematisch modifizierte Prädikabilien." *ibid.*, p. 260; trans. adapted from
Gibson, p. 301.

ting acts, ... originally 'constituting' objects. They are necessary
sources of various regions of being and, consequently, of the
ontologies that belong to them." [1] Thus Husserl says that e-
valuational consciousness constitutes axiological objects, which
form a region of reality formally different from simple objects,
a region which has certain rules, syntactical modifications, formations, and the like, proper to itself.

However, the very fact that such characteristics are objectivated means that they can then be made the objects of simple,
unmodified intentions. After evaluational noeses deposit an
objective sense of value in certain things, this value can be
contemplated simply as an objective reality; I can thematize it
by simple intentionality. In this way, it can be classed as an
ordinary object and as such it becomes subsumed under the rules
of ordinary formal logic or formal ontology All this is possible
because of the objectivation undergone by the noematic characteristics. The result is the universal applicability of the rules of
formal logic. Anything that is objectivated must be subject to
these rules. "Here lies the deepest source from which the universality of logic, and ultimately the universality of the predicative judgment, is to be clarified.... From this viewpoint we
can also understand the ultimate basis for the universality of
the supremacy of logic itself." [2] It is true that treating axiological
or esthetic values as simple elements of formal logic neglects
what is specific to them and puts them on a par with colors,
things, and any other objects, but it is not the function of formal
logic or formal ontology as such to account for the specific nature
of the objects they treat. This is done by regional ontologies or
regional logics. Formal logic and formal ontology must be supplemented by other disciplines before the fullness of reality can be
accounted for, but the basic structures they propose are the
necessary nucleus, the bare but indispensable rules of rationality

[3] "... Alle Akte überhaupt – auch die Gemüts- und Willensakte – [sind] 'objektivierende,' ... Gegenstände ursprünglich 'konstituierende,' notwendige Quelle verschiedener Seinsregionen und damit auch zugehöriger Ontologien." *ibid.*, p. 290;
trans. adapted from Gibson, p. 332.
[1] "Hier liegt die tiefste der Quellen, aus denen die Universalität des Logischen,
zuletzt die des prädikativen Urteils aufzuklären ist, ... und von da aus versteht sich
auch der letzte Grund der Universalität der Herrschaft der Logik selbst." *ibid.*, p.
291; trans. adapted from Gibson, p. 333.

which all objects of consciousness and reason must comply with, simply because they are objects of consciousness.

10. Husserl's noetic-noematic studies still leave the basic sense of an object unexplained

It should be noted that all these noetic-noematic correlations described by Husserl, even if carried to utmost detail in analysis, would never suffice, in themselves, to reconstruct the totality of a given experience. They are still formal analyses, and have nothing to say about the material objects to which they apply. For example, suppose I analyze the correlations involved in the perception of a tree. By reason of the perception noesis, the object acquires the sense of a "perceived" tree, and has the modal sense of a "real" tree, whose existence we spontaneously posit. If we evaluate the tree or admire it, it acquires further the sense of being a "good" or "beautiful" tree. None of these noeses, however, have yet given us any correlation for the material sense of "tree" itself, and hence we do not yet have any phenomenological explanation of the constitution of tree as such. We have explained the senses of "perceived," "good," "beautiful," but these are all formal attributes. We have not explained, phenomenologically, the constitution of "tree."

To find some sort of explanation, some correlation to the sense of tree, we can turn to the hyletic dimension of analysis, which Husserl considers far inferior to the noetic aspect. There we find something for the noema "tree" and its constitution, because the hyletic pattern of sensations correlative to trees is different from the pattern correlative to stones, dogs, houses, or men. However, the hyletic analysis is not enough to give an exhaustive phenomenological explanation of the material sense of tree. We do not differentiate between trees and men and animals simply because each of them has a different sensory pattern. The difference lies deeper than this. It presupposes the hyletic pattern, but it demands more. Not only the sensory form, but the "reality" and the objective sense of tree must be explained. Nothing we have discussed in Husserl's theory of constitution has yet been found which is capable of explaining this sense. This problem will arise again and be more satisfactorily answered in Husserl's study of reason and reality in the last section of *Ideas* and in his theory of genetic constitution, but even then there will be a certain facticity, a certain givenness of the content of reality, that is not explained by subjectivity.

11. Reason and reality. The constitution of reasonable encounter and real objects

Husserl's studies so far have concerned intentionality in general. The structures and constitutional performances he has described hold for all types of consciousness. A subclass of intentionality in general is what he calls "reasonable" intentionality. Certain acts we perform are called reasonable, authentic, or valid, and they bear this name because they are supposed to reveal to us what is "real" or "true." Through them, we encounter reality. Such encounters obviously hold a special place in our intentionality, as opposed to consciousness which is merely illusory, unfounded, erroneous, or imaginative. In section four of *Ideas*, entitled "Reason and Reality," Husserl attempts a phenomenological analysis of reasonable encounter and the reality which it constitutes. "Moving forward in this direction and, on the other hand, reflecting on the parallel noeses, we eventually strike the question of what the 'claim' of consciousness to be 'really related' to something objective, to have objective 'relevance,' properly means; how 'valid' and 'invalid' objective reference is to be clarified phenomenologically, according to noesis and noema. And thus we stand before the great problems of reason...." [1]

It should be noted that these investigations are still carried out in the phenomenological attitude, and therefore Husserl still must refrain from concurring, as a phenomenologist, in those reasonable but world-orientated judgments which he is now to describe. Reasonable encounter is something that takes place in the natural attitude, and the reality of things can be asserted only if we still naively posit the existence of a real world. For the phenomenologist, reasonable encounter is something to

---

[1] "Denn in dieser Richtung fortschreitend und andererseits auf die parallelen Noesen reflektierend, stossen wir schliesslich auf die Frage, was die 'Prätention' des Bewusstseins, sich 'wirklich' auf ein Gegenständliches zu 'beziehen,' 'triftiges' zu sein, eigentlich besage, wie sich 'gültige' und 'ungültige' gegenständliche Beziehung phänomenologisch nach Noesis und Noema aufkläre: und damit stehen wir vor den grossen Problemen der Vernunft...." *ibid.*, p. 315; trans. adapted from Gibson, pp. 360-61.

be reflected upon, and the reality constituted in it is to be treated simply as a phenomenon.[1]

In order to explain reasonable constitution as such, Husserl must clarify some structural elements in intentionality which he has not stressed very much until now. Up to this point, most of his analyses have been concerned with explaining a noematic or objective unit as constituted by a manifold in the noesis or in the hyletic moment of experience. Now he brings in the fact, which we have briefly mentioned above, that there is a unity-manifold opposition within the noema itself. It consists in the structure by which a manifold of senses or meanings is attributed to a single object. The unit in question is the object and the plurality is the series of senses attributed to it; speaking grammatically, the unit is the subject, the manifold a series of predicates belonging to the subject. "As the central noematic moment, there is set apart: the 'object of reference,' the 'object,' the 'identical element,' the 'determinable subject of its possible predicates' – the pure X in abstraction from all predicates – and it is set apart from these predicates, or more exactly, from the predicate noemas." [2] Intentional encounter does not consist simply in a succession of predicates or senses; the various senses follow one another in the flow of experience, but they are all related to a single object. Their manifold converges on the unity of the object, the carrier, to which they are all attributed.

Such a noematic structure is found in all intentional consciousness. For instance, in pure phantasy I can think about an entity which looks like a stone, then changes into a living creature, then becomes invisible and dimensionless. There is one subject for all these characteristics, and the manifold of senses (extended, brown, inanimate; then animated, breathing; then suddenly not visible but capable of being heard, capable of causing things to

[1] Cf. *ibid.*, pp. 225-26: "...Wir gestatten aber kein Urteil, das von der Thesis des 'wirklichen' Dinges, wie der ganzen 'transzendenten' Natur Gebrauch macht, sie 'mitmacht.' Als Phänomenologen enthalten wir uns all solcher Setzungen. Wir werfen sie darum nicht weg, wenn wir uns 'nicht auf ihren Boden stellen,' sie 'nicht mitmachen.' Sie sind ja da, gehören wesentlich mit zum Phänomen. Vielmehr wir sehen sie uns an; statt sie mitzumachen, machen wir sie zu Objekte...."

[2] "Es scheidet sich als zentrales noematisches Moment aus: der 'Gegenstand,' das 'Objekt,' das 'Identische,' das 'bestimmbare Subjekt seiner möglichen Prädikate' – das pure X in Abstraktion von allen Prädikaten – und es scheidet sich ab von diesen Prädikaten, oder genauer, von den Prädikatnoemen." *ibid.*, p. 321; trans. adapted from Gibson, pp. 365-66.

happen, etc.) are all predicates of this one subject. Let us now consider the strange series of predicates which we have attributed to our imaginary entity. There is nothing objectionable if I merely contemplate something which has all these attributes successively. Reasonableness does not come into question as long as I do not assert anything. However, there is something objectionable in saying or thinking that such an entity exists in the world of our encounter.[1] If I were to state that such a thing exists, or that I have really encountered such a thing, I would be told that such a thing *could not* exist, could not be a part of reality, and that my encounter was unreasonable. Why should such an accusation be made? It can be made because reality and reasonable encounter involve certain apriori patterns which must be maintained in the series of senses or predicates which we attribute to a given subject. Certain predicates must accompany certain others, and at the same time must exclude still other predicates. If we try to join irreconcilable predicates, or if we try to separate essentially conjoined ones, then we are breaking the rules of reason. The subject of predicates which break the rules of reason cannot be said to exist; it cannot be a real entity. Reality and reason go together.

In the example we have just given, we were able to recognize that to posit the reality of such an entity as we have described would be unreasonable. If we recognize irrationality, we must know something about its positive correlate, rationality. We must be able to state positively what constitutes rationality and its noematic counterpart, reality. To do this is the phenomenological task which Husserl now undertakes, and which he recognizes as "a major turning point of our investigations."[2] The problem is to determine the patterns of attributes which are necessary for reasonable encounter, and which warrant our assertion of the reality of the subject towards which our intentionality is directed. "The question then is, how in the spirit of phenomenological science we are to describe, noetically and noematically, all the interconnections of consciousness which render necessary a plain object (which in the sense of common

---

[1] In other words, we could not make such a noema part of an assertion, as Husserl calls it, a *Satz*. *Satz* does not mean "sentence," but means the unity of a sense with a thetic character, a sense which is posited or affirmed. Cf. *ibid.*, p. 324.

[2] "einen grossen Wendepunkt unserer Untersuchungen." *ibid.*, p. 331.

speech always means a real object) precisely in its character as real." [1]

12. The rules for reasonable noemas are to be found in acts of evidence. The role of perception

Where are we to find the rules for rational encounter? Husserl proposes that we look to certain paradigm cases, to certain forms of encounter in which we have what he calls "evidence." Such cases, he claims, are instances of rational intentionality. By subjecting them to phenomenological analysis, we will see what constitutes rational encounter.

Does this introduction of evidence help us? Husserl's concept of evidence is not that of something which is given to us in a thing, a quality of some sort, nor is it a criterion which enables us to judge whether we have found the truth or not. As he explains it, it is simply "the unity of a rational assertion with that which essentially motivates it." [2] Evidence is simply a reasonable, warranted assertion that is carried out in conjunction with those elements which are its motivations, its guarantee. He calls it a "special mode of asserting." [3] When an assertion is carried out in this way, it is said to be made with evidence. Various forms of evidence are possible, of course, depending on the type of act and type of object involved. Each will demand its own proper sort of motivation. Evidence means one thing in our knowledge of people, another in our knowledge of things, still something else in mathematical knowledge. The point is, however, that "evident" acts are not different in structure from "reasonable" acts, except that the qualification of evidence stresses that the assertion made in a reasonable act is made *in the presence of* its motivating factors, the factors which guarantee the reasonableness of the assertion in question. [4]

[1] "Die Frage ist also, wie in phänomenologischer Wissenschaftlichkeit all die Bewusstseinszusammenhänge noetisch, bzw. noematisch zu beschreiben sind, die einen Gegenstand schlechthin (was im Sinne der gewöhnlichen Rede immer einen wirklichen Gegenstand besagt) eben in seiner Wirklichkeit notwendig machen." *ibid.*, p. 332; trans. adapted from Gibson, p. 377.

[2] "Die Einheit einer Vernunftsetzung mit dem sie wesensmässig Motivierenden." *ibid.*, p. 336; trans. adapted from Gibson, p. 381.

[3] "Eigentümlichen Setzungsmodus." *ibid.*, p. 354.

[4] Cf. Eugen Fink, "Das Problem der Phänomenologie Edmund Husserls," p. 252: "Das Problem der Evidenz als die suchende Frage nach der Selbstgebung des Seienden ist für Husserl zur Frage nach den originären Bewusstseinsweisen geworden...

Thus Husserl does not clarify his problem of reasonableness by appealing to evidence. We cannot understand his notion of evidence until we have understood his concept of reason, because only then will we know what can serve as a guarantee, a motivation, for the authenticity of an actual assertion. Until this is achieved, we do not know what can be invoked as motivation. We still do not know what must be present in order that we can say we have evidence.

More light can be shed on our problem if we discuss, with Husserl, the case of acts of perception. These are the acts he chooses to analyze in order to show what he means by reasonableness in making assertions, because the character of rationality is most obvious in them. In perception, the object we know is immediately present to us; what we "mean" finds its fulfillment "in person," as Husserl says, and we are justified in asserting the object as it is given to us.[1] When we assert the reality of what we perceive, we are making a reasonable assertion. Such acts are acts of evidence, as Husserl understands the term.

However, perception is not a univocal term for Husserl. It does not simply mean seeing sensible qualities. I can perceive things, persons, tools, animals, works of art, and so on, and each of these objects calls forth a different series of noetic-noematic correlates. Perception is an act in which an object is originally present to me, but this presence is different, for example, for people and for things. In order that a tool be present to me, in all its reality, it may be necessary for me to learn how to use it. It is not enough just to be able to see its shape and color, for when that is all I perceive, then I see simply a material thing before me, not a tool.

Thus in order to find out what sort of evidence is relative to a certain thing, we must investigate the perception we make of that object. The manner in which the object is originally presented to us will illustrate the factors that make up the rationality associated with that object. "To every region and category

Offenbar ist 'originär' ein solches Wissen, das in sich selbst nicht mehr zurückverweisend ist und in Rückweisen seinen Sinn nimmt als Modifikation-von, sondern das eben das Ziel aller Rückweise ist und allen Modifikationen den in ihnen abgewandelten Sinn gibt."

[1] Cf. *Ideen I*, p. 335: "Dasselbe besagt: die Setzung hat in der originären Gegebenheit ihren ursprünglichen Rechtsgrund."

of would-be objects corresponds phenomenologically not only a basic type of senses or assertions, but also a basic kind of original presenting consciousness for such senses, and, pertaining to it, a basic type of original evidence...." [1] When we investigate perception in this way, we will find what series of senses or predicates must be associated with an object of a given type, in order that the object can be asserted as real. To use the example to which Husserl always returns, material things are perceived as subjects of a whole series of predicates: extended, colored, causally related, and so on. Our original encounter of things presents them to us with these senses. The chain of senses then becomes the rule of reason concerning material things. The composition of noemas in perception prescribes a rule for the composition of assertable, and hence reasonable noemas in other types of acts besides perception. Because perception presents material things as causally related with other things, I cannot assert the reality of a noema in which I imagine, in pure phantasy, a stone which is in principle impervious to all natural causality. I would be acting unreasonably if I tried to assert this, because I would be breaking the rules of rationality as regards material things, rules which I have given to me by perception. Reality and its structure are given to us in perception.

The rules of reason and reality are thus not found in an apriori that antecedes all encounter; they can be found only by investigating encounter itself, and determining through phenomenological analysis what noematic constitution a given region of beings must have in order to be reasonable, to be assertable. The noematic analyses in turn require phenomenological clarification of their noetic correlates in order to give a full, phenomenological explanation for the constitution in question.

This is then the problem of constitution as envisioned in the context of reason and reality. It proposes to find what noematic pattern of sense must be attributable to a subject in order to be able to assert the reality of a given noema. It tries to fulfill its task by turning to those acts where the object in question

---

[1] "Jeder Region und Kategorie prätendierter Gegenstände entspricht phänomenologisch nicht nur eine Grundart von Sinnen, bzw. Sätzen, sondern auch eine Grundart von originär gebendem Bewusstsein solcher Sinne und ihr zugehörig ein Grundtypus originärer Evidenzen...." *ibid.*, p. 340; trans. adapted from Gibson, p. 386.

is originally given and where, consequently, we have original evidence for positing the object. Since various regions of being have different ways of being perceived, and consequently have different modes of evidence and reason, each region has to be investigated for itself, in its own proper way of being originally present to consciousness, in order to find the rules of reason that exist for it.[1]

13. "Real" noemas and methods of discursive thought or proof

These rules of reason, which are found in phenomenological description of direct encounter of the object in question, operate also when we leave the realm of direct perception and begin to build up logical arguments, proofs, deductions, or inferences concerning the object.[2] The type of deductions, proofs, or arguments we can make concerning people is different from the sort carried out concerning things. The noematic constitution of each region influences the type of reasoning which can be carried out in respect to it. The rate of fall of a body can be used to prove something about material things, but it does not serve as an argument to prove anything about persons as such, even though they too will fall at a certain rate of speed. Because of the noematic constitution of the reality we call "person," a factor like velocity in free fall does not enter essentially in the network of reasonings that can be built up concerning persons as such.

To illustrate this in another way, let us consider the different types of answers one might give to the two questions: "Why do you say that this crater was caused by meteors?" and "Why do you say that this object was formed by an intelligent creature?" In both cases, we are dealing with claims about reality, and therefore with assertions. Consequently, the claims must be reasonable. We do not have the evidence of direct perception in such cases, and so we must try to build up a system of proofs

---

[1] Cf. Emmanuel Levinas, *La théorie de l'intuition*, p. 187: "C'est en vertu du mode même de se présenter à la conscience, de telle ou telle catégorie d'objets, que se justifie la diversité – non seulement dans la méthode, mais même dans les problèmes – des sciences qui portent différents 'régions'."

[2] Cf. *Ideen I*, p. 377: "Damit verbinden sich aber die entsprechenden Forschungen, bezogen auf die Leistungen der höheren, im engeren Sinne sog. 'Verstandes-' oder 'Vernunftssphäre,' mit ihren explizierenden, beziehenden, und sonstigen 'logischen' (dann auch axiologischen und praktischen) Synthesen, mit ihren 'begrifflichen' Operationen, ihren Aussagen, ihren neuen, mittelbaren Begründungsformen."

for our claim. The structure of such proof, however, is derived
from what we "perceive" about the regions concerned. Two
different regions are in question: material reality and intelligent
beings, and this difference is reflected in the type of answers we
will look for to prove our assertions. In the first, we might
appeal to the depth and shape of the crater, types of rock found
nearby, the age of the crater, physical laws of impact and
reaction, and so on. In the second case, we would try to find what
sort of use the supposed tool or work of art served, the type of
society it must have come from, general noematic characteristics of tools and objects of art, etc. Different factors are relevant as "proofs" in each of the two cases. The type of argument,
the type of rationality called for in each question, is different,
and the difference stems ultimately from our direct perception
of the regions in question. The rules of reason are given in such
perception, through noematic analysis of the objects given originally in it.

*14. Noematic analysis demands further noetic studies for a com-
plete phenomenological explanation. Reappearance of a fundamental difficulty*

The structural basis for all these noematic phenomenological
studies is the composition object-predicates which we find in each
noema, and in particular those noemas which can be asserted as
real. "Object is for us always a title for essential interconnections
of consciousness; it emerges first as a noematic X, as the sense-
subject of various essential types of senses and assertions. It
appears further under the title 'real object' and is then the title
for certain interconnections of reason, eidetically considered, in
which the X that unifies the senses in them acquires its reasonable assertion." [1]

As Husserl has pointed out, the investigation of such noematic
constitution is a turning point in his phenomenological analyses.
Until it appeared, all his studies were directed along formal lines.

[1] "'Gegenstand' ist für uns überall ein Titel für Wesenszusammenhänge des
Bewusstseins; er tritt zunächst auf als noematisches X, als Sinnessubjekt verschie-
dener Wesenstypen von Sinnen und Sätzen. Er tritt ferner auf als Titel 'wirklicher
Gegenstand' und ist dann Titel für gewisse eidetische betrachtete Vernunftzusam-
menhänge, in denen das in ihnen sinngemäss einheitliche X seine vernunftmässige
Setzung erhält." *ibid.*, p. 356.

His description of noetic-noematic correlation, as we have mentioned, allowed him to explain phenomenologically certain formal "senses" in the noema, such as "valuable," "beautiful," "perceived," and the like, but it did not have anything to say about the material object to which these formalities are assigned. They have nothing to say about how trees, men, stones, etc. are constituted by subjectivity. The present noematic investigations do say something about such material constitution. They describe the series of predicates which belong to the constitution of objects.

Analyses of noematic constitution, furthermore, have repercussions on their noetic correlates, both in their hyletic and noetic dimensions. For instance, in giving a phenomenological analysis of the noematic sense of a material thing, Husserl includes as one of the predicates the extension which a thing must have. When he carries through his phenomenological study of extension, he must go into a detailed treatment of kinesthetic, tactile, and visual sensations. These are the noetic correlates, on the hyletic level, of the noematic sense of extension. They belong to a complete phenomenological analysis of the object "material thing." [1] Likewise, noematic constitution of other persons supposes noetic acts proper to these noemas, such as acts of empathy and comprehension of motives. Such noeses are indispensable for the constitution of the noema of person, and a noematic analysis of the predicates proper to persons necessarily refers back to further studies of the noetic correlates associated with them. [2]

Although the material, regional analyses supplement the more formal noetic ones, they still do not explain in full the constitution of an object and its senses. We are still left with the unexplained factor which makes itself felt even in the *Logical Investigations:* the various predicates or senses are described and distinguished from one another, but where do they come from in the first place? Husserl's analysis is static. It describes the various layers of sense which an object has, but it does not explain the sources of these senses themselves. In the *Investigations*, we saw

[1] Cf. *Ideen II*, pp. 29-32, 56-57, 152-59; *Ideen III*, pp. 120-24.
[2] Cf. Theodor Celms, *Der phänomenologische Idealismus Husserls*, p. 415: "Die Schichten der Objektivität können also nur aus ihren Zusammenhang mit den Schichten der sie konstituierenden Erlebnisse verständlich gemacht werden." Also p. 419: "Alle Konstitutionsfragen führen also letzten Endes auf die Probleme der noetischen Konstitution zurück, wobei die konkreten Noesen, d.h. die Noesen, 'mitsamt ihren hyletischen Momenten,' gemeint werden."

that the meanings contained in intentional acts are posited, but their origins are not given. They are always assumed as already there. The same is true in the noematic analyses of the *Ideas*, where the senses of things are all posited as ready-made in perception. In our perception, we find such and such predicates belonging to one region, others belonging to another. But how are these senses constituted in themselves? Where do they arise from?

Thus Husserl does not explain the content of the senses or objects constituted by intentionality. The content is accepted as a simple facticity, as something that consciousness is faced with. Husserl does not explain where such contents come from when he analyzes the perception we make of them; all he does is describe what subjective activity is necessary to allow the sense and object in question to emerge.

If we recall what was said during our study of Husserl's fundamental meditation, we now see the reason why we claimed that, for Husserl, subjectivity is only a *sine qua non* for the emergence of sense, and not a sufficient cause of it. If subjectivity "created" sense and objects when it constitutes them, then their contents should be explained by subjectivity. This is not the case; the contents are simply given as facticity, and not as something essentially deducible from subjectivity and its operations. Therefore, subjectivity does not cause or create senses and objects. It merely allows them to come about. It is their condition, and not their cause; consequently, Husserl's doctrine of constitution should not be interpreted in too idealistic a manner.

When Husserl introduces the problem of genetic constitution into his phenomenology, there will arise a possibility of explaining the contents of meanings and objects, and the impression of idealism will be even greater than it is in the *Ideas*. Nevertheless, even in genetic constitution there is a certain facticity about what is constituted, as we shall see, and the accusation of idealism still cannot be unequivocally made.

15. Temporal constitution as a deeper form of constitution. The problem of absolutes

We have traced Husserl's treatment of the problem of constitution in all its essential steps as found in *Ideas I*. He begins by showing the relationship of constituted reality to absolute subjectivity as found through the phenomenological reduction, he shows the noetic-noematic correlations as part of the constitution problem, and finally he treats constitution in the framework of reality and reason. In following his development, we omitted treatment of his brief discussion of constitution and time. Let us now turn our attention to this subject.

Husserl mentions the problem of time only to state that he will not discuss it in *Ideas*. "Time is furthermore . . . a title for a completely self-contained problem sphere, and one of exceptional difficulty." [1] His presentation of phenomenology as a science has to neglect the question of time "in order to keep free of confusion that which first appears only in the phenomenological attitude." [2] To bring in the dimension of time at the beginning of phenomenology would confuse presentation of what we find when we first adopt the phenomenological attitude.

An interesting remark follows, in which Husserl says that the apodictic field of inner experience, which we have gained by reduction, is not really the ultimate absolute: "The transcendental 'absolute' which we have set up through the reductions is in truth not the ultimate; it is something which constitutes itself in a certain profound and wholly unique sense, and which has its primal source in an ultimate and true absolute." [3] Husserl does not deny that subjectivity is absolutely given to consciousness, but he says that there is still another deeper absolute, of another sort, given to consciousness. An anticipation of this is given right in Husserl's fundamental meditation leading to the possibility of the transcendental reduction. He observes that things are always given to us in profiles, but that inner objects do not have profiles. However, he continues, "Even an experience is not, and never is, perfectly perceived. It cannot be

[1] "Zeit ist übrigens . . . ein Titel für eine völlig abgeschlossene Problemssphäre, und eine solche von ausnehmender Schwierigkeit." *Ideen I*, p. 197; trans. adapted from Gibson, p. 236.

[2] "um unverwirrt zu erhalten, was zunächst allein in phänomenologischer Einstellung sichtig ist." *ibid.*, pp. 197-98; adapted from Gibson, p. 236.

[3] "Das transzendentale 'Absolute,' das wir uns durch die Reduktionen herauspräpariert haben, ist in Wahrheit nicht das Letzte, es ist etwas, das sich selbst in einem gewissen tiefliegenden und völlig eigenartigen Sinn konstituiert und seine Urquelle in einem letzten und wahrhaft Absoluten hat." *ibid.*, p. 198; trans. adapted from Gibson, p. 236.

grasped adequately in its full unity. It is essentially a stream...."[1]
Experiences are also units constituted in a manifold, a manifold
of temporal phases, hence there is a certain incompleteness in the
way they are given at any moment. This inadequacy is different
from that found in the encounter of material things, however,
and Husserl feels that it does not destroy the apodicticity of
inner experience.

What is the "final absolute" of which Husserl speaks? He
does not explain the term, but since he is dealing with subjectivity as a stream of inner temporality, it must refer to the source
of this flow, to the immediate present. Just as objective reality
is only relative and thus depends on an absolute, subjectivity,
so subjectivity itself, the noeses and hyletic data which are the
real components of subjectivity, are again "relative" and depend
for their possibility of phenomenological existence on a still
deeper absolute. As Celms says in this context, "By the problem
of objective constitution, we ask: what structure must consciousness have, to make objectivity possible? But here the question
is: how is this structure itself possible? ... Consciousness as a
real unity is the stream of experiences. Now we ask: how is
something like a stream of experiences possible?" [2]

The question here is thus not how to explain noemas. Their
constitution is explained by noeses and hyletic data. The problem
is to explain these noeses and sensations themselves. As we have
seen in our analysis of Husserl's lectures on time, these two real
components of consciousness are constituted by being spread
out in temporal phases. By virtue of this constitution, they
acquire phenomenological individuality and the possibility of
being experienced. They are all constituted immanent objects,
and depend upon the one absolutely ultimate unit which Husserl
says is not constituted, the individual temporal phase of
consciousness, and especially the immediate, present phase. This

[1] "Auch ein Erlebnis ist nicht, und niemals, vollständig wahrgenommen, in seiner
vollen Einheit ist es adäquat nicht fassbar. Es ist seinem Wesen nach ein Fluss...."
ibid., p. 103; trans. adapted from Gibson, p. 140.
[2] "Beim Problem der objektiven Konstitution wird gefragt: Welche Struktur
muss das Bewusstsein haben, um die Objektivität zu ermöglichen? Hier aber ist die
Frage: Wie ist diese Struktur selbst möglich? ... Das Bewusstsein als reelle Einheit
ist der Erlebnisstrom. Es fragt sich nun: Wie ist so etwas wie ein Erlebnisstrom
möglich?" *Der phänomenologische Idealismus Husserls*, pp. 418-19. See also Eugen
Fink, "Die phänomenologische Philosophie Husserls in der gegenwärtigen Kritik."
Kantstudien, 38 (1933), pp. 375-76.

is the final absolute of which Husserl speaks here. Rudolf Boehm says, "It can only mean that this absolute consciousness itself draws its own absoluteness in itself out of a source that is more fundamental than this same consciousness: the source of flowing time. Without this antecedent, original, and enduring, flowing presence of time, without this 'livingly flowing present' [*lebendig strömende Gegenwart*] ... no consciousness could constitute itself." [1]

16. Temporality and genetic constitution

Husserl goes on to summarize some of the important conclusions of his Göttingen lectures on time, but does not attempt to incorporate them into his investigation of constitution in the *Ideas*. The noetic and noematic analyses are carried out in abstraction from their temporal dimension. This does not result in their falsification, but it does result in a certain incompleteness which may be connected with the chief defect we have already noted in Husserl's studies. He always finds noematic senses, and hence their noetic counterparts also, as ready-made, and also as unchanging. For example, his analyses would find no difference in the predicates constituting the noema "father" as realized in the consciousness of a person who is only ten years old, and the noema as constituted by the same person when he is sixty years old. The dimension of historicity is absent; it is the dimension that will be accounted for in Husserl's theory of genetic constitution.[2]

This deficiency would not be remedied by simple incorporation of the ideas developed in the lectures on time, for they do not treat genetic constitution either. The temporal analyses in the lectures are purely formal. That is, they analyze the temporal dimension of immanent objects and real things, but they have nothing to say about the material element in them:

---

[1] "Het kan alleen maar betekenen, dat dit absolute bewustzijn zelf zijn absoluutheid in zich zelf uit een bron put die oorspronkelijker is dan dit bewustzijn zelf: de bron van de stromende tijd. Zonder deze voorafgaande, oorspronkelijke en voortdurende stromende aanwezigheid van de tijd, zonder deze 'lebendig strömende Gegenwart' ... zou geen bewustzijn zich kunnen konstitueren." "Zijn en tijd in de Filosofie van Husserl," p. 251.

[2] Cf. Levinas, *La théorie de l'intuition*, p. 220: "La philosophie paraît, dans cette conception, aussi indépendant de la situation historique de l'homme que la théorie cherchant à tout considérer sub specie aeternitatis." This will no longer be true after Husserl introduces the problem of genetic constitution.

the quality of acts and the material content of sensations, as well as the content of objective senses and objects. As a result, a given object or a given meaning can reappear more than once in the same flow of consciousness, but Husserl does not show how this reoccurrence changes the sense of the object or meaning. At most, the only change which could be explained would be the fact that the noema is recognized as something we are already acquainted with, but the content remains otherwise untouched by this. Likewise, the noetic correlate to the noematic sense reappears each time the same. The fact that it has a history does not penetrate into the sense of the noema, nor does it penetrate into the noesis or hyletic patterns which constitute the noema. This is so because Husserl's principles of temporality affect only the temporal character of objects, not their content. His principles are purely formal.

However, the concepts in the lectures on time have to be combined with those of the *Ideas* in order that genetic constitution can appear as a problem. This is especially true of the concept of the ego as a continuing time flow, which constitutes itself in temporality. Only when this is brought into the picture can Husserl begin to claim that noemas constituted at a given moment depend upon, and build upon, noemas which have been constituted earlier in the individual time flow. Then it will become clear that noemas do not simply reappear unchanged every time they occur in consciousness. A noema as it appears at a given moment bears the history of its past occurrences within itself, and it appears in the way it does because of this history, this genesis. By tracing the genetic constitution of a given noema, we will be able to give a new type of phenomenological explanation of it, a type of explanation which structural analysis, and even static noematic analysis, cannot furnish.

Since noemas are constituted by noeses and hyletic data, this genetic inquiry will also have an effect on them. They too will bear their history in themselves. When they recur, they will have a different internal pattern evolving on the basis of their past occurrences. Of course, they will be always formally the same: they will be noeses functionally animating hylectic data and thus constituting noemas, but the actual inner pattern of noeses and sensations corresponding to a given noematic content will be modified because of its location in time. This whole dimension is neglected by Husserl in the *Ideas*.

Once the historical dimension is brought in, Husserl will be forced to treat the first establishment (*Urstiftung*) of a given meaning or type of object. Genetic constitution points back to first occurrences as a particularly important problem, which does not make itself felt as long as we remain in static analyses. The theory of genetic constitution thus provides the first possibility of solution for a problem and a defect in Husserl's phenomenology which appears as far back as the *Logical Investigations*. Husserl's probe back into the very beginnings of a meaning or object as established will bring into relief the role of sensory data as the stuff from which it arises, and in which it must somehow be pre-formed before it actually appears. In this way, he will be able to give a certain explanation of the origins of the content of the senses and objects constituted by intentionality.

17. Conclusion

In the first volume of *Ideas*, Husserl is concerned with establishing phenomenology as a rigorous, presuppositionless science. The first task is to find a starting point for this science, a field of experience which is free of presuppositions. Husserl discovers this in transcendental subjectivity, and finds reality included within this field as the correlate, the "constituted" object of intentionality. By virtue of its constitution, therefore, reality can be included within phenomenology, it can be "explained" by Husserl's new apodictic science.

The sense of the term "constitution" and its relationship to the transcendental reduction are determined by what we have called the second theme in Husserl's fundamental meditation, the theme which is a forerunner of his ontological way to reduction. Reality, claims Husserl, cannot be conceived apart from subjectivity because it acquires its sense from subjectivity; subjectivity is the source of all sense. In this way, reality is relative to and constituted by subjectivity. We have discussed the meaning of this relativity; it does not signify that consciousness causes or makes objective meanings, but only that consciousness is a necessary condition for the emergence of the world as real, as possessing a sense.

Furthermore, Husserl maintains the transcendence of the world in relation to subjectivity. Reality is not reduced to consciousness; it remains transcendent and separate from the mind, and yet, in this very transcendence, it is accessible to consciousness. This is what Husserl calls the riddle or enigma of transcendence. It is at the same time the enigma of constitution, for intentionality constitutes an object which transcends itself, which acquires an existence and a sense that become independent of subjectivity. The theory of constitution is not an attempt to dissolve this enigma, but an endeavor to see what can be said about it. In describing the constitution of various objects, Husserl will show what subjective conditions are necessary for the emergence of their transcendent sense; he will show what subjectivity has to do in order that their particular type of transcendence can come about.

After introducing the transcendental reduction and including constitution as a dominant theme in his rigorous science, Husserl goes on to describe the structure of consciousness. As he explores various levels of this structure, the concept of constitution acquires fuller and deeper meaning. He goes through the hyletic aspect of constitution, then into various forms of noetic-noematic correlation; finally, in a turning point of his analyses, he treats the problems of reason and reality by describing the structure of the noema itself and the patterns it must have in order to be included in "reasonable" encounter. This last section of the *Ideas* is devoted basically to the problem of noematic constitution. Husserl's structural analyses are given to provide the framework for the great task he envisions for phenomenology: the clarification, through description of their constitution, of all the regions of human experience.

Husserl still uses the schema of noetic form animating hyletic matter to speak about the objectivity which is constituted by intentionality, the same schema we found in the *Investigations*. However, he admits that from the deeper point of view of inner time, this schema is unwarranted. Despite this fundamental inadequacy of the schema, he uses it on the higher levels of intentionality because he still has no other way of expressing the constitution of objectivity. Only with the introduction of genetic constitution will this contradiction be resolved, and the temporality of consciousness will be integrated into his higher level analyses.

We have also observed that Husserl's analyses of sense and objects as constituted by consciousness are purely static. He does not show how temporality can influence even the content of what we know. Once again, this is a failure on his part to integrate the temporality of consciousness into the higher level analyses of constitution that he carries out.

Finally, Husserl does not account for the origins of the various levels of sense which he describes. They are simply accepted as being present in perception as a facticity that subjectivity is faced with. To a certain degree, this failure to explain the content of what is constituted will be changed in genetic constitution, for Husserl will try to show the genetic origins which lead to the contents we encounter, and once again we will find genetic phenomenology providing a solution for the lacunae of static analyses. However, even in genetic constitution there will be a certain facticity, a certain element which is not explained by subjectivity. This failure of phenomenology to explain thoroughly the content of constitution is not a defect, because Husserl does not set before himself the task of deducing everything from consciousness. Subjectivity is only a necessary condition for the emergence of sense and objectivity, it is not their sufficient ground or cause. Therefore it is to be expected that a certain "givenness" from the part of reality will be present throughout phenomenology. Various senses and objects are simply given, and the study of their constitution is only the investigation of what subjective structures or processes are required as necessary conditions for the emergence, the coming-to-be of their specific forms of transcendence.

CHAPTER V

GENETIC CONSTITUTION

1. Introduction of the problem of genetic constitution into "Formal and Transcendental Logic"

We have seen how Husserl's development, from the beginning of his philosophical reflections to his composition of *Ideas I*, leads naturally into problems of genetic constitution. In order to close our study of his concept of constitution, let us briefly examine how genetic phenomenology is presented in *Formal and Transcendental Logic* [1] and, subsequently, in the *Cartesian Meditations*.[2] It is present in definitive form in these two works, and study of them will show how Husserl's early doctrine of constitution finds the final term of its evolution.

The problem of constitution appears as an explicit theme only in section two of *Formal and Transcendental Logic*, which is entitled, "From Formal to Transcendental Logic." [3] In the first section, Husserl has presented his theory of formal systems and investigated both formal ontology and formal apophantics, the theory of judgment that is correlative to formal ontology. After discussing the rules, elements, problems and methodology of formal systems, Husserl asks whether we as philosophers can consider our task concerning formal logic finished.[4] In his introduction, Husserl had proposed to study logic in order to find a basis for theoretical thought, to fashion the ultimate, self-justifying science.[5] Has the study of formal systems achieved

---

[1] *Formale und transzendentale Logik* (Halle a.S.: Max Niemeyer, 1929).
[2] *Cartesianische Meditationen* (The Hague: Martinus Nijhoff, 1950). This volume also contains Husserl's *Pariser Vorträge*. There is an English translation of the *Cartesian Meditations* by Dorion Cairns (The Hague: Martinus Nijhoff, 1960). We will use Cairns' translation for quotations from this work, but to keep uniformity with the rest of our study, we will also give the original German in footnotes.
[3] "Von der formalen zur transzendentalen Logik." *Form. trans. Log.* p. 133.
[4] Cf. *ibid.*, p. 133-34.
[5] Cf. *ibid.*, p. 14.

this? He answers negatively and begins his phenomenological analysis of subjectivity as a necessary supplement to his formal analyses.

Husserl organizes his problem in a manner reminiscent of the *Investigations* and the *Philosophy of Arithmetic*. He stresses the ideal existence of logical entities as something given to us in evidence and bases his proof of such ideal existence on the fact that we can encounter numerically the same ideal, logical entity in a multitude of different acts.[1] When we do encounter a logical entity, however, we are not passive before it; the presence of the logical entity is brought about by an active, constructive performance on our part. Husserl speaks of an "originally engendering activity as the self-giving of logical formations."[2] His analysis of formal systems neglects this aspect of logical entities, for it considers them as ideal objects which are simply and unquestionably given to us. Formal analysis is therefore incomplete; it leaves unsaid the problem of the origins of logical elements.

In order to remedy this defect, Husserl proposes a transcendental logic which will consist in "uncovering the hidden subjective methods of formation."[3] Its procedure will be to repeat the subjective activity which forms logical entities, but to do so in reflective awareness of what is performed in subjectivity. In this way we will carry out "exploration of the methods through which the 'basic concepts' of analysis are originally engendered."[4] Such investigations must be performed on the basic concepts of logic and on those of all sciences, in order to provide a foundation for them.[5] For example, by bringing a judgment to evidence, to self-givenness, and by being reflectively aware of what occurs in subjectivity when this is done, we will understand the origins of the logical entity known as "judgment." Such an investigation will bring to light the presuppositions concealed in logical entities.[6]

---

[1] Cf. *ibid.*, p. 138.

[2] Ursprünglich erzeugende Aktivität als die Selbstgebung der logischen Gebilde." *ibid.*, p. 149.

[3] "Enthüllung der verborgenen subjektiven Bildungsmethoden." *ibid.*, p. 159.

[4] "Erforschung der Methode, durch die die 'Grundbegriffe' der Analytik ursprünglich erzeugt werden." *ibid.*, p. 160.

[5] Cf. *ibid.*, p. 161.

[6] Cf. *ibid.*, p. 177: "...Evidenz [ist] zunächst eine naive betätigte und 'verborgene Methode,'... die nach ihrer Leistung befragt werden muss, damit man weiss, was man in ihr, als einem Bewusstsein im Modus der Selbsthabe, wirklich selbst hat und mit welchen Horizonten."

In the *Logical Investigations*, we would then expect Husserl to proceed with a structural analysis of intentionality and the acts whose performance brings logical entities into being. In *Formal and Transcendental Logic*, he pursues his problem in quite a different manner. His chief interest is no longer structural analysis alone, but analysis of the *sense* of judgments and logical entities in general. Judgments as ready-made are the result of a genesis: "It is the essential property of such products that they are senses which bear a sort of historicity in themselves as the sense implications of their genesis; that in them a sense refers back by degrees to an original sense and to the noematic intentionality belonging to it; and that we can therefore investigate every sense formation for the sense history essential to it." [1]

Thus the "hidden achievements" of intentionality which are supposed to be clarified by phenomenological analysis are no longer structural elements. They are now the hidden implications of meaning, the assumed senses and contexts (horizons) which are present in judgments. They are present as the result of previous acts of evidence, but now they are hidden from our direct, explicit awareness. To bring these implications and assumptions to full awareness is the task of phenomenology as Husserl sees it in this work.[2]

Although Husserl begins his phenomenological studies in *Formal and Transcendental Logic* with the problem of logical entities, he does not limit himself to them. Once we have realized that one type of object, logical entities, are the result of subjective, constituting performance, we can expand this conviction to cover all types of objects of consciousness, even "real" things. They too owe their sense to subjective constitution.[3] All objects

---

[1] "Es ist eben die Wesenseigenheit solcher Produkte, dass sie Sinne sind, die als Sinnesimplikat ihrer Genesis eine Art Historizität in sich tragen; dass in ihnen stufenweise Sinn auf ursprünglichen Sinn und die zugehörige noematische Intentionalität zurückweist; dass man also jedes Sinngebilde nach seiner ihm wesensmässigen Sinnesgeschichte befragen kann." *ibid.*, p. 184.

[2] Cf. *ibid.*, p. 185: "Alle intentionalen Einheiten sind aus einer intentionalen Genesis, sind 'konstituierte' Einheiten, und überall kann man die 'fertigen' Einheiten nach ihrer Konstitution, nach ihrer gesamten Genesis befragen und zwar nach deren eidetisch zu fassender Wesensform. Diese fundamentale Tatsache, in ihrer Universalität das gesamte intentionale Leben umspannend, ist es, die den eigentlichen Sinn der intentionalen Analyse bestimmt als Enthüllung der intentionalen Implikationen, mit denen, gegenüber dem offen fertigen Sinn der Einheiten, ihre verborgenen Sinnesmomente und 'kausalen' Sinnesbeziehungen hervortreten."

[3] Cf. *ibid.*, p. 233: "Diese Frage, einmal an einer Art von Objekten gesehen, wird

have a certain ideality, a transcendence which is correlative to subjective constitution.[1] Even a material thing, as present to consciousness, carries senses which are the result of subjective activity and must be brought to light by genetic constitutional analysis.

2. The intentional process of genetic constitution

How does Husserl conceive the process which he calls genetic constitution? He claims that once a judgment is performed on a given object, the object thereafter carries a sense that is the result of the judgment. If, in an original judgment and on the basis of encounter, I judge that S is p, from then on S will appear to me as carrying the sense p. "At the same time there is co-engendered the categorical resultant Sp: that is, p emerges as a 'deposit' in the sense of S, as now determined in this way."[2] Sp can then become the subject of a further predication, Sp is q, in which the new predicate is a development or determination of the first one. The predicate q depends on the predicate p. If p had not been predicated earlier, q could not have been predicated now. The process can be continued indefinitely, and the result is an object with a multiple layer of senses, $Spqrt \ldots$, each of which presupposes those which have gone before.

The condition that each layer of sense presupposes those which arise before it is essential to genetic constitution. The senses or predicates $pqrt \ldots$ are not simply juxtaposed. They build upon each other in a step by step progression; one is the "motive" or the "cause" to those which follow it.[3]

However, one judgment does not sprout immediately out of another, even if dependent upon it. Judgments come from an encounter with reality. To put it schematically, let us suppose we have already made the judgment, "S is p." Before we can move on to the genetically posterior judgment, "Sp is q," we must again encounter the reality of S. From this new encounter there

sofort zur allgemein: ist nicht alle und jede Objektivität, mit allem Sinn, in dem sie uns je gilt, in uns selbst zur Geltung kommende oder gekommene, und das mit dem Sinn, den wir uns selbst erworben haben?"

[1] Cf. *ibid.*, p. 148.

[2] "Hierdurch ist zugleich miterzeugt das kategoriale Ergebnis Sp: d.h. das p ist als 'Niederschlag' in den Sinn des S, als nunmehr so bestimmten, getreten." *ibid.*, p. 275.

[3] Cf. *ibid.*, p. 185.

will result a subsequent judgment, which will add a new sense to the subject *S*.

The consciousness of the reality of *S*, which intervenes between two judgments, is not random. When we encounter *S*, we no longer stand before it as though we were perceiving it for the first time.[1] By virtue of the first judgment, "*S* is *p*," we now "see" the object with the sense we have given to it. We encounter *Sp*, not simply *S*. It is precisely because we encounter *Sp* that our experience is pre-formed, determined, and also enlightened in such a way that we are able to arrive at the subsequent judgment, "*Sp* is *q*." It is through the intermediary of encounter that the sense in one judgment is said to "cause" or "motivate" the sense of the next. In his theory of genetic constitution, Husserl thus gives an alternating and reciprocal influence to judgment and encounter. Judgments arise from our encounter with reality, but they also determine and illuminate our subsequent encounter out of which further judgments arise.

The development followed by a given genesis is teleological.[2] Judgment and encounter work alternatively to build a sense. Furthermore, the growth of such a sense is not a chance oc-curence conditioned only by certain historical conditions. It is necessary; transcendental subjectivity must develop along the lines uncovered by genetic analysis. Husserl's theory of genetic constitution keeps the characteristics of a necessary, apriori science. However, the necessity in question is not something that is deducible from subjectivity as such. It is a necessity that comes from our perception of reality, and as such supposes a certain facticity or givenness on the part of objectivity. Within this facticity and our encounter of it, there are certain apriori interconnections of sense which govern the development of the content of knowledge. [3]

---

[1] Cf. *ibid.*, p. 195.

[2] The term "teleological" is used by Husserl. Cf. *ibid.*, pp. 216, 232. It is also found in *Ideas I*, but has a different sense there; it means the ordering of sense data in the constitution of a given object.

[3] Cf. Suzanne Bachelard, *La logique de Husserl*, pp. 251-52: "Il ne faudrait pas croire que ce dévoilement des implications intentionnelles soit livré à la contingence d'une démarche empirique. En effet, 'le flux de la synthèse intentionnelle est le règne de structures typiques de nature essentielle' et ces structures typiques essen-tielles ne peuvent se révéler qu'à un examen qui recherche les essences et qui, comme nous allons le voir, se dégage de tout attache aux faits." Because genetic analysis discovers the pattern which encounter and judgment must have, it can be used to criticize our actual encounter, as Bachelard points out on p. 229.

It is important to note, finally, that a full-grown sense or meaning can be present only *after* a judgment is made. A fixed sense which has the consistency and solidity to reappear in different acts as the same ideal entity appears for the first time in judgment. We might say that "concepts" arise only in judgments. Before the categorical act of judging takes place, there are only the fluid anticipations of meaning or sense, but such anticipations are not the same as fixed senses. They are only the "lived" pre-conceptual or pre-categorical foreshadowing of the type of object we call a sense, and they can be understood only teleologically, that is, in function of the terminal sense they anticipate. There is no crystallized meaning in pre-predicative encounter.

3. *The method used in phenomenological analysis of genetic constitution*

When we encounter an object whose sense we have not phenomenologically analyzed, claims Husserl, it always carries within itself the layers of senses deposited by previous judgments. Schematically expressed, we encounter $Spqr$.... If we make an original judgment about this object, we do so on the concealed basis of such hidden layers of meaning. We make the judgment, "$Spqr$ is t," and the encounter leading to the predicate t has been motivated, determined, and enlightened by the implied but operative senses pqr.... These senses are the sediment of previous judgments, the implied horizons or contexts which exert a decisive influence on our present judgment and encounter.[1] The task of phenomenology is to uncover these deposits of sense and to show how they work upon the encounter and judgment that follow them, how they work upon our present intentional activity. In order to explain the object $Spqrt$, phenomenology will describe how t depends on pqr, how r depends on pq, and how q depends on p. It will show what categorical formations have been constituted along this history of sense, and what sort of encounter with reality took place between them.

Husserl gives a heuristic principle which governs the method

---

[1] Cf. *Form. trans. Log.*, p. 221: "Erst durch dieses Apriori erweist sich, und in einem tieferen Sinne, was im voraus schon gesagt worden ist, dass in dem, was die Analyse als intentional Impliziertes der lebendigen Sinnkonstitution enthüllt, eine sedimentierte 'Geschichte' liege."

phenomenology will use to do this.[33] He claims that it is possible
for us to reactivate the encounter which leads to a given
judgment. Instead of simply accepting the object Sp, "... I can
really reactivate it, genuinely re-produce it, engender it, the
very same thing, in renewed and real activity. I can take the
Sp that simply comes to mind and change it back into S is p,
and thereby, in renewed activity and thus originally, constitute Sp." [31] In this way, by going through the layers of sense
which an object possesses, we will gradually clarify the hidden
implications present in it. We will do so by performing ourselves
the constituting encounter and judgment through which the
sense was originally deposited in the object.[3]

4. The nature of pre-predicative constitution

In uncovering the genesis of a given sense, particular attention
must be paid to the sphere of pre-predicative encounter. Husserl
says, "... That which is first *in se* in a theory of evident
judgments ... is to lead predicative evidence genetically back
into non-predicative evidence, which is called encounter." [4]

It is easy to see why Husserl places so much importance on
the question of pre-predicative intentionality. In attempting to
analyze the origins of a meaning, we are continually led from
completed judgments to the encounter from which they arise.[5]
The place in which discovery of a new sense, a new predicate

[1] Cf. *ibid.*, p. 217: "Freilich musste dazu die Methode erst eröffnet werden, weil
die Entdeckung der Intentionalität durch Brentano merkwürdigerweise nie dahin
geführt hat, in ihr einen Zusammenhang von Leistungen zu sehen, die in der jeweils
konstituierten intentionalen Einheit und ihrer jeweiligen Gegebenheitsweise als eine
sedimentierte Geschichte beschlossen sind, eine Geschichte, die man jeweils in
strenger Methode enthüllen kann."

[2] "... Ich kann es auch wirklich reaktivieren, es ernstlich re-produzieren, es,
dasselbe, in erneuter und wirklicher Aktivität erzeugen, das auftauchende Sp zurück-
verwandeln in S ist p und dabei das Sp in erneuter Aktivität, also ursprunglich
konstituieren." *ibid.*, p. 284.

[3] Cf. Jacques Derrida's introduction to his translation of Husserl's *L'origine de
la géométrie* (Paris: Presses universitaires de France, 1962), p. 53: "On ne peut ainsi
éclairer le sens pur de la praxis subjective qui a engendré la géométrie que réctro-
activement et à partir de son résultat. Le sens de l'acte constituant ne peut se dé-
chiffrer que dans la trame de l'objet constitué."

[4] "... Das an sich erste in einer Theorie der evidenten Urteile ... ist die genetische Rückführung der prädikativen Evidenzen auf die nichtprädikative Evidenz,
die da Erfahrung heisst." *Form. trans. Log.*, p. 186.

[5] Cf. *ibid.*, p. 278: "Hierbei zeigt es sich, ... dass die Originalform des Bewusstseins, die der 'Erfahrung' im weitesten Sinn, ... nicht nur statisch sondern auch
genetisch bevorzugt ist gegenüber ihren intentionalen Abwandlungen."

occurs, is in pre-predicative awareness; the encounter with reality that happens there is the origin of the new sense. The series of discoveries forcing the growth of a sense arise in the encounter spaced between the judgments that mark each perceptible step in the history of a meaning. Genetic constitution is not simply deductive explicitation of the content of our concepts; it is the result of a continually repeated encounter between subjectivity and reality.

Such encounter is particularly important when we come to the limit of the history of a sense. Following the genesis of a sense ultimately leads us to its very beginning, and here the first anticipations of the sense we wish to understand will be found in the pre-predicative encounter which was the basis for a first categorical formation. This is the apogee of the quest for the origin of sense.[1]

Husserl proposes to describe encounter in what he calls "transcendental aesthetics." "As the basic level there functions 'transcendental aesthetics,' taken in a new sense. . . . It deals with the eidetic problem of a possible world in general as the world of 'pure encounter,' as it precedes all science in a 'higher' sense. It is thus eidetic description of the universal apriori without which unified objects could not appear in simple encounter, before categorical acts; . . . the apriori without which the unity of a nature in general, the unity of a world, could not be constituted as a passive, synthesized unity." [2]

An important characteristic of pre-predicative intentionality is that objects are given to us through it. "Encounter is the achievement in which encountered being 'is there' for me, the

---

[1] Cf. Jacques Derrida, *L'origine de la géométrie*, p. 33: "Leur historicité est donc une de leurs composantes eidétiques, et il n'y a pas d'historicité concrète qui n'implique nécessairement en elle le renvoi à une 'Erstmaligkeit'."

[2] "Als Grundstufe fungiert die in einem neuen Sinne 'transzendentale Aesthetik.' . . . Sie behandelt das eidetische Problem einer möglicher Welt überhaupt als Welt 'reiner Erfahrung,' als wie sie aller Wissenschaft im 'höheren' Sinn vorangeht, also die eidetische Deskription des universalen Apriori, ohne welches in blosser Erfahrung und vor den kategorialen Aktionen, . . . einheitliche Objekte nicht erscheinen und so überhaupt Einheit einer Natur, einer Welt sich als passive synthetische Einheit nicht konstituieren könnte." *Form. trans. Log.*, pp. 256-57. Husserl gives a few examples of what a study of transcendental aesthetics would involve. He limits himself to showing how certain intentional modalities, which so far have been attributed only to judgments, are realized in pre-predicative consciousness. Bachelard, in *La logique de Husserl*, p. 212, correctly observes that Husserl's description of transcendental aesthetics is very brief in this volume. She uses *Erfahrung und Urteil* as a supplement.

encountering subject...." [1] As a sense develops through genetic constitution, it is carried by an object. The object itself is constituted as object in the type of awareness described in transcendental aesthetics. "Encounter is the primary establishment of the 'being-for-us' of the objects of its objective sense." [2] In pure encounter, we achieve the presence of objects before any sense is deposited in them by judgment. It is the region of consciousness in which we have "presence" but not yet any fully crystallized, conceptual "sense." [3]

Because encounter is fixed on concrete objects, the judgment that immediately arises from it is always an individual judgment. Universalization comes only later.

Husserl observes that even on this rudimentary level of consciousness, there is a history. Even the constitution of objects in pre-predicative encounter occurs as a development. In the *Cartesian Meditations*, he points out that in childhood we have to learn to "see things." "With good reason it is said that in infancy we had to learn to see physical things, and that such modes of consciousness of them had to precede all others genetically. In 'early infancy,' then, the field of perception that gives beforehand does not as yet contain anything that, in a mere look, might be explicated as a physical thing." [4] Learning to "see things" does not involve any categorical activity. It does not suppose the constitution of any judgments, for it takes place in what Husserl calls "passive genesis," which is the term he uses in *Cartesian Meditations* to name pre-predicative constitution. [5] Even on this level, however, there is a teleological sequence governing our consciousness.

The dominating factor in transcendental aesthetics is association. "The universal principle of passive genesis, for the consti-

[1] "Erfahrung ist die Leistung, in der für mich, den Erfahrenden erfahrenes Sein 'da ist.'..." *Form. trans. Log.*, p. 206.

[2] "Erfahrung ist die Urstiftung des Für-uns-seins von Gegenständen ihres gegenständlichen Sinnes." *ibid.*, p. 147.

[3] The contraries "sense" and "presence" are used by Alphonse De Waelhens, *Existence et signification* (Louvain: Nauwelaerts, 1958), p. 18.

[4] "Mit gutem Grund heisst es, dass wir in früher Kinderzeit das Sehen von Dingen überhaupt erst lernen mussten, wie auch, dass dergleichen allen anderen Bewusstseinsweisen von Dingen genetisch vorangehen musste. Das vorgebende Wahrnehmungsfeld in der frühen Kindheit enthält also noch nichts, was in blossem Ansehen als Ding expliziert werden könnte." *Cart. Med.*, p. 112; Cairns p. 79.

[5] "Passive genesis" is opposed to "active genesis," which is the constitution carried out in categorical acts.

tution of all objectivities given completely prior to the products
of activity, bears the title association." [1] Husserl tries to purify
the concept of its empiricist connotations and to give it a strictly
phenomenological sense.[2] Association, he claims, is part of the
structure of intentionality and is given as such in our consciousness along with structural elements like temporality or horizons.

After we have constituted a judgment, association functions
when we return to contact with reality in subsequent encounter.
When we make such a return, we do not find the objects of our
intentions in the same situations they were found in before, and
sometimes we are faced with entirely new objects. Despite this
change in what is given, the constituted sense still can be applied
by association. New situations and new intentional objects are
organized in our perception according to patterns previously
constituted. Our earlier constitution thus affects subsequent
encounters.[3]

The principle of association works also in a deeper region of
constitution, in the organization of sensations. Husserl observes
that it includes the problem of "sensuous configuration in coex-
istence and succession."[4] Thus it would operate in the field of
perception which precedes any presence of things. Sensations are
not given to us chaotically even when we experience some which
are entirely new and unfamiliar. Even these are organized, by
association with past sensory formation, into some sort of coherent order. Such organization is only preliminary and must be
followed by a more determined constitution which will be specific to the new situation or objects. We must break away from
mere association, but the beginning of rationality in a new situ-

[1] "Das universale Prinzip der passiven Genesis für die Konstitution aller den
aktiven Gebilden letztlich vorgegeben Gegenständlichkeiten trägt den Titel Assoziation." *Cart. Med.*, p. 113; Cairns p. 80.
[2] The empiricist sense of association, as Husserl sees it, conceives sense data as
material things which gravitate together by virtue of certain laws of association.
Both the data and the laws are taken as "real" facts or events. For Husserl, neither
sensations nor the laws of association belong to the real world when considered from
a phenomenological point of view. They are factors in transcendental subjectivity,
part of the structure of pure consciousness.
[3] Cf. *Form. trans. Log.*, p. 279: "Das hängt damit zusammen, dass jede originale
Gegebenheitsweise eine doppelte genetische Nachwirkung hat.... Fürs Zweite die
'apperzeptive' Nachwirkung, der gemäss in ähnlicher neuer Situation das wie immer
schon konstitutiert Vorliegende in ähnlicher Weise apperzipiert wird."
[4] "Die sinnliche Konfiguration in Koexistenz und Sukzession." *Cart. Med.*, p. 114;
Cairns p. 80.

ation is nevertheless based on it. In describing the genetic constitution of a given sense, therefore, we would be led ultimately to this preliminary organization of sensations, which is the first tenuous trace of its history.

We have spoken of a state of pure sensation, a state in which there are as yet no "things" in our field of perception. In discussing this theme, we rejoin the remarks made towards the end of our discussion of Husserl's lectures on time.[1] As we saw there, he gradually became convinced that there can be non-intentional sensations. We now see how sensations fit in the theory of genetic constitution. They are a state of awareness that antecedes the presence of things, and thus makes up the most rudimentary level of awareness and constitution. If we wish to probe back to the earliest appearance of a sense, we must not only trace it to the judgment which deposits the sense in our subjectivity, but also follow it into its earliest anticipations in such a state of sensation as is described here.

5. Husserl's rejection of his former schema for intentional structure

In our discussion of pre-predicative encounter, we have not yet said anything about the structure it is supposed to have. In Husserl's earlier works, the structure of intentionality is conceived according to the following schema: sense data are given as real elements in subjectivity, and they are animated by noeses. By virtue of such "apprehension," the sense data, which in themselves are non-intentional, are objectivated; that is, through them we are enabled to encounter something objective and transcendent to the flux of immanent sensations and acts. Objectivity is "constituted" in such apprehension. The schema involves two real components of consciousness, noeses and sense data, whose union results in the appearance of an ideal component, the noema. Meanings and objects are parts of the noema, and as such they arise in our consciousness only with the advent of noeses. Sensations in themselves have neither meaning nor objectivity.

In *Formal and Transcendental Logic*, Husserl drops this schema. In a criticism of psychologism, he says that it is incorrect to picture elements in consciousness as ready-made objects,

[1] Cf. *supra*, § 14 of Chapter III.

simply given as component parts in subjectivity. One would fall into this error, he claims, if "one were to distinguish, within this sphere of objects which already exist in advance, between sensory data and intentional experiences as different types of data." [1] Husserl thus includes his own earlier schematism of sense data and apprehension under the condemnation of psychologism.

He continues, "Not as though this last distinction were to be rejected entirely." [2] We do not have to reject it entirely, for there is a sense in which it can be useful. What is this sense? It can be useful only as a pedagogical aid. It is easier to begin phenomenology, or to explain it to beginners, by taking intentions and sense data as two distinct, fixed objects in subjectivity. "One can, as ego, focus on immanent objects as objects of immanent encounter, i.e., as objects of immanent time, and that is obviously the first step for the beginner in phenomenology." [3] This was, continues Husserl, the procedure followed in the *Ideas*. The easier, higher level of subjectivity was investigated first, and on this level it is legitimate to distinguish between apprehension and sense data, but this provisional distinction could be made only because the deeper layer of subjectivity, the layer of temporality, was explicitly neglected in order not to confuse.

While writing the *Ideas*, Husserl was already aware that the distinction between sense data and noeses could not hold if we were to probe deeper into the temporal structure of subjectivity. When he introduces this distinction, he says it is valid only if we limit ourselves to a superficial view of subjectivity, one that does not go into the deep and final region of temporality. [4] When we do descend into the temporal sphere of subjectivity, we reach the point where apprehensions and sense data are no longer accepted as ready-made objects, nor can we treat them

---

1 "... [Wenn] man innerhalb dieser Späre im voraus schon seiender Gegenstände zwischen sinnlichen Daten und intentionalen Erlebnissen als andersartigen Daten unterscheidet." *Form. trans. Log.*, p. 252.

2 "Nicht als ob die letztere Unterscheidung völlig zu verwerfen wäre."

3 "Man kann sich als Ego auf die immanenten Gegenstände als Gegenstände der immanenten Erfahrung, das ist als solche der immanente Zeit einstellen, und das ist offenbar das Erste für den phänomenologischen Anfänger." This pedagogical use of the schema is found in *Phänomenologische Psychologie*, pp. 166-67.

4 Cf. *supra*, Chapter IV, p. 140, n. 2.

as distinct from one another. We realize here that both spring from a common source and are both constituted by subjective performance. "But in the immanent 'internality' of the ego, there are no objects given in advance...." [1] In the *Cartesian Meditations*, the same idea is repeated: "But, when descriptive theory of consciousness begins radically, it has before it no such data and wholes, except perhaps as prejudices." [2] Thus when we surpass pedagogical considerations and reach the ultimate state of things as they really are, we find that the distinction between intention and sense data no longer exists. On this level, there is nothing which is first "given " and then "apprehended" by intentionality, no "matter" which is "informed" by noeses. There is no longer any duality.

If there is no duality, what is there? We have already seen the answer in our study of the lectures on time: there is only immanent temporality, the sequence of primal intentions identified with temporal phases. There is only the flow of inner time building immanent objects, which from this point of view cannot be distinguished into the two groups of sensations and intentions. [3] In itself, a temporal phase or primal intention is undifferentiated. There is no duality in it, and when we look at immanent objects from this level, there is no duality in them either. There is just the series of elapsed primal intentions which are held in retention.

Thus the schema "sensations – intentions" does not apply to the most fundamental level of intentionality, nor does it apply to the constitution wrought on this level. Husserl had already mentioned the possibility of this in a note to his lectures on time, where he said that not every form of constitution need have the schema. [4] Another expression of this opinion is found in a manuscript dating from 1932: "Is not my original conception of the immanent sphere with immanent data, which ultimately come

---

[1] "Aber es gibt auch in der immanenten 'Innerlichkeit' des Ego keine Gegenstände im voraus...." *Form. trans. Log., p.* 253.

[2] "Aber die radikal anfangende deskriptive Bewusstseinslehre hat nicht solche Daten und Ganze vor sich, es sei denn als Vorurteile." *Cart. Med.,* p. 77; Cairns, p. 38.

[3] Cf. Rudolf Boehm, "Deux points de vue: Husserl et Nietzsche," p. 174: "Cependant, le dépassement et l'abandon du 'schema contenu – acception' signifia seulement la reconnaissance du fait que, sur le plan fondamental de la constitution du temps 'immanent' et donc en dernière analyse, il n'y a point de 'sujet' ou d' 'objet' prédonnés."

[4] Cf. *supra,* Chapter III, p. 95, n. 2.

to 'apprehension' only through the passive execution of association, still a remnant of the old psychology and its sensualistic empiricism?" [1]

One of the clearest expressions of Husserl's criticism of his schema is found in an addition made to *Ideas I*, dating from shortly before 1928. The remark is made in reference to § 88, where he talks about noeses as opposed to noemas. Concerning noeses he says, "Only on page 239 is it mentioned in passing that 'noesis' means the same as 'concrete, complete intentional experience' with stress on its noetic 'components.' Thus the hyletic moments belong to the noeses insofar as they bear functions of intentionality, undergo a giving of sense, and help to constitute a concrete, noematic sense." Thus Husserl stresses that sensations are "within" noeses, and not distinguished from them. There is no duality between intention and hyletic data. He continues: "But this must be stated sooner and with appropriate embellishment. I fell into uncertainty myself because, earlier, noetic and hyletic moments were distinguished from one another." [2]

Husserl admits therefore that at one time he did use this schema even in the sphere of immanent temporality, where it does not belong. In *Formal and Transcendental Logic* he admits that it was incorrect, and calls it a form of psychologism. He no longer maintains the structure of intentionality which was the norm for his earlier works.

---

[1] "Ist nicht meine ursprüngliche Auffassung von der immanenten Sphäre mit den immanenten Daten, die am Ende erst durch die passive Leistung der Assoziation zu 'Auffassung' kommen, noch ein Rest der alten Psychologie und ihres sensualistischen Empirizismus?" Mss. B I 13 I, p. 8. Cited, but with reference to the wrong manuscript, in Gerd Brand, *Welt, Ich und Zeit* (The Hague: Martinus Nijhoff, 1955), p. 27.

[2] *Ideen I*, p. 218; the note itself is on p. 478. "Erst Seite 239 ist im Vorübergehen gesagt, dass 'Noesis' so viel besagt wie 'konkret vollständiges intentionales Erlebnis' unter Betonung seiner noetischen 'Komponenten.' Zur Noesis gehören also die hyletischen Momente, sofern solche Funktionen der Intentionalität tragen, Sinngebung erfahren, einen konkreten noematischen Sinn konstituieren helfen. Das muss aber früher mit entsprechender Feierlichkeit gesagt werden. Ich bin selbst ins Schwanken gekommen, da ja früher noetische und hyletische Momente unterschieden wurden."

Cf. Hermann Asemissen, *Strukturanalytische Probleme der Wahrnehmung in der Phänomenologie Husserls* (Cologne: Cologne University Press, 1957), pp. 24-25. Asemissen correctly claims that Husserl does not examine sensations in themselves, only in their function as material for animating sensations. He concludes that the matter-form structure is an unwarranted hypothesis, but he does not mention that Husserl saw this difficulty himself and tried to correct it in his later works.

6. Impact of Husserl's rejection of his earlier schema: objectivity is now explained genetically, not structurally

What impact does this change of mind have on Husserl's doctrine? The schema was used to explain objectivity. It was brought in to show what element in our consciousness is responsible for the intrusion of objective, transcendent noemas within the flow of constantly changing, immanent experience. Now that the schema is abandoned, must we conclude that Husserl denies the objectivity of logical entities, meanings, and things?

We cannot draw this inference, because in *Formal and Transcendental Logic* he affirms as strongly as he ever did that such objects are indeed transcendent to subjectivity. For instance, in criticizing Hume, he says that Hume missed the true problem of constitution because of his blindness towards the objectivity of what we encounter. "Through his naturalistic sensualism, which sees only a mass of data floating in an emptiness devoid of any essence and is blind to the objectivating function of intentional syntheses, he falls into the absurdity of a 'philosophy of the *as if*'." [1] Thus far from rejecting objectivity, he makes it the essential factor in the problematic of phenomenology.

The change is that objectivity is now explained in a different way. Structural explanation is no longer valid, because by its very nature it supposes ready-made structural elements as explanatory factors. A structural element, apprehension, is no longer acceptable as explanation for the "origins" of transcendent, ideal objectivities because it is not radical enough. A structural element itself points back to more ultimate origins.

Instead of using structural explanations, Husserl now employs genetic ones. Instead of showing what structural elements constitute objectivity, he reveals what genetic process has taken place to form such constitution. Husserl now tries to reveal the genealogy of logical entities and of objects in general. In order to explain the origins of a given meaning or object, he will show what pre-predicative encounter must have gone on in order to lead to them.

Objectivity is no longer conceived as something that can be

---

[1] "Durch seinen naturalistischen Sensualismus, der nur einen in wesensloser Leere schwebenden Haufen von Daten sieht und blind ist für die objektivierenden Funktionen der intentionalen Synthesis, gerät er in den Widersinn einer 'Philosophie des Als ob'." *Form. trans. Log.*, p. 227.

turned on and off abruptly in our consciousness by the introduction or removal of noeses. Objectivity is now conceived as the
solidifying of a part of our intentional life in a judgment. In the
judgment there is constituted a sense that immediately breaks
off from the perpetual flow of consciousness and becomes an
ideal entity transcending the life and temporality from which it
arose. To explain the objectivity and transcendence which this
sense has, therefore, we no longer can simply state that an
"objectivating apprehension" illumines our sensations. All we
can do is trace the pattern of encounter which precedes the
constitution of the objective sense and leads to it.

What is the advantage of Husserl's new explanatory project?
His genealogical research will not suffer from the weakness that
pervaded his structural analyses, because it will not suppose any
ready-made, immanent structural elements such as intentions
or sensory data. They are not necessary any longer. The explanation now takes the form of showing how a categorically fixed
sense, a sense that is solidified in judgment, has arisen out of
earlier encounter. Husserl will now trace the history of a sense
from its rudimentary, pre-meaningful stages in encounter up to
its defined stage in judgment. In this way, the sense is traced
from its primitive origins in the "now instant" to its final state
in judgment, where it becomes a permanent possession in our
intentional life, a deposit that remains thereafter in our subjectivity.

What happens, in this perspective, to sensations and intentions?
Are they still not presupposed as subjective correlates that also
develop genetically in correlation to the sense? Does Husserl not
distinguish, even on this deep level of consciousness, between
cogitatum and *cogitatio*? There is indeed a subjective correlate
which evolves with the objective sense, and it is described in
transcendental aesthetics. However, this correlate is no longer
distinguished into two "real" components, sense data and noeses.
If we go deeply enough into subjectivity, says Husserl, we see
that such a distinction is false. There is only one subjective time
flow, or as Husserl now chooses to call it, one "conscious life"
which evolves. This conscious life is so fashioned that, if we look
at it superficially, we can distinguish sensations and intentions,
but in reality the stuff it is made of is not so distinguished.

Such genetic analysis must replace structural analysis if Husserl is to be consistent with the discoveries he made, in his lectures on time, concerning the nature of immanent temporality. In this respect, the *Ideas* suffer from an inherent contradiction, and that is why he could not integrate the doctrine on time with his analyses of that work. In the deepest level of intentionality, he admits a perpetual flow of time phases in the *Ideas*, but on the higher level of intentionality he uses static, ready-made structural elements which escape the flow of time. The static superstructure has to be destroyed if the inner temporality is to be taken seriously, and this is accomplished in *Formal and Transcendental Logic*, where the static structure is replaced by a genetic process. Thus the genetic constitution described in this work does justice to immanent temporality and accounts for it even on the level of intentionality. Temporality now pervades all of subjectivity.

7. *Husserl's new concept of subjectivity and phenomenology*

Husserl's rejection of the schema "apprehension – sensations" must be viewed in the context of his new conception of phenomenology as genetic analysis, and in the context of his new conception of how subjectivity objectivates itself. It is thus a symptom of a profound change in his thought; or more precisely, an integration of ideas which until now stood next to one another without ever being successfully harmonized. Once he adopts the theory of genetic analysis, reconciliation of temporality with objective constitution becomes possible.

Husserl's new concept of genetic analysis also enables him to overcome some of the formalism we have found in his earlier doctrine. We have noticed that his structural analyses of intentionality had little to say about the specific contents of various objects. When he analyzes constitution in his new manner, he is able to remedy this to some extent. His aim now is to take an objectivated sense, a solidified, "conceptualized" meaning, and discover its origins in the pre-predicative consciousness that leads to it. He will take, for instance, our defined, conceptualized senses of space or color and show how they arise from the nameless, "lived" space and color which we experience in our conscious life before the categorical achievement of judgment takes place.

He will bring this nameless anticipation of meaningfulness to light. "Its beginning is the pure – and, so to speak, still dumb – encounter, which now must be made to utter its own sense with no adulteration."[1] In performing this genetic analysis, he will show what sort of pre-predicative encounter is required *specifically* for colors, space, trees, stones, etc., and thus will show the origins of the contents proper to each. A step was made in this direction in Husserl's studies of reason and reality in the *Ideas*, but the framework of genetic constitution allows a still more developed treatment of the content of what is constituted.

It is not accidental that Husserl begins to use the term "conscious life" abundantly in *Formal and Transcendental Logic* and the *Cartesian Meditations*.[2] His new theory of constitution and subjectivity has much in common with a "life philosophy" such as that elaborated by Dilthey or even Nietzsche.[3] In the heart of consciousness there is a spontaneous flow of temporality which Husserl now calls the life of consciousness, and which continually objectivates itself in categorical entities. Categorical entities, and the meanings that crystallize in them, break off from the life of consciousness and transcend it, but they can be understood only as off-spring of this life. Furthermore, the conscious life itself can be analyzed only by first accepting its objectivated products and searching back into the life which engendered them. Indirectly, therefore, even for Husserl, the conscious life can become aware of its own concrete possibilities and structure only by objectivating itself. The history of conscious life is what reveals this life to itself.

Husserl's last philosophy is dominated by this new conception of subjectivity, objectivity, and phenomenology, and his concept of *Lebenswelt* arises from it. The *Lebenswelt* is what issues directly from pre-predicative encounter. It is the complex of primitive meanings that are constituted before any scientific conceptualizing is carried out on the world, and thus serves as the basis on which such scientific theorizing is founded.

---

[1] "Der Anfang ist die reine und sozusagen noch stumme Erfahrung, die nun erst zur reinen Aussprache ihres eigenen Sinnes zu bringen ist." *Cart. Med.*, p. 77; Cairns, pp. 38-39. We have slightly altered Cairns' version.

[2] Cf. *Form. trans. Log.*, p. 278; *Cart. Med.*, pp. 80-82.

[3] Cf. Hans Georg Gadamer, *Wahrheit und Methode* (Tübingen: J.C.B. Mohr, 1960), pp. 232-33; Rudolf Boehm, "Deux points de vue: Husserl et Nietzsche."

8. Comparison of the structure of the "Cartesian Meditations" with that of "Ideas I"

Our study of genetic constitution has been centered on *Formal and Transcendental Logic* so far, but the *Cartesian Meditations* make an extensive use of it also, although in a different perspective. The *Cartesian Meditations* are presented as an introduction to phenomenology, and in this respect they are similar to *Ideas I*. For the sake of comparison, and to see what influence the concept of genetic constitution has, let us briefly analyze the structure of Husserl's *Meditations*.

The aim is to establish philosophy as an authentic science, and to imitate Descartes' quest for "a complete reforming of philosophy into a science grounded on an absolute foundation." [1] In the interpretation of this first point, however, the *Meditations* already differ from the *Ideas*. In the *Ideas*, the rigorous science has the characteristics of adequateness and apodicticity; in the *Meditations*, it must have only apodicticity. The propositions of philosophy, Husserl now claims, must exclude all doubt and thus be apodictic, but they need not be adequate, that is, they need not express the sense and structure of their subject exhaustively.[2] There is room for growth, precision and development in philosophy. At any stage of its realization, phenomenology may have a certain incompleteness, its intentions may be encircled with "unfulfilled components, with expectant and attendant meanings" [3] which are still unexplored, but what it does succeed in saying must be said apodictically. Thus the idea of phenomenology brought to perfection, to complete adequation, is an ideal. [4]

Philosophy must be apodictic and self-justifying. Such a science cannot be grounded in the real world, because its existence is not apodictic but doubtful in principle. Doubtfulness of real existence vitiates any science based upon it. Therefore,

---

[1] "eine völlige Reform der Philosophie zu einer Wissenschaft aus absoluter Begründung." *Cart. Med.*, p. 43; Cairns, p. 1.

[2] *ibid.*, p. 55; Cairns, p. 14.

[3] "Komponenten unerfüllter Vormeinungen und Mitmeinungen." *ibid.*, p. 55; Cairns, p. 15.

[4] Cf. *ibid.*, pp. 90-91; Cairns, p. 54: "Doch wir sagen besser, es handle sich hier um eine unendliche regulative Idee. Das in evidenter Antizipation vorauszusetzende System möglicher Gegenstände als solcher möglichen Bewusstseins sei selbst eine Idee ..."

says Husserl, we turn to subjectivity, where we find the desired basis for a rigorous science. "At this point, following Descartes, we make the great reversal that, if made in the right manner, leads to transcendental subjectivity: the turn to the *ego cogito* as the ultimate and apodictically certain basis for judgments, the basis on which any radical philosophy must be grounded." [1] The transcendental experience we have of our subjectivity is apodictic and can serve as the basis for apodictic judgments which will make up our ultimate science.[2] Even this experience is not adequate, however, because of the temporality of the ego. The present moment is given to us adequately when we experience it, but the content of its temporal horizons, the content of our stream of consciousness which reaches into the past or future is not adequately given.[3]

What do we have apodictically given to us? Besides the existence of subjectivity, we also have the "universal apodictic encounter-structure of the ego." [4] But in telling us what this structure is like, Husserl nowhere mentions the schema of sense data and apprehensions. Instead, he says that subjectivity is essentially temporal, that it is directed towards a *cogitatum*, that each *cogitatum* is a unit correlated to a subjective manifold, to a synthesis of subjective phases succeeding one another in time.[5] All these are apodictic structural factors in subjectivity; they are an "innate apriori." [6]

Husserl then proposes, as constitutional analysis, that we examine the subjective syntheses which correspond to various types of objects.[7] Finally, he proposes the task of "reason and reality," the study of subjective correlations to objects which make up the real world. The first three meditations thus follow

---

[1] "Hier machen wir nun, Descartes folgend, die grosse Umwendung, die in rechter Weise verstanden zur transzendentalen Subjektivität führt: die Wendung zum *ego cogito* als dem apodiktisch gewissen und letzten Urteilsboden auf den jede radikale Philosophie zu begründen ist." *ibid.*, p. 58; Cairns, p. 18.

[2] Cf. *ibid.*, p. 61; Cairns, p. 22.

[3] Cf. *ibid.*, p. 62; Cairns, pp. 22-23.

[4] "die universale apodiktische Erfahrungsstruktur des Ich." *ibid,.* p. 67; Cairns, p. 28. We have made a slight alteration in Cairns' version.

[5] Cf. *ibid.*, pp. 67, 71, 77, 79; Cairns, pp. 28, 32-33, 39, 41.

[6] Cf. *ibid.*, p. 114; Cairns, p. 81. These structural elements do not fall under the criticism of psychologism expressed in *Formal and Transcendental Logic*, because they are not static components or parts of intentionality. They express the temporal structure of intentionality; they are not parts, but developmental structures.

[7] Cf. *ibid.*, p. 90; Cairns, p. 54.

rather closely the pattern, and in general the doctrine, we have seen in *Ideas I*. The concept of genetic constitution is not conspicuous so far, although there are some elements which prepare the ground for it.

9. *Introduction of genetic constitution into the "Cartesian Meditations"*

In the fourth meditation, Husserl introduces the problem of genetic constitution by means of concepts we have not met in his earlier works. His manner of presenting genetic constitution is also different from that in *Formal and Transcendental Logic*.

Up to this point, says Husserl, our investigations have been centered on the objective pole of intentionality. Intentionality has been investigated as orientated towards objects and its structure has been described as the condition of possibility for the constitution of objects.[1] Husserl now proposes to turn to the other pole of intentionality, the ego in the structure *ego-cogito-cogitatum*. Let us study consciousness as related to the ego, the identical subject of the whole stream of intentional acts.

What is this ego? "But it is to be noted that this centering ego is not an empty pole of identity. . . . Rather, according to a law of 'transcendental generation,' with every act emanating from him and having a new objective sense, he acquires a new abiding property."[2] In the *Logical Investigations*, the ego is simply the stream of conscious experiences.[3] In the *Ideas*, it is presented as the empty identity pole to which all intentional acts are referred, but which is unaffected by them.[4] In the *Cartesian Meditations*, it is something of a compromise between these two concepts: the ego retains its identity throughout the flux of consciousness and thus transcends this flux, but at the same time it is not unaffected by what transpires in consciousness. Husserl's new

[1] Cf. *ibid.*, pp. 99-100; Cairns, p. 65.
[2] "Aber nun ist zu bemerken, dass dieses zentrierende Ich nicht ein leerer Identitätspol ist,... sondern vermöge einer Gesetzmässigkeit der transzendentalen Genesis mit jedem der von ihm ausstrahlenden Aktes eines neuen gegenständlichen Sinnes eine neue bleibende Eigenheit gewinnt." *ibid.*, p. 100; Cairns, p. 66.
[3] Cf. *Log. Unt.*, p. 331; 2nd ed., II, 1, p. 353: "Es ist selbstverständlich, dass das Ich nichts Eigenartiges ist, das über den mannigfalten Erlebnissen schwebte, sondern dass es einfach mit ihrer eigenen Verknüpfungseinheit identisch ist."
[4] Cf. *Ideen I*, p. 195: "Von seinen 'Beziehungsweisen' oder 'Verhaltungsweisen' abgesehen, ist es völlig leer an Wesenskomponenten, es hat gar keinen explikabeln Inhalt, es ist an und für sich unbeschreiblich: reines Ich und nichts weiter."

concept of the ego involves the use of another new concept, that of habitualities.

To explain the concept of habitualities, Husserl uses the example of decisions made in our will. When we make a certain decision, we are modified by it. We exist thereafter with a certain conviction, which becomes a lasting characteristic of ourselves. Such a conviction is not an act; it is established by an act when it is first formed, but thereafter it remains not as an act, but as a modification of subjectivity, an abiding *habitus*. What Husserl describes for voluntary activity is also true of intellectual acts: "This, my activity of positing and explicating being, sets up a habituality of my Ego...." [1] Intellectual convictions are also established as habitualities of the ego. The ego is now defined not only as the identity-pole of intentional acts, but also as the permanent substratum of habitualities. The ego and its habitualities, taken together, form the "monad." The monad is an ego as it concretely exists. [2]

The concept of habitualities has already been mentioned in Husserl's structural analysis of intentionality in the third meditation, but its implications for genetic constitution were not expressed. [3] The concept refers to the same thing Husserl describes in *Formal and Transcendental Logic* when he says that categorical acts deposit a sense which remains in objects and has an effect on the way we subsequently encounter such objects. The categorical act which constitutes the sense as a predicate is equivalent to the act which establishes our conviction, and the deposited sense is equivalent to the conviction itself. Considering such senses as convictions or habitualities is simply to consider their subjective orientation.

At this point, we are brought to the problem of genetic constitution. "With the doctrine of the Ego as pole of his acts and substrate of habitualities, we have already touched on the problems of phenomenological genesis and have done so at a significant point. Thus we have touched the level of genetic phe-

[1] "Diese meine Aktivität der Seinssetzung und Seinsauslegung stiftet eine Habitualität meines Ich..." *Cart. Med.*, p. 102; Cairns, p. 68.
[2] The monad is still conceived in a transcendental sense; it is not a psychophysical ego, but the transcendental ego conceived together with the products of constitution that it has carried out.
[3] Cf. *Cart. Med.*, pp. 95-96; Cairns, pp. 60-61.

nomenology." [1] Whereas the structural analyses carried out in the first three meditations gives us an eidetic, formal description of subjectivity, the problem will now be to describe subjectivity as it concretely exists. The principle Husserl uses is that not all habitualities are compossible in a given ego at a given time. "But in a unitarily possible ego not all singly possible types are compossible, and not all compossible ones are compossible in just any order, at no matter what loci in that ego's own temporality." [2] As we have seen in *Formal and Transcendental Logic*, there is a certain historicity, a certain necessary sequence, which occurs. Tracing this history and showing the motivation of one conviction on those which follow is the work of genetic phenomenology.

Husserl says in both *Formal and Transcendental Logic* and the *Cartesian Meditations* that phenomenology should now be considered as the explicitation of the transcendental monad. Everything is present in it: not only the essential structure which intentionality must have, but also the noematic senses which are its correlates and, in addition, the entire history and ultimate sources of these senses. The monad is the totality of conscious life and its objectivating constitution.

10. Other influences of genetic constitution on Husserl's phenomenology

Genetic constitution is a symptom of Husserl's turn to a philosophy of life. Objectivity and its senses are now conceived as solidifications of the life of consciousness in judgments, and they are explained by showing what pre-predicative encounter leads to them. Structural explanation, the appeal to noeses and apprehensions as objectivating elements, are no longer used. However, besides this fundamental influence of genetic constitution on phenomenology, there are other effects which should be mentioned.

The fact that Husserl now demands apodicticity, and not

---

[1] "Mit der Lehre vom Ich als Pol seiner Akte und als Substrat von Habitualitäten haben wir schon, und in einem bedeutsamen Punkt, die Problematik der phänomenologischen Genesis berührt und damit die Stufe der genetischen Phänomenologie," *ibid.*, p. 103; Cairns, p. 69.

[2] "Aber zu einem eigentlich möglichen ego sind nicht alle einzelnen möglichen Typen kompossibel, sind es nicht in beliebiger Ordnung, an beliebigen Stellen seiner eigenen Zeitlichkeit." *ibid.*, p. 108; Cairns, p. 74.

adequacy, for his phenomenology is one of these effects. As long as he was only concerned with structural analysis or with static constitution, as in *Ideas I*, Husserl could still claim that his phenomenology gives an adequate picture of subjectivity. All the structural elements in intentionality and the static layers of sense in noemas can be adequately seen in reflective, phenomenological analysis. They are all immediately present to us when we reflect on subjectivity. However, once we begin to look into the history of the ego and try to reactivate the content of acts which are already past, we cannot claim adequateness any more. These acts are no longer immediately present to us, even in reflective analysis; they lie at a temporal distance from the immediate present. Furthermore, even when we do reactivate a past judgment, it still will be encircled with a horizon of attendant senses and assumptions which date from still earlier judgments and which, consequently, are not explicitly given even in the reactivation. We can still claim apodicticity for this investigation, for we still deal with apriori, essential relationships of sense, but the claims of adequateness have become an ideal no longer achieved in fact. Genetic constitution makes it no longer possible to claim adequateness as a characteristic of phenomenological investigation.

Another effect of genetic phenomenology is to bring the problem of intersubjectivity to the fore. It is true that Husserl began to discuss intersubjectivity as early as 1910-1911, but this theme was not introduced into the *Ideas*.[1] The concept of genetic constitution, although not the direct cause for the problem of intersubjectivity, forces Husserl to integrate it into his whole system of phenomenology. The genetic origins of the layers of sense in our noemas are not all created originally by the individual transcendental ego; each ego accepts many of them as tradition from his culture. In order to uncover the genetic origins of our intellectual convictions, we are forced sooner or later to investigate the first constitution of them performed in human history. This problem is especially well brought out in Husserl's last period by his essay on the origin of geometry.[2] Both

---

[1] Cf. *Form. trans. Log.*, p. 215, n. 1.

[2] "Die Frage nach dem Ursprung der Geometrie als intentional-historisches Problem," *Revue internationale de Philosophie*, 1 (1939), pp. 203-25. Reprinted in the Louvain edition of *Krisis*, pp. 365-86.

Formal and Transcendental Logic and the *Cartesian Meditations*, furthermore, are concerned with the problem of intersubjectivity. Finally, it is by virtue of genetic constitution that Husserl's phenomenology acquires the historical perspective which is so important in his last thought and is the basis for his *Crisis of the European Sciences.* [1]

The concept of monad, the ego taken together with all its habitualities, is also a direct result of the problem of genetic constitution, as we have seen in our discussion of the *Cartesian Meditations*.

11. Husserl's genetic constitution still leaves room for a certain facticity in the content of constitution

Although Husserl now becomes concerned with explaining the sense and content of what is constituted by subjectivity, his analyses still retain a certain formalism. He does not explain the content exhaustively; the content is not explained *totaliter* as a product of subjectivity. For instance, his genetic analyses do not tell us why we encounter men, animals, plants, and matter with all the characteristics proper to them, nor does it explain why human beings have acts of perception, desire, evaluation, hatred, and so on. These actual developments of the transcendental ego are given as a facticity. Phenomenology does not explain why human knowledge branches off into the paths it does follow. The branches of science, of constitution, are not deducible from the transcendental ego

This facticity is stressed by Husserl's claim that we must encounter reality between the stages of a genetic development. We have to return to what is *given* and allow it to reveal itself to us; it does not simply emanate from consciousness.

If this is the case, what does Husserl have to say about the content of constitution? He provides, once again, the conditions of possibility for the genetic emergence of sense and objects. We have already seen how he gives such conditions of possibility by analyzing the structure of consciousness in his early works. In

---

[1] Walter Biemel seems to move too quickly from the concept of constitution in *Ideas* to that in *Crisis*, where history is studied by Husserl. He neglects the introduction of genetic constitution in the intervening works; genetic constitution is the basis for the historical interest in the *Crisis*. Cf. "Die entscheidende Phasen der Entfaltung von Husserls Philosophie," p. 211.

the *Cartesian Meditations* and *Formal and Transcendental Logic*, he gives us some structural analysis again, but it is different; it is orientated towards genetic study, and shows how pre-predicative experience can lead into predication and conceptualization. It is a structural analysis of the movement of consciousness, not a structural analysis of what components or parts are found in consciousness.[1]

Furthermore, he also analyzes the conditions of possibility that meanings exercise in regard to one another. He shows how one sense is presupposed, as a *sine qua non*, by another sense which follows it. For example, Euclidian geometry can be considered as a necessary condition for a geometry of more than three dimensions, and the lived consciousness of space is a necessary condition for both of these. Newtonian mechanics is a necessary prior step before quantum theory, and the lived awareness of causality in general is a necessary condition for both again. A primitive moral code based on selfish motives is a prior condition for more sophisticated morality based on justice.

In these and many other cases, a prior habituality is a necessary condition for an ulterior one, and a lived sense is a *sine qua non* for a conceptual habituality. It is an indispensable antecedent, and as such is said to "motivate" what comes after it. If the prior sense were not achieved, then the ulterior one could not emerge, could not be constituted.

However, a prior sense is never claimed by Husserl to be the sufficient cause for what follows it. There is a difference between Newtonian physics and quantum mechanics, and the difference is not simply one of clearer deduction or simple emanation. Quantum mechanics presupposes classical mechanics, but it goes beyond it, and simply from knowing classical mechanics, a phenomenologist could not *predict* that quantum theory would come after it. The new theory comes not directly from classical mechanics, nor from the ego that possesses classical mechanics as a habituality; it comes from perceiving reality. It is a facticity which the ego meets. Just as in the *Ideas*, therefore, phenomenology studies subjectivity as the condition of possibility for the emergence of sense and reality, not as the adequate cause and

[1] To posit ready-made component parts in intentionality is now judged to be psychologism by Husserl.

sufficient reason for what is constituted. The difference between genetic constitution and the static constitution of *Ideas* is that Husserl now looks for the genetic, the historical conditions, and not simply the structural ones.

12. Conclusion

The effects of genetic constitution on Husserl's thought are far reaching and upset some of his earlier doctrines. Most important, it allows Husserl to drop the schema of sense data and apprehensions which so dominated his earlier concept of constitution. However, genetic constitution is provoked by his earlier work and is a logical development of it, in the sense that it remedies some of the weaknesses that were present in his earlier phenomenology.

The chief service performed by genetic constitution is to provide a framework within which a better explanation can be given for the sources of the contents of consciousness, and not merely its structure. The pattern of explanation which is supposed to achieve this is no longer structural analysis nor simply study of noetic correlates, but inquiry into the history of the content of consciousness. By reactivating the intentional activity which once constituted a sense, we are supposed to be able to understand the sense. In principle, we should be able to push our examination back into the earliest stages of the origins of sense, even to the lived awareness which precedes the presence of objects. The ultimate ideal of such investigation will be to understand all the senses we encounter, and thus to understand the structure and sense of the entire world as it is presented to us. Even such fundamental concepts as those of "thing," "person," or "extension" have a genesis which must be revealed in this way.

Husserl says that a sense is constituted in two related stages, first in the passive genesis or pre-predicative constitution, and then in active genesis or categorical, predicative constitution. The alternating and mutually dependent operation of these two stages of constitution causes the genetic development of a sense. Passive genesis takes place as a part of our conscious life, and active genesis (judgment) results in ideal objects which "break off" from this life and transcend it and its temporality.

The most obvious value of Husserl's study in genetic constitution is its power of criticism for our judgment and encounter. It makes us aware of the hidden senses and implied contexts which affect our intentional activity and which must be uncovered if we are to understand our own conscious achievements.

In such analysis, Husserl presents the genetic conditions of possibility for the development of the world as it becomes real for us; he does not claim to deduce all the content and progress of our knowledge from the transcendental ego. There is still room for facticity in the paths that the evolution of our knowledge follows.

CHAPTER VI

THE PLACE OF CONSTITUTION
IN HUSSERL'S PHENOMENOLOGY

1. Constitution and absolute subjectivity

The central role which constitution plays in phenomenology is shown by its relationship to the phenomenological reduction. The reduction is the starting point of phenomenology; it is supposed to make us adopt the point of view proper to it, and to see how phenomenology alone can be a rigorous, presuppositionless science. We have distinguished two patterns of thought or themes in Husserl's argument leading to the reduction. The first of these is to find a region of experience which bears its justification within itself, a region where we can make assertions that are warranted solely and completely on the basis of what is presented to us. This region, claims Husserl, is transcendental subjectivity. It is given without profiles and consequently, he claims, apodictically and absolutely. We make no assumptions or presuppositions when we speak about subjectivity, because the way it is given to us guarantees what we say about it. The whole real world, on the other hand, is capable of warranting only presumptive assertions because of the profile continua which, in principle, characterize the way material reality is given to us. We mention in passing that Husserl admits subjectivity is only a provisional absolute, one rooted in a final and true absolute; we will return to this question.

The second theme in Husserl's argument leading to reduction is that of the "giving of sense." The entire world is relative to subjectivity in this respect, because it can have a sense, it can have "reality," only if there exists a consciousness; only consciousness can give meaning. Without consciousness, there is no sense. Subjectivity itself does not suppose the existence of a real world for its own sense, however. It does not demand any "thing" in order to be real, to be given, in the mode proper to

itself. For this reason, it is again called "absolute," but this
time it merits this name for a different reason from that used
in the first theme. Here it is absolute because it does not need
any other reality to have a sense; in the first theme it is absolute
because it is given apodictically and adequately, without spatial
profiles.

Thus by virtue of his first theme, Husserl arrives at a region
of absolute givenness which, by virtue of the reasoning in the
second theme, is also seen to be the "source" of all sense and
meaning. Husserl uses the term "constitution" to name the way
in which subjectivity carries out its function of giving sense. The
concept of constitution is therefore primarily associated with the
second theme, the one which, in the course of Husserl's development, later acquired the name of the "ontological way to reduction." In *Ideas I*, as we have shown, this "ontological" theme
is not sufficiently distinguished from the so-called "Cartesian"
train of thought, but the two themes are fundamentally different.
They are based on different arguments and issue in different
results (as is shown by the two types of "absolutes" arrived at
by them).

In his reasoning concerning reduction, Husserl sets up the
fundamental relationship that exists between reality and
consciousness, as this relationship is to be understood in phenomenology. We have already seen one factor in this relation:
reality requires consciousness in order to be "real." Husserl also
insists, however, that reality cannot be reduced to consciousness.
The two are wholly different, and Husserl says that an "abyss"
of sense separates the two. Reality is radically transcendent to
subjectivity and any attempt to assimilate one into the other is
a μετάβασις εἰς ἄλλο γένος. Real being is irreducible to
consciousness, *Sein* is in principle not *Bewusstsein*.[1] Transcendence, therefore, is the other qualification of the relationship
between reality and consciousness.

Thus when we say that subjectivity gives reality its sense, we
must not neglect this aspect of transcendence. The sense which
consciousness constitutes is an objective, transcendent sense,

---

[1] In the region of inner temporality, however, "being" is identified with "being
conscious." Husserl says, "Denn hier fällt ja Sein und Innerlich-bewusst-sein zusammen." *Zeitbewusstsein*, p. 471, Beilage VIII.

one radically alien to the manner of being which marks subjectivity. Both the dependence of reality and its transcendence towards subjectivity have to be retained if we are to give Husserl's concept of constitution the philosophical value and balance which belong to it. If we concentrate too much on the side of dependence, then we interpret constitution in the sense of a creation, where subjectivity simply produces reality out of its own self; the senses and distinctions found in reality would be conceived as something made by consciousness. If we were to overemphasize transcendence, subjectivity would become superfluous for the emergence of reality.

There is little danger of falling into the second error in interpreting Husserl. His forms of expression lead much more easily into the first; his strong statements about the relativity of the world can readily be taken in such a way as to forfeit what he says about its transcendence. The interpretation given by Fink to Husserl's phenomenology is orientated in this direction. In an explanation of constitution, for instance, Fink says, "In Husserl, the meaning of 'transcendental constitution' fluctuates between formation of sense and creation." [1] On the basis of what Husserl says about the transcendence and objectivity of sense, Fink's interpretation should be restricted.

In order to restrict it, and thus to save the transcendence of reality, the "relativity" which Husserl attributes to the real world should be interpreted as the relativity of something which depends on subjectivity as a necessary condition. Without subjectivity, the real world cannot acquire its sense; however, subjectivity is not a sufficient cause for the meaning of the world. It neither "forms" nor "creates" the sense and objectivity which the world has, as Fink claims, but "gives" the world its sense by making it possible for this sense to come about. Understanding consciousness as a simple condition *sine qua non* is required by the transcendence and radical alienation of the world towards

---

[1] "Bei Husserl schwankt der Sinn der 'transzendentalen Konstitution' zwischen Sinnbildung und Creation." "L'analyse intentionelle et le problème de la pensée spéculative," *Problèmes actuels de la phénoménologie* (Paris: Desclée de Brouwer, 1952), p. 78. In general, Fink makes Husserl says that "being" is equivalent to "givenness" and nothing more. Cf. *ibid.*, p. 70: "Sie dekretiert einfach, das Seiende ist gleich dem 'Phänomen,' gleich dem sich zeigenden und sich darstellenden Seienden." Also p. 72: "Das Seiende hat sich ins Phänomen verwandelt.... Vielmehr steht die Entscheidung jetzt fest: das Seiende ist Gegenstand und weiter nichts."

consciousness. Otherwise, the meanings and senses in the world would share in the ontic status of subjectivity, because they would be its products; they would be fundamentally the same type of existent as consciousness is.

Concretely, our interpretation is verified by the fact that Husserl's analyses of constitution always possess a certain formalism. They leave room for a facticity in what is consti-tuted, and do not explain away, by means of subjectivity, the content of what is the object of intentionality. The types of acts which are performed by subjectivity (the "quality" of such acts), the content of noemas, and the material aspect of sensations, are all taken as factually given, as something simply there. They are not shown to be "explained" in their content by means of subjectivity. If such contents were entirely the work of consciousness, if they were caused or created by it, then they should be explicable in terms of consciousness. They would be deducible from the nature of subjectivity, from the apriori immanent in consciousness and its activity. This is not the case, and the fact that contents are not explained by phenomenology is by no means a cause of regret for Husserl. On the contrary, the appearance of a variety of data gives him the opportunity to perform varied descriptions, to show how each of these requires a subjective correlate proper to itself as a condition for the possi-bility of appearing as an objective sense.

Even in genetic constitution, the element of facticity remains. Genetic constitution does provide Husserl with a method to probe into the contents of senses and objects, and thus to a certain degree the formalism of his static analyses is surpassed. When he makes a genetic analysis, he tries to explain how this or that particular sense has arisen out of earlier senses, or how a conceptualized, fixed sense arises from pre-predicative encounter. Thus the content of constitution becomes his concern; the sense we give to houses will call forth a different history than the sense we give to men or animals. Nevertheless, the ultimate origins of all such meanings are in pre-predicative encounter and, as Husserl shows, the characteristic of such encounter is that in it we are faced with reality, we accept what is given to us in facticity. This contact with facticity is what provides the stimulus for the growth of a sense. Subjectivity does not manufacture the contents of the concepts it forms in judgments, but forms its judgments on the basis of what is given to it in perception.

Thus when we say that there are necessary, apriori relationships between the stages of evolution that a sense goes through, this means simply that earlier stages are required as necessary conditions for later ones. A certain conceptualization is required if our perception of reality is to be enlightened and motivated sufficiently and properly to yield a further, more advanced conceptualization and understanding. But the earlier concept does not cause the subsequent one in the sense of accounting for the totality of its content. The content of our further concepts comes from encounter with the world, from the givenness and facticity we are faced with. There is more in the content of our later concepts that there is in earlier ones, and the increment does not only come from what subjectivity does, but from the world which reveals itself to consciousness. It is always true, of course, that subjectivity has to act on its objects. It has to carry out intentional performances if reality is to manifest itself, but once again this is a necessary condition and not a cause of the growth in knowledge. Subjectivity does not create what it sees.

Thus Husserl does not claim to be able to deduce the development of knowledge from subjectivity by means of his phenomenology. He always takes what is already acquired in constitution and probes back into the steps it must have taken to get where it is. The guideline is what is already there, what has already issued from intentional contact with the world; Husserl does not start with subjectivity and then show where it must go. Subjectivity alone cannot account for the facticity of what we have constituted; it only provides the conditions of possibility, both static and genetic, for what is constituted.

2. Constitution and the final absolute in time

The absolute which we attain through reduction is not the ultimate goal of phenomenology. It points back to something still more fundamental, says Husserl, the truly final absolute. Thus the stream of consciousness is now seen to be itself "relative" to another "absolute," one which is absolute in a new sense. We have seen that this final point of reference in phenomenology is the immediate, flowing now-instant, or as Husserl calls it, the "livingly flowing present" (*lebendig strömende Gegenwart*).[1]

The motive that makes Husserl go beyond subjectivity into the absolute present is the same that has motivated the transcendental reduction: the quest for a rigorous science. He will push his inquiry until it reaches the very beginning and origin of experience, the point at which all presuppositions become impossible. Consciousness, although it does not have spatial profiles, still has temporal ones. It is essentially a flux or stream, and points on this stream can lie at a temporal distance from the present moment at which we reflect on subjectivity. As a stream, as a manifold of temporal phases, consciousness itself depends on an ulterior condition of possibility, which is the present instant out of which the flow of time issues.

Just as subjectivity is required as the condition of possibility for the real world, the present instant is required as the condition for subjectivity. Without the flowing present, there can be no consciousness. The present, with its characteristics of retention and protention, is what makes the objects of inner experience possible, the same immanent objects which will in their turn be the conditions for constitution of transcendent objects and senses. Only when Husserl reaches this point can he say that he has truly founded the possibility of his rigorous science, and established a base of final apodicticity for philosophy as he conceives it.[2]

Once again, Husserl uses the term "constitution" to name the way in which an "absolute" (in this case, the flowing present) allows its corresponding "relative" term to come about. Immanent objects are constituted in temporal phases which flow from the immediate present. On the other hand, as we have stressed, the immediate present is not constituted in any way; it is the only element in Husserl's entire phenomenology that has

---

[1] An interesting implicit commentary to this is found in the additions Husserl made to the text of *Ideas I* between 1923 and 1928. In some passages where the 1913 edition speaks of subjectivity as absolutely given, he adds, at the later stage of his thought, "as the immediate present." For example: *Ideen I*, p. 107: "Aber mein Einfühlen und mein Bewusstsein überhaupt ist *als strömende Gegenwart* originär und absolut gegeben...." (The words added are here italicized by us.) Also, p. 108: "In dieser absoluten Sphäre *lebendiger, immanenter Gegenwart* hat Widerstreit, Schein, Anderssein keinen Raum."

[2] Cf. Rudolf Boehm, "Zijn en tijd in de filosofie van Husserl," pp. 269-74.

this characteristic. As such it is truly an absolute in an ultimate sense. It is given in a final evidence which is the ground for all other evidences that occur for subjectivity, the condition for all objects, whether immanent or transcendent.

In this way, we find that Husserl uses constitution as the way of expressing the relationship between absolutes and relatives. An absolute *qua* absolute is not constituted; the relative is constituted by virtue of its relativity, and it is constituted by the absolute on which it depends. The manner in which such dependence occurs is called constitution.

Nevertheless, we must again place a restriction on what is achieved by constitution, even in the sphere of inner time. There is still a certain formalism in Husserl's theory of inner temporality, for the temporal constitution of inner objects does not explain the diversity of acts or sensations which we experience. The fact that we perform acts of perception, desire, or imagination, is still a pure fact for Husserl's phenomenology. We do not deduce such acts from the evidence of the immediate present. In other words, temporal constitution does not explain the quality of acts, the material aspect of sensations, or the content of meaning and objects which we constitute. All this is simply given, and illustrates once again that Husserl does not try to find the sufficient cause for constitution when he looks for the absolute on which it is based. He is simply trying to uncover the necessary condition which allows constitution to take place. The immanent constitution achieved by temporality allows us to experience inner objects, and in doing so it allows these objects to exist, but it does not explain them totally.

3. The basic model for constitution

The remarks we have made so far have been of a general and fundamental nature. They were concerned with the relationships between consciousness and reality and time, which comprise the basic framework supporting Husserl's phenomenology, the framework within which all other elements in his thought have to be situated in order to be seen in correct perspective. We have shown how constitution fits into this pattern. Let us now return to a more concrete analysis of constitution. It is supposed to express the relationship between the absolute and relative in

Husserl's phenomenology; how is this expression actually carried out? What images, concepts, or schemas does Husserl use? In particular, can we determine how Husserl started his concept of constitution and find which expression of it governed his early thinking on the subject?

It is often said that mathematical entities and, in a more general way, categorical or logical objects were the first things to be explained by constitutional analysis. Husserl concurs in this opinion when he says that his analysis of numbers and groups in the *Philosophy of Arithmetic* was the first instance of constitutional clarification.[1]

It is correct to say this, but we cannot infer too much from it. Although numbers and categorical objects are the first stimulus to constitutional analysis, the basic model for constitution, the schema which dominates Husserl's first systematic conception of it, is not the process of categorical activity leading to such objects. The most basic image which Husserl uses to express constitution and to explain it is the schema of sense data apprehended or interpreted by intentions. The schema of intentional "form" animating sensory "matter" is the most fundamental way in which the concept of constitution appears in Husserl's phenomenology.

Thus Husserl observes that through the flow of subjective experiences, it is possible for us to have consciousness of something objective, of a transcendent, identical object, which serves as the focal point which all our experiences intend. What occurs to make this possible? The answer, says Husserl, is that our sensations, which in themselves are not intentional, are animated, informed, or interpreted in such a way as to become representants for an objective reality. Such an explanation for objectivity is a structural one and supposes the presence of two basic and distinct elements, sensations and intentions, in subjectivity. It was the common way of explaining our awareness of objectivity in the psychological and philosophical literature of the time when Husserl composed the *Logical Investigations*. [2]

The schema appears explicitly first in the *Logical Investigations*, where Husserl presents his first systematic study of the

---

[1] Cf. *supra*, p. 6.
[2] Cf. *supra*, p. 57.

nature and structure of intentionality.[1] The aim Husserl has in mind when he uses it is to explain how we can become conscious of objectivity, how transcendence can appear to consciousness. It is his way of solving the enigma and mystery of "the relationship between the subjectivity of knowing and the objectivity of the contents of knowledge." [2]

Thus it would be incorrect to say that Husserl first develops his theory of constitution for categorical objects and then expands it from them to all of reality. Such an opinion would claim that the primitive model and paradigm for constitution is the formation of logical entities, and that Husserl subsequently tries to treat all of reality in a manner analogous to the way he treats them. It would claim that Husserl takes something proper to logical entities and tries to force it on all objects of consciousness, including real things – a procedure whose justification is far from evident.[3] But Husserl does not do this. He does not start with logical entities and expand his concept of constitution to all of reality. The first model and paradigm for constitution is simply the constitution of objectivity, of transcendence, and it does not matter whether this objectivity is logical, real, imaginary, or simply intended in an unfulfilled meaning. There is no question of an *expansion* of this concept of constitution; from the beginning, it is large enough to encompass all objectivity. The only essential aspect in it is that consciousness

---

[1] Is the schema found in the *Philosophy of Arithmetic?* In that work, Husserl does not yet have a systematic theory of intentionality, and the schema does not appear as it will in the *Logical Investigations*, where such a theory is developed. However, when he introduces the schema in *Ideas I*, Husserl makes reference to his book on arithmetic and says that his concept of "primary contents" (i.e. hyletic data) is already found there. The reference is made to the section of the *Philosophy of Arithmetic* where Husserl introduces the concept of psychic relationships; cf. *Ideen I*, p. 208. In a sense, psychic relationships can be considered as a foreshadowing of the schema, because they imply a given datum which is informed, interpreted, or animated by intentionality; intentionality brings something to the datum which the latter does not have in itself (i.e., the relation).

[2] Cf. *supra*, p. 39.

[3] One of the strongest statements of such an interpretation can be found in Fink's remarks concerning Biemel's talk in *Husserl* (Cahiers de Royaumont), p. 64: "En d'autres termes le concept de constitution est d'abord orienté vers la constitution d'objets dits idéaux. Et ensuite vous avez dit que ce concept de constitution avait été étendu. J'objecterais seulement qu'à parler rigoureusement il ne s'agit pas d'une 'extension' mais bien d'une transformation.... C'est d'abord au modèle des idéalités que Husserl emprunte le concept de constitution et ensuite, dans cette transformation particulière, il l'applique simplement à toutes les choses; il me semble que c'est un pas important et en même temps contestable...."

reaches something transcendent to its own immanent experience, and that it does so by virtue of the apprehension of sense data. The matter-form schema, and not the formation of logical entities, is the paradigm for constitution. Categorical entities are said to be constituted only *qua* objectivities, not *qua* logical entities.

Categorical constitution is wholly subordinated to the matter-form schema in the *Investigations*. This is clearly shown by Husserl's attempt to apply the schema to categorical constitution by looking for a sensory representant to serve as the "matter" that will be animated by an intentional form and thus allow us to perceive the categorical object. The attempt is a patent failure, and in the second edition Husserl disowns it; but the attempt itself is a sign of how much he was convinced that the schema is essential to the constitution of all objectivity in our consciousness. Thus categorical constitution is not the first model for Husserl's concept of constitution.

Besides this structural explanation of constitution, however, Husserl, in the *Logical Investigations*, also speaks of a process which is related to constitution. First, there is an intentional process involved in categorical constitution, for various partial intentions and simple acts build upon one another until there is formed a categorical act in which a categorical object is constituted. Secondly, Husserl says that in the perception of a material thing, a series of partial intentions coalesce to constitute the material object as actually given. Both these forms of constitution, although differing in type from one another, are processes, and as such they present a picture for constitution which is basically different from the structural analysis that predominates in the *Investigations*. Ultimately, it is their form of constitution that will survive through Husserl's development even after the structural analysis is surpassed, but at this early stage of his thought they are thoroughly subordinated to the structural schema.

4. Weakness of Husserl's matter-form schema and its gradual replacement

In the lectures on time, Husserl at first stands by his structural schema. He explains the constitution of objective things by the objectivating apprehensions which sensations undergo. Furthermore, he is tempted to use it even on the level of immanent temporality, when he tries to show how primal sense data are constituted. His first tendency is to say that a non-temporal, material moment of such data is apprehended and temporalized by intentionality, and thus constituted into an immanent object.

However, Husserl's studies of inner time gradually showed him that the schema has no place in this sphere, and led him to see that constitution has to be conceived in another way. We have seen, in our analysis of his lectures on time, three cases of constitution which could not be expressed in terms of the matter-form dichotomy. They are: (1) the constitution of intentions as inner objects. In the intention itself, there is obviously no sensory element. (2) The constitution of sensations as immanent objects. To posit a duality in them would lead to an infinite regress. (3) The constitution of objective time. It is impossible to claim that there is such a thing as "temporal sensations" which will be animated by an intention, for all inner temporality comes from the intentional moment itself, according to Husserl's principles of inner time. The reasoning by which he comes to these conclusions, which we have explained above, is too intricate to be repeated here; we simply observe that Husserl was forced to admit that not every type of constitution has the schema "sensations – intentions."

On the level of inner temporality, therefore, constitution acquires a new image or model, that of a flow of elements (partial intentions or temporal phases) which gradually builds up an immanent object. There is no duality in it, no matter-form dichotomy of intention and sensations. Instead, it is again the image of a process bringing about constitution.

There is still a more important result of Husserl's study of inner time. It begins to throw doubt on the value of the matter-form schema, not only in the sphere of inner time, but also in the higher level of consciousness, the level at which Husserl distinguishes between noeses and hyletic data. Both of these elements are now seen to flow from the same source, to be made out of the same "stuff." They are both constituted by a manifold of temporal phases emanating from the immediate present. If this is so how can they still differ from one another? On what basis can they be distinguished? They cannot be distinguished any longer; from the point of view of inner time, which is the decisive point of view for Husserl, sensations and intentions cannot be conceived as two distinct elements. With this conclusion, the very possibility of the schema is destroyed, and Husserl cannot justly use it any longer as a true phenomenological explanation of the constitution of objectivity.

The case of *Ideas I* is especially interesting, because it contains an unresolved tension between the two schemas which Husserl has developed. On the higher level of intentionality, he still adheres to the dual image, but he admits that the distinction between noeses and sensations does not hold if we go deeper into intentionality, into the region of inner time, where there is no duality but only the unified stream of temporal phases. On the level of acts, he posits static, ready-made structural elements, noeses and sensations, while in the immanent sphere he affirms an unending process where nothing can be assumed as static or ready-made. The two schemas do not fit one another, as Husserl himself admits. It is contradictory to say that on one level there is duality and static structure, while on the other, more basic level there is simplicity and constant change. As long as Husserl maintains his static structure and the distinction between noeses and hyle, it remains impossible for him to integrate his doctrine on inner time and its constitution with that of the higher level constitution achieved in acts.

The tension in *Ideas I*, between the higher and lower levels of intentionality, is resolved in *Formal and Transcendental Logic*, where Husserl replaces the static structure of acts with a genetic process, and thus allows the process of inner time to reach into the higher levels of intentionality. In this work, objectivity is no longer explained by structural elements and their composition, but by a process in our conscious life that, beginning from the now instant, finally solidifies into the constitution of things and categorical objects. To explain objectivity, Husserl now traces the pre-objective, lived anticipations of it in our conscious life.

In this way, the evolution of Husserl's thought is brought to its culmination. Each step consists in replacing the static structural schema by a genetic process; the use of a process is already present in categorical constitution, it appears strongly in the sphere of immanent time, and finally reaches the constitution of all objectivity in Husserl's concept of genetic constitution.

5. Husserl's final concept of constitution and its advantages over the first

The image of constitution and subjectivity which prevails in Husserl's last period has much in common with a "life philosophy," and Husserl now frequently uses the term "life" to express the consciousness of the ego. Consciousness is conceived as a flow of temporal phases or primal intentions that emanate from the flowing present moment.

The first level in the development of this life is called "passive genesis" and is characterized by the absence of any categorical activity on the part of the ego. Various sub-levels can be distinguished in this region. There is first a stage of pure sensation, then a stage in which sensations are externally spatialized, when they are constituted into what Husserl calls "phantoms," and finally a stage in which things are constituted: fixed identity points that solidify within the world of phantoms. The objective correlate to this level of conscious life is a world in which there is the presence of things, but no judgment or predication, and consequently no firmly defined, conceptualized sense. Within passive genesis, however, there are already anticipations of sense and the development which subjectivity undergoes to this point leads on, teleologically, into active genesis, where permanent senses or meanings are constituted.

When the ego makes judgments on the things it has encountered, when it carries out active intentional performances on the world of things, it thereby deposits fixed, permanent senses in the world. On the basis of such senses, the ego finds its subsequent encounter of the lived world modified, determined, and enlightened, so that it can go on to make further judgments and deposit further senses which depend on the prior ones. Thus a whole network of interdependent, "scientific" senses is constituted. Each of these senses has its roots in the pre-predicative encounter which precedes it, and if we are to explain a sense, we must trace its anticipations in such encounter. This means tracing it first to its anticipation in our encounter of things, then more deeply to its realization in the world of phantoms, and finally to the world of pure sensation springing from the immediate present. Such investigation is genetic analysis and is the way in which Husserl now conceives phenomenology.

There are many reasons why this new method of analysis is more advantageous than the structural method of inquiry, with its matter-form schema, used earlier by Husserl. It accounts for the temporality of the ego even on the higher level of consciousness, where acts occur. It allows Husserl to integrate what he says about inner time with his analysis of intentional constitution. The objective senses and things constituted by subjectivity are put into motion; they are shown to have a historicity within their very contents. The factor of time, which Husserl claims is the central element in subjectivity, is thus given its proper extension into all levels of consciousness. The genetic schema has the advantage of being applicable to all problems of constitution, whereas the matter and form schema, as we have seen, has only a limited application; there are cases of constitution to which it cannot be applied.

The factor of time and historicity in the contents of what is constituted makes it possible for Husserl to bring many interesting philosophical problems into the open, and to provide a rich and varied description of the activity of consciousness towards reality. It is a more fruitful method of inquiry. Each type of experience and encounter has its own way of developing, and goes through stages of evolution proper to itself. Genetic constitution will allow such individual differences to come to the fore. Most important, it will allow us to see how each region of being becomes conceptualized on the basis of pre-predicative encounter. It gives us a framework in which we can show, for example, how ethical concepts become fixed in judgments, and what pre-predicative consciousness has preceded them; then we would be able to contrast this form of conceptualization with the fixation of concepts proper to science or esthetics, for example. Thus the sources from which these regions of reality and encounter arise can be studied, and the great complexity and richness that lies in the "lived encounter" at the base of our concepts can be revealed. The subtle and complicated details of experience that motivate the formation of concepts can thus be brought into the light, and the danger of reductionism, of trying to standardize all human experience into one form of consciousness or another, is removed. Furthermore, the constant interplay of conceptualized senses with pre-predicative encounter, and the stimulus this has on the growth of constitution, is also stressed.

In contrast, the type of inquiry made possible by Husserl's earlier schema is relatively limited. The chief limitation is that it always starts with meanings or senses as already present, already constituted in intentionality. It is too abrupt. It neglects the encounter that leads into meanings, and in doing so it hammers out many of the fine nuances of experience and anticipations of sense which are important in the coming-to-be of our knowledge in its actual state. This weakness and crudeness is due to the nature of the schema itself; its way of explaining the advent of sense and objectivity is too abrupt. It achieves its explanation by claiming that sensations are animated by noeses, and that objects and meanings thus become present to us. But the whole question of how they came to be what they are, how they acquired the content and status they enjoy, is left aside.

Finally, the matter and form schema is subject to the chief criticism which Husserl makes of it himself. He says that it is a form of psychologism, which he defines as follows in *Formal and Transcendental Logic:* "The prevalent data-sensualism in psychology and epistemology... consists in the fact that it builds up the life of consciousness out of data that are taken as what might be called ready-made objects." [1] He goes on to classify the matter and form schema of intentions and sensations as an example of such psychologism, for it posits the ready-made existence of immanent objects that are supposed to be present to the ego as something simply given, as an existence that appears without any activity or performance, without any evidence carried out by subjectivity. [2] They are said to exist as phenomena for the ego, but to do so independently of the ego. In other words,

---

[1] "Der allherrschende Daten-Sensualismus in Psychologie wie Erkenntnistheorie ... besteht darin, dass er das Bewusstseinsleben aus Daten aufbaut als sozusagen fertigen Gegenständen." *Form. trans. Log.*, p. 252.

[2] Cf. *ibid.*, p. 253: "Aber es gibt auch in der immanenten 'Innerlichkeit' des Ego keine Gegenstände im voraus und keine Evidenzen, die nur umgreifen, was im voraus schon ist. Die Evidenzen als das Seiende konstituierende Funktionen ... vollziehen die Leistung, deren Ergebnis da heisst seiender Gegenstand. So schon hier und so überall."

they are posited as phenomena that exist for consciousness without having their condition of possibility explained. One falls into such psychologism by not explaining the conditions of possibility on which noeses and sensations depend in order to be experienced, in order to exist as immanent objects. One falls into such psychologism when the matter-form schema is accepted as the ultimate datum, the final principle in consciousness, when one neglects the "final and true absolute" that is more fundamental than the schema itself. In order to avoid this error, we must show how both noesis and hyletic data are themselves constituted in inner temporality, by the process engendered from the immediate present. We must show the condition of possibility for their existence, and show what sort of "evidence" and constitution bring them about. Husserl does this in his analysis of inner temporality.

6. The problem of sensations

A good example which illustrates the development Husserl follows from static to genetic constitution, and which shows the improvement achieved by the latter, is the case of sensations. Even in the *Philosophy of Arithmetic*, Husserl states that sensations have a role to play in determining the "logical content" of concepts, but he does not have a theory of intentionality capable of showing how sensations could perform such a function. In the *Logical Investigations* and in *Ideas I*, the role of sense data is incorporated into a theory of intentionality, under the matter-form schema. Sensations are the raw material which serves as the basis for the constitution of objects and meanings. The intentional and meaningful moment in consciousness comes from noeses; and yet, continues Husserl, we are not completely free in forming objects and senses. We are limited by what is given in sensation, for the passive, material element imposes restrictions on the activity of intentionality. The manner in which this happens, however, is not explained. It calls for an explanation, because it is not self-evident how sensations, which are radically different from noeses, can enter into the realm of intentions and exercise an effect on them. No explanation is forthcoming as long as we hold to the schema, because the correlation of sensations and noeses has to be simply accepted as a fact expressed in this schematism. The schema is accepted as an ultimate datum; Husserl does not take us a step beyond the datum and show us how the schema itself is possible, and especially how the influence of sensations on noeses is possible.[1]

The perspective changes when Husserl extends his doctrine on temporality throughout all of consciousness, and envisions the problems of genetic constitution. Sense data and noeses are no longer conceived as two distinct elements; they are now seen to be one immanent reality, one inner flow of consciousness. By conceiving the structure of subjectivity in this way, Husserl dissolves the problem we have raised above by removing the dichotomy which gives rise to it. Sense data can have an effect on constitution because they are no longer conceived as distinct from intentionality.

It is true that Husserl still speaks of a state of pure sensation which precedes objectivation, but now this is conceived in a new perspective.[2] The state of pure sensation is a step in genetic constitution. It is the most primitive step in transcendental aesthetics or pre-predicative consciousness, and leads gradually into the more developed steps in which external space and finally external things are constituted. However, the pure sensation already possesses inchoate senses, it has anticipations of sense which will gradually develop into full, fixed meanings in predication. It thus influences the constitution of sense and objectivity by the teleological development of which it is the first stage. By means of this genetic schema, the concept of constitution envisioned as a process, the place of sensations in the growth of sense and meaning is explained. Husserl is able to show how sensations can influence meaning.

---

[1] Merleau-Ponty criticizes what he calls an "intellectualist" way of explaining knowledge, according to which perception, meaning, and objectivity come into our experience by a spiritual act radically distinct from sensations. Cf. *Phénoménologie de la perception* (Paris: Gallimard, 1945), p. 40: "On le verra mieux en examinant le rôle que joue dans son analyse ıa notion de jugement. Le jugement est souvent introduit comme ce qui manque à la sensation pour rendre possible une perception." The criticism that Merleau-Ponty makes of this position would not apply to Husserl's genetic phenomenology, but, because of the sensation-intention schema he uses in his earlier thought, his first writings are subject to it.

[2] Cf. *supra*, Chapter III, § 14.

7. Phenomenology and material logic

An immediate value which Husserl's analyses of constitution have is their value of criticism. In analyzing the constitution of a certain type of objects or a certain region of being, Husserl gives us a "material logic" appropriate to it. He shows what sort of encounter is necessary for a certain object and what type of reasoning can be built up concerning it. In doing so, he supplements purely formal logic with a material logic which is absolutely necessary if we are to account for the structure of discursive reasoning as it takes place concretely in our life. A material logic, based on analysis of how certain objects are constituted in consciousness, must be elaborated if we are to see why we can use certain arguments in respect to one type of reality and not in respect to another. It is also necessary to show what sort of perception we must try to carry out in order to deepen our knowledge of a given object. We cannot use any type of argument or any type of scientific experiment, which is simply controlled perception, in each and every context of research. Constitutional analysis, especially as developed in the section of "Reason and Reality" in *Ideas I*, can provide a standard of criticism for our methodology.

In this matter of material logic, Husserl's constitutional studies have much in common with the philosophy of linguistic analysis. Wittgenstein's theory of language games, regions of discourse which have an internal logic specific to themselves, is closely parallel to the material logic uncovered in the study of reason and reality.[1] Wittgenstein and those who use his general method raise many problems which Husserl would call problems of constitution, but have never elaborated a systematic theory of subjectivity as a base for their investigations.

The theory of genetic constitution provides another area in which we can find rules for criticism of our experience and argument. Here Husserl tries to uncover the genetic presuppositions in which our present encounter or use of discourse is couched. A physicist, for instance, approaches his experiments with certain convictions concerning matter, force, space, or motion.

---

[1] For example, see *Philosophical Investigations*, sections 31, 72-75, 139-40, 143-49, and the entire second part of the work. On the question of material logic, cf. Stephen Toulmin, *The Uses of Argument* (Cambridge: The University Press, 1958).

They are the result, the sedimentation of prior acts of judgement, but are they justified? To what extent are they motivating his present controlled perception, so that he sees only what his convictions let him see? A phenomenological analysis of the senses of concepts he assumes may help free him from unwarranted presuppositions and make his experience of reality more genuine. Studies in the history of scientific concepts can be carried out with this aim in mind.[1] A similar case is that of the philosopher reflecting on a problem or attempting to understand a new system of philosophy. On a wider scale, the problem of hermeneutics, the interpretation of texts, is still another example. What convictions (habitualities) do we bring with us when we attempt to decipher the sense of a document? Genetic constitution may help us to criticize our procedure and make us aware of our own presuppositions.

The critical value of constitutional analysis, however, is only a secondary advantage of phenomenology. Even apart from this pragmatic use, such analysis has a value in itself. It makes us understand reality, claims Husserl, with an understanding that is apodictic and final, philosophical.

In his later thought, Husserl became aware of certain limitations in the apodictic and ultimate nature of what he achieves through his transcendental reduction. During the course of his lectures given in 1923-24, he realizes that the reduction has been carried out in a certain naiveté, and that it is necessary for him to work out a theory or phenomenology of the reduction itself. This would amount to a "metaphenomenology," a phenomenological investigation and critique of phenomenology, and would comprise an ultimate sort of "First Philosophy." [2] The new problems faced here could be treated in terms of constitution, for they would consider phenomenology as something that is itself constituted. Husserl dealt with this subject extensively during the last fifteen years of his life, but at least in the works that have been published so far, he does not discuss it explicitly

---

[1] For example, Norwood Hanson, *Patterns of Discovery* (Cambridge: The University Press, 1958), which is carried out in the context of linguistic analysis, and Hermann Weyl, *Philosophy of Mathematics and Natural Science* (Princeton: The University Press, 1949).

[2] Cf. Rudolf Boehm's introduction to *Erste Philosophie II*, pp. xxxvii-xlii; also pp. 217-18, 252 of the same volume.

as a problem of constitution; it would be treated more appropriately in a study of his later theory of phenomenological reduction.

8. *Husserl's choice of the term "constitution"*

Why does Husserl make use of the particular term "constitution" to name the intentional process we have been discussing? It seems certain that he took the term from the neo-Kantians, and more particularly from Paul Natorp, who had such a great influence on Husserl's thought. Natorp uses the word frequently, as a noun, verb, or adjective. For instance, he speaks of "the unity of consciousness which, in the unity of laws, constitutes the unity of the object." [1] He mentions "the activity of science, which everywhere constitutes the object in law." [2] In another work, he devotes a section to: "The constitution of objects of encounter according to the basic laws of dynamic unification." [3]

The general sense of the term in Natorp is the constitution of objects of encounter by the application of certain subjective categories or apriori laws to immediately given sense data. Constitution of objects of encounter takes place in subjectivity. He claims, "that even the thought of objectivity, even the constitution of an object on the base of law-governed connections of appearances, ultimately is given simply 'in us,' in thinking, or more correctly, in knowing; but at any rate in consciousness, in our subjectivity alone." [4] What he considers philosophical psychology is the determination of the apriori elements necessary for such constitution, an investigation similar to Kant's deduction of the categories.[5] Constitution is thus the process by which sub-

[1] "die Einheit des Bewusstseins, ... welche in der Einheit des Gesetzes die Einheit des Gegenstandes konstituiere." *Einleitung in die Psychologie nach kritischer Methode*, p. 108. Husserl made a careful study of this work before writing the *Logical Investigations*.

[2] "die Tat der Wissenschaft, die überall im Gesetze den Gegenstand konstituiert." "Über objektive und subjektive Begründung der Erkenntnis," *Philosophische Monatshefte*, 23 (1887), p. 260.

[3] "Die Konstitution des Erfahrungsgegenstandes gemäss den Grundgesetzten der dynamischen Verknüpfung." *Philosophische Propädeutik* (Marburg: N.G. Elwert, 1903), p. 28.

[4] "dass auch der Gedanke der Objektivität, auch die Konstituierung des Gegenstandes auf Grund des gesetzmässigen Zusammenhanges der Erscheinungen zuletzt bloss 'in uns,' im Denken, richtiger im Erkennen, jedenfalls aber im Bewusstsein, in unserer Subjektivität allein gegeben sei." *Einleitung in die Psychologie nach kritischer Methode*, p. 108.

[5] Cf. *ibid.*, p. 129: " 'In der Tat' entspricht aber Kants Verfahren der subjektiven Deduktion sehr genau dem, was wir als die rekonstruktive Methode der Psychologie

jectivity forms objectivity by virtue of its own activity; Natorp often speaks of the objectivating function of consciousness.[1]

Natorp was not the only neo-Kantian to use the term. It is found frequently in Cohen, again in connection with the problem of how objects of encounter are formed for consciousness, how sensations are objectivated. The term appears especially in his study of Kant's Analogies of Experience: "The principle we must clarify is an analogy, which must serve as transcendental basis for natural laws; objects are constituted as instances of these laws, and consequently as objects of encounter.... The principle must nevertheless first constitute the object as object, and indeed as object of encounter." [2]

Kant himself uses the term, but, it seems, only as an adjective; he uses the word "constitutive" in opposition to "regulative." Quite in opposition to Cohen, however, he says that the term does not apply to Analogies of Experience, but only to the Axioms of Intuition and the Anticipations of Perception, in other words, to the mathematical principles: those which deal not with the existence or objectivation of things, but with the apriori possibilities of space and time that precede objectivation.[3] The term is rare in Kant, however, and given the interest Husserl had in Natorp's writings, in which "constitution" frequently appears, it would be reasonable to conclude that he acquired it from them.

Husserl's first use of the word is especially close to the neo-Kantian sense, for he speaks of consciousness "informing"

definierten, ja die letztere ist wirklich nichts Anderes als die Verallgemeinerung des tatsächlichen Vorgehen Kants in dem betreffenden Teile seiner Untersuchung."
    [1] Cf. *ibid.*, pp. 94-95, 100.
    [2] "Der Grundsatz, den wir zu beleuchten haben, ist eine Analogie, welche als transzendentale Grundlage zu dienen hat für die Naturgesetze, als deren Fälle die Gegenstände und somit als Gegenstände der Erfahrung konstituiert werden.... Der Grundsatz soll jedoch den Gegenstand als Gegenstand und zwar als Gegenstand der Erfahrung allererst konstituieren." Herman Cohen, *Kants Theorie der Erfahrung* (Berlin: Dümmler, 1885), p. 452. See the entire chapter 12, pp. 406-500, where the term is frequently used. Cohen did not have much of an influence on Husserl; we cite him only to show that the term "constitution" was commonly used in the neo-Kantian school. We were unable to find the term used by German psychologists before the turn of the century.
    [3] Cf. *Kritik der reinen Vernunft* (Hamburg: Meiner, 1956), A 179-80, B 221-23. H.J. Paton, in *Kant's Metaphysic of Experience* (London: George Allen & Unwin, 1961), vol. II, p. 179, observes that to be "constitutive" always implies the possibility of construction for Kant, and construction implies in turn the possibility of immediate certainty or evidence.

sensations by means of apprehension, and thus constituting objectivity. His method of looking for an explanation for objectivity in subjective structure and processes bears much similarity with the general project of the neo-Kantians. There is an important difference, however, for the Kantian tradition maintained the idea of fixed subjective categories that are imposed upon sensation, while Husserl never accepted this. For the neo-Kantians, strictly speaking, it is the categories that constitute the object, and this process of constitution takes place in subjectivity; for Husserl, on the other hand, subjectivity itself constitutes the object. In his conception of constitution, whatever categories are constituted are the *result* of encounter; they are never found before encounter and imposed on it. Husserl's subjective apriori is not as rigid and predetermined as the Kantian system of apriori elements is.[1]

To add a few more remarks concerning vocabulary, it is significant that the term "constitution" is used both in the active and reflexive forms when it appears as a verb in Husserl's writings. Consciousness constitutes its objects, but reality, things, meanings, etc., are also said to "constitute themselves" in consciousness. The reflexive form should be considered in the light of what we have said about subjectivity as a simple condition of possibility for the emergence of the real. Consciousness does not cause its objects and their contents; they can be said to "constitute themselves." Such an expression is not used for things which are totally caused by something else. For instance, we do not say that a manufactured product constitutes itself, but that we make or cause it, or that machines make it. Husserl's grammatical expression can be taken to indicate the element of facticity in what is given to consciousness, to indicate that reality also has a contribution to make in the process of constitution.

---

1 We do not wish to describe the entire influence of Kant and the neo-Kantians on Husserl's concept of constitution; our remarks concerning them are made only to show the source from which Husserl probably acquired the *term* "constitution." For an exhaustive study of this subject, see Iso Kern, *Husserl und Kant*. Kern attributes a great influence of Natorp in the formation of Husserl's concept of genetic constitution. Besides this external influence, however, we feel that the internal development of Husserl's thought led to the theory of genetic constitution.

The expression, "to manifest itself" *(sich bekunden)* also carries such an implication.[1] It is used by Husserl as a synonym for constitution and connotes at least the fact that reality brings something to consciousness. Husserl uses other synonyms which have a much more active sense, and seem to simply that subjectivity produces objects. Such terms as *erzeugen* (to produce or engender), applied to the activity of constitution, or *Geblide* (products or formations), which designates that which is constituted, carry such an overtone. However, words of this sort are usually applied to categorical constitution, where it is more correct to speak of a "creation" or "production" on the part of subjectivity. Categorical objects are objects which have undergone a logical formation, and the categorical element in them is clearly the result of a subjective activity that could be called "causal." However, even in the case of categorical constitution, we are not entirely free in what we can bring about, because the contents in categorical objects remain determined by what is given in pre-predicative encounter.

In order to paraphrase the constitution of meaning and objects, it seems that a neutral term like the "coming-to-be" of such objects and senses would be best. It must be understood that they cannot "come into being" without the presence and concurrence of consciousness, which is the necessary condition for becoming real; in static constitution, consciousness is required as their correlate, and in genetic constitution, the step by step development of conscious acts of evidence, with the deeper conceptualization and insight it brings, is necessary as a historical condition for the gradual emergence of what is genetically constituted. However, consciousness is not the sufficient cause of all that transpires in constitution. There is a facticity and givenness in the actual content found in objects and senses when they come to be.

---

[1] Cf. *Die Idee der Phänomenologie*, p. 70, and especially the passage in *Ideen I*, p. 174: "Die Kategorienlehre muss durchaus von dieser radikalsten aller Seinsunterscheidungen – Sein als Bewusstsein und Sein als sich im Bewusstsein 'bekundendes,' 'transzendentes' Sein – ausgehen, die, wie man einsieht, nur durch die Methode der phänomenologischen Reduktion in ihrer Reinheit gewonnen und gewürdigt werden kann."

9. *Criticism of Husserl's phenomenology as providing the philosophical foundation for reality*

We have stressed throughout our study that Husserl's concept of constitution supposes two elements: subjectivity as a condition of possibility for constitution, and also a certain facticity in what is actually constituted. There are two sources for constitution. However, in his phenomenology, Husserl has really elaborated only one of these; he has exploited subjectivity as the *sine qua non* for the real, and he has made of it the dominating principle of explanation for his "first philosophy." As a result, his philosophy becomes too much orientated towards subjectivity.

In providing only subjectivity as a condition of possibility, Husserl is left with the content of constitution as an unexplained residuum, a pure facticity which escapes the principles of his philosophy. We suggest that it would be necessary for him to complete his thought with investigation of another "condition of possibility," one which would encompass the facticity of what is actually given in constitution. Husserl's philosophy needs an examination of what the condition *sine qua non* is for reality to reveal itself, in constitution, as that which it actually is. In other words, the fundament in reality which allows reality to emerge in constitution has to be investigated.[1] As long as this is not done, the content of constitution remains outside the sphere of philosophy. It has no principle of philosophical explanation, and must be accepted as a brute, irrational fact, something which philosophy is powerless to treat.

The problem of constitution, viewed in this bilateral perspective, is now said to suppose two "sources" or two foundations. Instead of seeing constitution exclusively as the problem of subjectivity, we consider it as the problem of subjectivity and objectivity in their mutual rapport. Constitution is not simply the evolution of subjectivity (the idealist extreme), nor only the evolution of reality as a closed process independent of consciousness (the empiricist position), but the development of

---

[1] Thus Heidegger tries to account for this by treating what he calls *das Sein der Seienden*. Cf. Alphonse De Waelhens, *Phénoménologie et vérité* (Paris: Presses universitaires de France, 1953), p. 57: "Notre thèse à ce sujet est que Husserl a négligé de développer l'ontologie nécessaire à sa propre doctrine et que Heidegger a comblé cette lacune."

reality and subjectivity in their fundamental relationship to one another. The real cannot be conceived apart from its manifestation to subjectivity, but consciousness cannot be conceived without its tendency to the real, and both dimensions must be retained in giving the philosophical basis for constitution. Constitution is the product of the dialectic between these two poles, each of which must be posited if a true dialectic is to exist. Philosophical explanation of constitution would then demand not only that we show how subjectivity makes encounter with reality possible, but also that we describe what it is in being that makes revelation possible. Both foundations of the dialectic must be clarified, and "transcendental logic" must be based equally on subjectivity and reality.

Why does Husserl center on only one locus for philosophical clarification? It is his quest for a rigorous science that leads him to this. Reality is rejected because it is only presumptive, while consciousness, and consciousness alone, is accepted as a philosophical principle because it alone, claims Husserl, is apodictically (and, in his early thought, absolutely) given. This is the criterion which Husserl uses as a guide for his philosophy, and it leads him to only one principle of philosophical explanation.

Even if we accept Husserl's criterion of apodicticity as the final test of what is going to be accepted as a point of departure for philosophical explanation, we need not be led to his conclusion. There is a way in which the real existence of the world can be asserted apodictically. Even if we concede that a certain amount of error or doubtfulness is possible concerning individual things in the world, we can still say that the world itself is not doubtful. The existence of the world as a transcendent horizon for our experience and encounter is apodictic; it is the background against which all individual instances of knowing take place, and although we may be misled in certain cases of knowledge, we cannot be misled about the background of knowledge itself.

We can consider such a world as the general, undifferentiated "real" that is first given to our consciousness. But consciousness, or intentionality, cannot be conceived apart from such a real, "worldly" correlative. The intentionality of consciousness is ordered towards what is. When we define intentionality as "consciousness of" something, this "something" is not imaginary or fictitious; it is reality. Intentionality is not conceivable as nothing more than an undifferentiated intending, as though it made no difference what it intended. Rather, intentionality is essentially orientated to discovering the real world, and so this real world is a necessary correlate to consciousness. Reality thus gives consciousness its sense. Consciousness cannot be understood apart from its orientation, not simply to any object at all, but to the world. True, we perform acts that intend unreal, fictitious, or imaginative objects, but such acts make sense only as derivative forms of "real" intentions. Consciousness necessarily demands the world as its correlative; this is as apodictic in phenomenology as the claim that the sense of the world requires consciousness as a correlative supplement to itself. Thus for phenomenology, the reality of the world cannot be doubtful "in principle," but is apodictic and necessary, and must be given its part in the fundamental starting point of this form of philosophy.[1] It too is a necessary condition for constitution.

In claiming that the real world has a fundamental place in phenomenology and constitution, we have not yet said anything about how it carries out its role as a basis for knowledge. In order to discuss this, we must bring in another point which Husserl develops in this context, the fact that material reality presents itself to us through profiles (*Abschattungen*.) This point must be considered, because Husserl uses it as the reason for attributing doubtfulness "in principle" to material reality.

It cannot be denied that material things are given to consciousness through profiles; this much is a fact of experience. But what interpretation can we make of this fact? Do we have to follow Husserl in saying that it renders all our knowledge of material reality doubtful?

Because material reality is given through an aspect continuum, we can never have adequate evidence of individual things. There is always room for a deepening and explicitation of what we know about them. But there is still an apodictic,

[1] Cf. De Waelhens, *ibid.*, p. 45: "Un tel monde n'est nullement présomptif et, si l'on y tient absolument, on peut lui appliquer la malheureuse notion que développaient les *Méditations cartésiennes;* il bénéficie d'une évidence apodictique puisque la conscience ne se conçoit pas sans lui."

adequate judgment we can make about material reality on the basis of its givenness through profiles: we can say that material things *exist* in profile continua. That is, we can affirm that they exist in a mode of change. When we make such an assertion, we are not going beyond the evidence that we have. We simply assert or posit material reality in the mode in which it is given to us. Hence such an assertion, even though it is an assertion of existence, is just as apodictic and adequately justified as the assertion of the existence of transcendental subjectivity. It posits no more than is actually given to consciousness, and thus according to Husserl's criterion it is a justified and evident assertion. Both assertions of existence are warranted by the immediate experience or encounter on which they are based. Thus besides being able to say that the real world is a necessary correlate to consciousness, we can also state something about the way in which it exists, and we can do so apodictically. We do not make any "presumption" whatsoever when we state that material reality exists under an aspect continuum. Such a statement is apodictic, and can be introduced as a principle, as an "axiom" in Husserl's rigorous science.

The profile continuum which we encounter in our consciousness of reality, as Husserl readily admits, is not the result of the way we happen to see things, it is not the result of the psychological makeup of human nature. We do not put profiles into things; they are present in the change which things constantly undergo.[1] A static, changeless world, if such a thing can really be conceived, would neither possess a continuum of aspects or profiles, nor would it present one to our consciousness.[2]

Interpreting the fact of profile continua in this way, we have been able to state something about the way material reality exists. In addition, we now have something to say about how reality can contribute its part to the process of constitution. As Husserl has shown, the only way consciousness can constitute

[1] It is interesting to note that even in his thought experiment in § 49 of *Ideas I*, where Husserl performs an imaginary "annihilation" of the world, he does not claim to annihilate the phenomenon of change as something "really" existing, nor does he remove the world as an all-encompassing horizon intended by consciousness.
[2] We do not mean to identify reality with change, for there must remain some elements of stability and permanence in it. But both fixity and change have to be taken into consideration in our awareness of the material world; neither can be neglected.

reality is through a stream of profiles. But this is not only a characteristic of subjectivity; it also tells us something about the second condition of possibility that we have introduced for constitution. It tells us that reality cannot constitute itself in subjectivity unless it exists in profiles as well. Reality cannot manifest itself to consciousness unless it exists in change. Material things manifest themselves, or constitute themselves, in the activity and change that they carry out, and to use Husserl's terminology, an objective "achievement" (*Leistung*) is just as necessary for the constitution of sense as a subjective one is. A static universe would make constitution just as impossible as a non-temporal consciousness would; changing reality is a condition *sine qua non* for intentional constitution. Thus we have an insight into the fundament in reality which allows the emergence of sense.

To express this in other terms, the concept of constitution presupposes, as its ultimate condition of possibility, two flows of temporality: the historicity of subjectivity and the change of reality. Both are necessary for the coming-to-be of what is real. The problem of constitution then studies how the two streams of temporality or change interact in the growth of sense and presence.[1]

In this connection, it should be noticed that Husserl never exploits the constitution of objective time as much as he does the constitution of inner time, which he makes the basis of his theory of genetic constitution. The fruitfulness of his doctrine of inner time comes from his success in integrating time with the being of subjectivity. He shows that the ego is not simply an object around which time flows, like a rock in a stream, but that the very being of subjectivity involves temporality. He does not succeed in doing the same for real objects. Real objects are conceived as too much distinct from the objective time which "contains" them. Their time is too much simply the measure of their "before and after" in our encounter, and not enough the expression of the changeability that is as much a part of their reality as their existence is. The basic phenomenological situ-

---

[1] Einstein's space-time continuum has led recent thinkers to stress the fundamentally temporal nature of physical reality. Cf. Milic Capek, *The Philosophical Impact of Contemporary Physics* (Princeton: Van Nostrand, 1961), pp. 209, 360-80.

ation, given in the apodicticity which Husserl demands, comprises two distinct flows of time in necessary rapport with one another, issuing in the common process called constitution.

* * *

In following the development of Husserl's concept of constitution, we have, in effect, been tracing the evolution of his concept of phenomenology itself. There is no other concept that reflects in itself the totality of his thought so completely and so well. The philosophical value of his theory of constitution is the philosophical value of phenomenology as a whole, and the weakness and difficulty attached to this concept are the weakness and difficulty inherent in phenomenology as a philosophical method. Besides its historical interest for an understanding of Husserl's thought, moreover, the study of constitution leads us to many questions, problems, and insights which are truly fundamental for the philosophy of any age.

HUSSERL'S DESCRIPTION OF THE ORIGIN OF A
SYMBOLISM FOR NUMBERS.[1]

According to the *Philosophy of Arithmetic*, the concept of number differs from that of multiplicity in that it specifies the precise form of multiplicity involved in a given case. When faced with a group of objects, it is enough to know that there is a multitude there to have the concept of multiplicity apply. In order to apply the concept of number, we must be able to say how many objects there are; that is, we must specify which of the forms of multiplicity is present in this case.

When we are limited to authentically given numbers, we have only a handful of such forms to deal with. Only a few numbers are actually given in direct consciousness. It would be easy to decide on a few names or signs to represent them symbolically. Now that symbolically given multitudes are introduced, however, the picture changes. We know that a specific number corresponds to each multitude that can be symbolized, but now there is no limit to the diversity of forms of multitudes that can be involved. The weakness of our imagination and memory and the limits of our ability to perform actual collective liaisons do not matter any more. We know that every number, every form of multiplicity, can be changed into another form simply by the addition of one number, and that this process can, theoretically, be carried out indefinitely. The only limitation on it is that imposed by our mental powers of collecting, and since we are no longer dealing with actually collected multitudes, this element of factual limitation falls away. Husserl says, "So the restrictions on the conception of number concepts fall away, together with the restrictions that check our presentation of multitudes. In a symbolical, but in a very determined way, we can speak of numbers even where an authentic presentation is forever denied us, and on this level we are even in a position to determine the ideal infinity of the realm of numbers." [2] Thus we are now faced with a limitless variety of forms of multitudes or numbers; what sort of symbolism are we to devise for them, so that, given the symbol, we will know exactly which form of multiplicity we are dealing with? The first problem is to devise an appropriate system of symbols.

What materials do we have to work with? We have the names of numbers which are authentically given to us. Let us say they go as far

---

[1] To § 10, Chapter I.

[2] "So sind wirklich mit den Schranken, die unser Vorstellen von Mengen hemmt, auch diejenigen für die Konzeption der Zahlbegriffe gefallen. In symbolischem aber ganz bestimmtem Sinne können wir von Zahlen sprechen, wo deren eigentliche Vorstellung uns für immer versagt ist, und wir sind auf dieser Stufe sogar in der Lage, die ideelle Unendlichkeit des Zahlenreiches festzustellen." *Phil. Arith.*, pp. 251-52.

as ten or twelve. We have the operations of addition and subtraction, and the relationship of more and less.[1] We have the principle that each number, each form of multiplicity, differs from its immediate predecessor and successor by one unit each; it is one more than its predecessor and one less than its successor.

One way of building a series of signs to symbolize all possible numbers, the first method studied by Husserl, would be to do so in an unsystematic way, through "systemless symbolization of numbers." [2] This could be done, he says, by taking the symbols for authentic numbers and adding them together to form complex symbols for new numbers which are not given in direct encounter. Thus "10 + 5," "9 + 6 + 8," "7 + 10 + 5," etc., could each be complex signs for numbers greater than those we encounter directly. The difficulties in such an unsystematic method are apparent. The complex symbols become very long and unwieldy once the numbers become large, and the strain on memory and imagination becomes very great. Also, it becomes difficult to determine whether two such complex symbols stand for the same number or not, and if they do not, it is hard to determine which of the two represents the larger or the smaller number. Thus the main purpose of numeration, to indicate which form of multiplicity we are dealing with in a given case, is not achieved by this method. This purpose can best be attained, says Husserl, by use of a systematic method of forming symbols.[3]

The systematic method Husserl adopts is developed as follows. Let our symbols be defined in a sequence running parallel to the sequence of number concepts. This means that each symbol will be introduced as being equal to its preceding symbol plus one, just as each number is equal to its predecessor plus one unit. This results in a sequence of symbols as follows:

$1; 2 = 1 + 1; 3 = 2 + 1; \ldots 9 = 8 + 1.$

This process can be continued indefinitely, and will generate a system of signs each of which corresponds to a given form of multiplicity, to a given number, since each number is also generated from its predecessor by the addition of one.

However, it should be noted that nothing we have said so far, none of the rules we have introduced, justifies our *repeating* the cycle of symbols, "1," "2," "3," etc., after we have passed beyond the number 9. Strictly speaking, we must find altogether new symbols for all the succeeding numbers. "Every new step in the symbolical formation of numbers demands a new step in naming them." [4] This would result in an unlimited

[1] Husserl explains the relationship of more-less after he treats the origins of authentic numbers, and uses this relationship to explain addition and subtraction, which he considers the two fundamental operations of arithmetic, the two to which all other operations can be reduced (*ibid.*, pp. 203-11). The explanation of the relationship more-less does not involve any principles different from those presented in Husserl's treatment of the origins of groups. The relationship arises, once again, as a result of psychic acts of relating, but in this case the things related are groups. In forming this relationship, we form a higher order group, we form a group of groups (p. 99). Once we relate two such groups, we can see, says Husserl, which is greater than the other. This is the origin of the relationship more-less.

[2] "Die systemlose Zahlsymbolisierungen." *ibid.*, p. 252.

[3] Cf. *ibid.*, p. 254.

[4] "Jeder neue Schritt der symbolischen Zahlbildung erfordert einen neuen Schritt der Bennenung." *ibid.*, p. 256.

number of symbols, each different from the others, generated by our series. The series would continue:

$$9; x = 9 + 1; y = x + 1; z = y + 1....$$

We would have as many different symbols as there are numbers. This result will not do, since the limits of memory and imagination once again make such a series of symbols useless.

The difficulty can be resolved by carrying on the sequence for a given distance, then repeating the same sequence over again, but indicating somehow that a repetition is being carried on. Thus we build up the first sequence,

1, 2, 3, 4, 5, 6, 7, 8, 9.

Then we repeat it, but add a "1" to each repeated symbol to indicate that we are now in the second phase of the cycle:

10, 11, 12, 13, 14, 15, 16, 17, 18, 19.

When we repeat the sequence another time, we add "2" to each symbol:

20, 21, 22, 23, 24...

and so forth, with appropriate changes made for hundreds, thousands, etc.[1]

This system of symbols satisfies all the requirements for a good set of signs for the number system. Each symbol differs from its predecessor by one unit, so the system of symbols is parallel to the system of numbers. Furthermore, we can tell at a glance which of two symbols represents the larger of two numbers, and how far apart they are in the number series. Thus these symbols serve to identify clearly which number, which form of multiplicity, we are dealing with in any given case.

If we accept the principle of a recurrent cycle of symbols for our number system, the question then arises, how long should each cycle be? How many units should it include? The only requirements imposed are (1) the cycle should not be too short, or else the symbols quickly become too complex and too long. If we repeat the cycle after only two or three units, for example, we would soon have very complicated symbols to deal with. (2) It should not be too long, or else we would have too many different basic symbols in the first cycle. For example, if the cycle extends over seventy-five different units before repeating itself, we would have to handle seventy-five different basic signs. Both of these requirements are imposed, once again, by limitations of our memory and imagination, perceptual discrimination, and other such psychological factors.[2]

The fact is that our number symbols repeat in cycles of ten units. There is no apriori necessity that dictates this. The cycle could just as conveniently have extended over, for example, twelve units before repeating, and Husserl observes that mathematically a number system based on twelve units would be more advantageous.[3] Husserl suggests a historical explanation for the choice of ten units in the basic cycle, referring to the fact that primitively ten fingers are used as the most common means of counting.[4]

---

[1] Cf. *ibid.*, pp. 260-63.
[2] Cf. *ibid.*, pp. 265-68.
[3] Cf. *ibid.*, p. 268.
[4] Cf. *ibid.*, p. 279.

CONSTITUTION IN THE *IDEA OF PHENOMENOLOGY*

The thought expressed in the *Idea of Phenomenology*, which dates from courses given in 1907, is much the same as that which we have found in *Ideas I*, especially concerning the concept of constitution. Husserl sets out to found his phenomenology as a science, and to describe the radically new method and attitude it must have.[1] He will focus his study on that which is absolutely given, which is the region of our conscious experience, the sum of our *cogitationes*.[2] In order to limit himself to this sphere, Husserl performs the transcendental epoche; the reduction is carried out in a Husserlian interpretation of Descartes' universal doubt.[3] Carrying out the reduction leaves us with the first impression that we are preparing for a science of the immanent elements of our experience: "It looks almost as though it were a question only of a science of the absolute *cogitationes*." [4] On closer inspection, however, we see that within the field left after reduction, there also remain the "transcendental objects" which we suspended in our epoche. They remain simply as objects given to consciousness, correlates to our *cogitationes*. These objects, which were formerly considered as completely transcendent to our consciousness, are now found to be present within the immanence of our consciousness. "We become puzzled when we look closer and consider how, in the experience of a tone, for example – even after the phenomenological reduction – appearance and that which appears stand opposed to one another, and do so within what is purely given, thus within genuine immanence."[5] Finally, this "transcendence" which remains in our immanent experience is said to be constituted, and the task of phenomenology is to describe what teleological pattern the *cogitationes* must have in order to constitute a given type of object.[6]

---

[1] *Die Idee der Phänomenologie*, pp. 24-26.

[2] Cf. *ibid.*, pp. 29-32, 71-72.

[3] Cf. *ibid.*, p. 30.

[4] "Fast scheint es, als käme es nur auf eine Wissenschaft von den absoluten *cogitationes* an." *ibid.*, p. 46.

[5] "Wenn wir näher zusehen und nun achten, wie im Erlebnis etwa eines Tones, auch nach phänomenologischer Reduktion, sich Erscheinung und Erscheinendes gegenübersetzen und sich gegenübersetzen inmitten der reinen Gegebenheit, also der echten Immanenz, so werden wir stutzig." *ibid.*, p. 11. Cf. Walter Biemel's introduction to this volume, p. viii: "Den Zugang zu der transzendentalen Betrachtungsweise bildet die phänomenologische Reduktion, sie ermöglicht den Rückgang auf das 'Bewusstsein'. In ihm erschauen wir, wie die Gegenstände sich konstituieren.... In den fünf Vorlesungen hat Husserl zum ersten Mal diese Gedanken, die sein ganzes späteres Denken bestimmen sollten, öffentlich ausgesprochen."

[6] Cf. *ibid.*, pp. 14, 73, 75.

This pattern of thought, and especially the inclusion of constituted objects within the region of pure subjectivity, is similar to that of *Ideas I*. Nevertheless, there are some notable differences between the two books. We will mention some of the more apparent ones. First, Husserl's motive for doubting the reality of transcendent objects, and for affirming the indubitability of immanent ones, is slightly different from the motive given in *Ideas*, where the decisive factor is that real things appear in profiles while immanent ones do not. In the *Idea of Phenomenology*, Husserl says he can doubt external objects simply because they are transcendent to consciousness, while immanent objects are not and therefore cannot be doubted. "The transcendence of the thing demands that we put it into question." [1] This same idea is expressed in *Ideas I* when Husserl observes that immanent objects belong to the same stream of consciousness as the reflective acts which know them, whereas real objects are outside this stream. The argument is completely subordinated in *Ideas*, however, to that based on profiles.

The reasoning by which Husserl includes "transcendent" reality within subjectivity is also slightly different. In the *Idea of Phenomenology*, Husserl performs the reduction and finds immediately that *cogitationes* are present in what remains. The next step, however, is a detour in comparison with the method followed in *Ideas*, for Husserl then goes on to show that universals are also present in the region of subjectivity. He argues that after the reduction, we can analyze eidetically our conscious experiences, and thus form universal concepts of them. These universal concepts then remain as data in subjectivity and are also absolutely given. [2] Thus through ideal universals, Husserl introduces the first type of "transcencence" within the sphere of immanent subjectivity.

Then the third step is to find that not only universals, but also everything which is given to consciousness is also retained, as given, within the sphere of subjectivity. [3] For instance even a color, as something given to consciousness in perception, is present as a pure phenomenon in subjectivity. [4]

Husserl never speaks of "absolute being" or "relative, intentional being" in the *Idea of Phenomenology*. These "idealistic" terms, which are so abundant and important in *Ideas I*, are not mentioned in the earlier lectures.

The meaning of the word "phenomenon" is ambiguous in the *Idea of Phenomenology*. [5] Husserl begins by applying it to the *cogitationes* which

---

[1] "Die Transzendenz des Dinges fordert, dass wir es in Frage stellen." *ibid.*, p. 49. Cf. also pp. 4-5, 43.

[2] Cf. *ibid.*, p. 10: "Wie weit reicht Selbstgegebenheit? Ist sie beschlossen in der Gegebenheit der *cogitatio* und der sie generell fassenden Ideationen?" Cf. also pp. 51, 56-57.

[3] Cf. *ibid.*, p. 11: "Also dasselbe, was wir auch beim Allgemeinheitsbewusstsein fanden, dass es ein Bewusstsein ist, das eine Selbstgegebenheit konstituiert, die nicht im Reellen enthalten ist und überhaupt nicht als *cogatitio* zu finden ist, das finden wir auch beim Phänomen der Wahrnehmung."

[4] Cf. Rudolf Boehm, "Zum Begriff des 'Absoluten' bei Husserl," pp. 214-16. Only once in the *Idea of Phenomenology* does Husserl approach the manner of speaking found in *Ideas I*, when he speaks of the cogito as "lautes pures Sein." Even this is not equivalent to saying that subjectivity is absolute, however. Cf. pp. 70-71.

[5] Cf. *ibid.*, p. 14: "Das Wort Phänomen ist doppelsinnig vermöge der wesentlichen Korrelation zwischen Erscheinen und Erscheinendem. Φαινόμενον heisst

are given in reflection after reduction is carried out, but later he applies it to the "transcendent" objects which remain as given within the sphere of subjectivity. He finally concludes that the authentic meaning for the word is the second one. Finally, there is a constant ambiguity in Husserl's use of the term "transcendent" in the *Idea of Phenomenology*. At first, it is referred to all that exists outside my stream of consciousness, to the realities in the world. Later it acquires the sense of that which is present in my consciousness, but only as given from outside, as something which constitutes itself in consciousness.[1] "Constitution" acquires its technical sense for Husserl in association with the second sense of "transcendence."

Despite the differences we have listed, the overall train of thought found in *Ideas I* is already prefigured in the *Idea of Phenomenology*. The search for an apodictic science, the determination of subjectivity as the object of this science, the reduction, and finally the concept of reality as something constituted by consciousness, are all found in Husserl's thought in 1907.

eigentlich das Erscheinende und ist aber doch vorzugswiese gebraucht für das Erscheinen selbst, das subjektive Phänomen...."

[1] Cf. Rudolf Boehm, "Les ambiguïtés des concepts husserliens d'immanence' et de 'transcendance'." pp. 487-92.

APPENDIX III

GLOSSARY

The following are the English-German correlatives that have governed our English version of Husserl's terminology.

GERMAN-ENGLISH

ablaufen,	*to elapse*
Abschattung,	*profile*
Anschauung,	*intuition*
Anzahl,	*cardinal number*
Auffassung,	*apprehension*
Ausdruck,	*expression*
Aussage,	*utterance*
Bedeutung,	*meaning (esp. word meanings)*
Begriff,	*concept*
Beseelung,	*animation*
Bildung,	*formation*
Deutung,	*interpretation*
eigentlich,	*authentic, genuine*
Einstellung,	*attitude*
Empfindung,	*sensation*
Erfahrung,	*encounter*
Erfüllung,	*fulfillment*
Erlebnis,	*experience*
Erscheinung,	*appearance*
erzeugen,	*to produce, engender*
Gebilde,	*formation*
Gegebenheit,	*givenness*
Gegenstand,	*object, object of reference*
Gegenständlich-keit	*objectivity*
Gegenwart,	*present*
Inbegriff,	*group*
Inhalt,	*content*

leibhaft,	*"in person"*
Lebenswelt,	*lived world*
Leistung,	*achievement, performance*
Mannigfaltigkeit,	*manifold*
objektivierende,	*objectivating*
prinzipiell,	*"in principle"*
Sachverhalt,	*state of affairs*
Satz,	*assertion*
setzen,	*to assert*
Sinn,	*sense*
sinnlich,	*sensory*
Stiftung,	*establishment*
Ur-(auffassung, -empfindung, etc.)	*primal, primitive*
Ursprung,	*origin*
ursprünglich,	*originary*
Urteil,	*judgment*
Verbindung,	*liaison*
Vernunft,	*reason*
Vielheit,	*multiplicity*
Vorstellung,	*presentation*
Wahrnehmung,	*perception*
Zahl,	*number*
Zusammenhang,	*interconnection*

ENGLISH-GERMAN

achievement,	*Leistung*	manifold,	*Mannigfaltigkeit*
animation,	*Beseelung*	meaning (esp.	*Bedeutung*
appearance,	*Erscheinung*	word meanings),	
apprehension,	*Auffassung*	multiplicity,	*Vielheit*
attitude,	*Einstellung*	number,	*Zahl*
assertion,	*Satz*		
(to) assert,	*setzen*	object,	*Gegenstand,Objekt*
		object of refer-	*Gegenstand*
cardinal number,	*Anzahl*	ence,	
concept,	*Begriff*	objectivating,	*objektivierende*
content,	*Inhalt*	objectivity,	*Gegenständlich-*
			keit
encounter,	*Erfahrung*	origin,	*Ursprung*
(to) engender,	*erzeugen*	originary,	*ursprünglich*
(to) elapse,	*ablaufen*		
establishment,	*Stiftung*	perception,	*Wahrnehmung*
experience,	*Erlebnis*	performance,	*Leistung*
expression,	*Ausdruck*	"(in) person"	*leibhaft*
		present,	*Gegenwart*
formation,	*Bildung, Gebilde*	presentation,	*Vorstellung*
fulfillment,	*Erfüllung*	(to) produce,	*erzeugen*
		profile,	*Abschattung*
genuine,	*eigentlich*	primal,	*Ur- (auffassung,*
givenness,	*Gegebenheit*		*-empfindung,*
group,	*Inbegriff*		*etc.)*
		"(in) principle,"	*prinzipiell*
"in person,"	*leibhaft*		
"in principle,"	*prinzipiell*	reason,	*Vernunft*
interconnection,	*Zusammenhang*		
interpretation,	*Deutung*	sensation,	*Empfindung*
intuition,	*Anschauung*	sense,	*Sinn*
		sensory,	*sinnlich*
judgment,	*Urteil*	source,	*Quelle*
		state of affairs,	*Sachverhalt*
liaison,	*Verbindung*		
lived world,	*Lebenswelt*	utterance,	*Aussage*

BIBLIOGRAPHY

This bibliography includes books and articles cited in our study and others directly relevant to it.

WORKS OF HUSSERL

Cartesianische Meditationen und Pariser Vorträge. Edited by S. Strasser Husserliana, I). The Hague: Martinus Nijhoff, 1959.

Cartesian Meditations. Translated by Dorion Cairns. The Hague: Martinus Nijhoff, 1960.

"Entwurf einer 'Vorrede' zu den 'Logischen Untersuchungen'." Edited by Eugen Fink, *Tijdschrift voor Philosophie*, 1 (1939), pp. 106-133; 319-339.

Erfahrung und Urteil. Edited by Ludwig Landgrebe. Hamburg: Claassen, 1954.

Erste Philosophie. Volume I. Edited by Rudolf Boehm (Husserliana VII). The Hague: Martinus Nijhoff, 1956.

Erste Philosophie. Volume II. Edited by Rudolf Boehm (Husserliana VIII). The Hague: Martinus Nijhoff, 1959

Formale und transzendentale Logik. Halle a.S.: Max Niemeyer, 1929.

"Die Frage nach dem Ursprung der Geometrie als intentional-historisches Problem," Edited by Eugen Fink, *Revue internationale de Philosophie*, 1 (1938-1939), pp. 203-225. Reprinted in Husserliana VI, pp. 365-386.

Ideas: General Introduction to Pure Phenomenology. Translated by W. R. Boyce Gibson. London: George Allen and Unwin, 1931.

Die Idee der Phänomenologie. Edited by Walter Biemel (Husserliana II). The Hague: Martinus Nijhoff, 1950.

Ideen zu einer reinen Phänomenologie und phänomenologische Philosophie. Volume I. Edited by Walter Biemel (Husserliana III). The Hague: Martinus Nijhoff, 1950.

Ideen zu einer reinen Phänomenologie und phänomenologischen Philosophie. Volume II. Edited by Marly Biemel (Husserliana IV). The Hague: Martinus Nijhoff, 1952.

Ideen zu einer reinen Phänomenologie und phänomenologischen Philosophie. Volume III. Edited by Marly Biemel (Husserliana V). The Hague: Martinus Nijhoff, 1952.

Idées directrices pour une phénoménologie. Translated by Paul Ricoeur. Paris: Gallimard, 1950.

Die Krisis der europäischen Wissenschaften und die transzendentale Phäno-menologie. Edited by Walter Biemel (Husserliana VI). The Hague: Martinus Nijhoff, 1954.

Logische Untersuchungen. Erster Band: Prolegomena zur reinen Logik. Halle a.S.: Max Niemeyer, 1900. Second, revised edition: Halle a.S.: Max Niemeyer, 1913.

*Logische Untersuchungen. Zweiter Band: Untersuchungen zur Phänome-
nologie und Theorie der Erkenntnis.* Halle a.S.: Max Niemeyer, 1901.
Second, revised edition in two parts, with the following subtitles:
*Zweiter Band: Untersuchungen zur Phänomenologie und Theorie der Er-
kenntnis,* I Teil. Halle a.S.: Max Niemeyer, 1913.
*Zweiter Band: Elemente einer phänomenologischen Aufklärung der Er-
kenntnis,* II Teil. Halle a.S.: Max Niemeyer, 1921.
Phänomenologische Psychologie. Edited by Walter Biemel (Husserliana
IX). The Hague: Martinus Nijhoff, 1962.
"Philosophie als strenge Wissenschaft," *Logos,* I (1910-1911), pp. 289-341.
Philosophie der Arithmetik. Psychologische und logische Untersuchungen.
Volume I. Halle a.S.: C.E.M. Pfeffer, 1891.
"Philosophie der Arithmetik," (Selbstanzeige), *Vierteljahrsschrift für
wissenschaftliche Philosophie,* 15 (1891), pp. 360-361.
"Psychologische Studien zur elementaren Logik," *Philosophische Manats-
hefte,* 30 (1894), pp. 159-191.
Ueber den Begriff der Zahl; psychologische Analysen. Habilitationsschrift.
Halle a.S.: Heynemann'sche Buchdruckerei, 1887.
Vorlesungen zur Phänomenologie des inneren Zeitbewusstseins. Edited by
Martin Heidegger. Halle a.S.: Max Niemeyer, 1928.

BIBLIOGRAPHIES

Eley, Lothar. "Husserl-Bibliographie," *Zeitschrift für philosophische For-
schung,* 13 (1959), pp. 357-367.
Patocka, Jan. "Husserl-Bibliographie," *Revue internationale de Philoso-
phie,* 2 (1939), pp. 374-397.
Raes, Jean. "Supplément à la bibliographie de Husserl," *Revue inter-
nationale de Philosophie,* 14 (1950), pp. 469-475.
Robert, J.D. "Elements de bibliographie husserlienne," *Tijdschrift voor
Philosophie,* 20 (1958), pp. 534-544.
Van Breda, H. L. "Bibliographie der bis zum 30. Juni 1959 veröffent-
lichten Schriften Edmund Husserls," in *Edmund Husserl, 1859-1959.*
Edited by H. L. Van Breda and J. Taminiaux. The Hague: Martinus
Nijhoff, 1959, pp. 289-306.

SECONDARY SOURCES

Adorno, Theodor. *Zur Metakritik der Erkenntnistheorie.* Stuttgart: Kohl-
hammer, 1956.
Asemissen, Hermann. *Strukturanalytische Probleme der Wahrnehmung in
der Phänomenologie Husserls.* (Kantstudien: Ergänzungshefte, n. 73).
Cologne: The University Press, 1957.
Bachelard, Suzanne. *La logique de Husserl.* Paris: Presses universitaires
de France, 1957.
Berger, Gaston. *Le cogito dans la philosophie de Husserl.* Paris: Aubier,
1941.
Biemel, Walter. "Die entscheidende Phasen der Entfaltung von Husserls
Philosophie," *Zeitschrift für philosophische Forschung,* 13 (1959), pp.
187-213. This article appears also, with a discussion following as: "Les

phases décisives dans le développement de la philosophie de Husserl,"
in *Husserl* (Cahiers de Royaumont, Philosophie III). Paris: Editions de
Minuit, 1959, pp, 32-71.

Boehm, Rudolf. "Les ambiguïtés des concepts husserliens d''immanence'
et de 'transcendence'," *Revue philosophique de la France et de l'étranger*,
84 (1959), pp. 481-526.

— "Deux points de vue: Husserl et Nietzsche," *Archivio di Filosofia*,
(1952), pp. 167-181.

— "Husserl et l'idealisme classique," *Revue philosophique de Louvain*, 57
(1959), pp. 351-396.

— "Zijn en tijd in de filosofie van Husserl," *Tijdschrift voor Philosophie*,
21 (1959), pp. 243-276.

— "Zum Begriff des 'Absoluten' bei Husserl," *Zeitschrift für philosophische Forschung*, 13 (1959), pp. 214-242.

Bosio, Franco. "Constituzione statica e constituzione genetica," in *Tempo
e intenzionalità*. Padua: Casa Editrice Dott. Antonio Milani, 1960, pp.
73-88.

Brand, Gerd. *Welt, Ich und Zeit*. The Hague: Martinus Nijhoff, 1955.

Bröcker, Walter. "Husserls Lehre von der Zeit," *Philosophia Naturalis*,
4 (1957), pp. 374-379.

Capek, Milic. *The Philosophical Impact of Contemporary Physics*. Princeton: Van Nostrand, 1961.

Celms, Theodor. *Der phänomenologische Idealismus Husserls*. (Acta Universitatis Latviensis, XIX). Riga: Walters and Rapa, 1928.

Cohen, Hermann. *Kants Theorie der Erfahrung*. Berlin: Dümmler, 1885.

De Muralt, André. *L'idée de la phénoménologie*. Paris: Presses universitaires de France, 1958.

Derrida, Jacques. Introduction to: *Edmund Husserl: L'orgine de la géométrie*. Translated by J. Derrida. Paris: Presses universitaires de
France, 1962.

De Waelhens, Alphonse. *Existence et signification*. Louvain: Nauwelaerts,
1958.

— "Phénoménologie et métaphysique," *Revue philosophique de Louvain*,
47 (1949), pp. 366-376.

— *Phénoménologie et vérité*. Paris: Presses universitaires de France, 1953.

Diemer, Alwin. *Edmund Husserl*. Meisenheim: Anton Hain, 1956.

Eigler, Gunther. *Metaphysische Voraussetzungen in Husserls Zeitanalysen*.
Meisenheim: Anton Hain, 1961.

Farber, Marvin. *The Foundation of Phenomenology*. Cambridge: Harvard
University Press, 1943.

Fink, Eugen. "L'analyse intentionnelle et le problème de la pensée spéculative," in *Problèmes actuels de la phénoménologie*. Edited by H. L. Van
Breda. Paris: Desclée de Brouwer, 1952, pp. 54-87.

— "Operative Begriffe in Husserls Phänomenologie," *Zeitschrift für
philosophische Forschung*, 9 (1957), pp. 321-337.

— "Die phänomenologische Philosophie Edmund Husserls in der gegenwärtigen Kritik," *Kantstudien*, 38 (1933), pp. 319-383.

— "Das Problem der Phänomenologie Edmund Husserls," *Revue internationale de Philosophie*, 1 (1938-1939), pp. 226-270.

Follesdal, Dagfinn. *Husserl und Frege*. Oslo: I Kommisjon Hoe H. Aschehoug, 1958.

Frege, Gottlob. "Dr. E. G. Husserl: Philosophie der Arithmetik," (Book review) *Zeitschrift für Philosophie und philosophische Kritik*, 103 (1894), pp. 22-41.

Gadamer, Hans Georg. *Wahrheit und Methode*. Tübingen: J. C. B. Mohr, 1960.

Hanson, Norwood R. *Patterns of Discovery*. Cambridge: The University Press, 1958.

Illeman, Werner. *Husserls vorphänomenologische Philosophie*. Leipzig: Hirzel, 1932.

Ingarden, Roman. "Le problème de la constitution et le sens de la réfléxion constitutive chez Edmond Husserl," in *Husserl* (Cahiers de Royaumont, Philosophie III). Paris: Editions de Minuit, 1959, pp. 242-264.

— Über den transzendentalen Idealismus bei E. Husserl," in *Husserl et la pensée moderne*. Edited by H. L. Van Breda and J. Taminiaux. The Hague: Martinus Nijhoff, 1959, pp. 190-204.

Kant, Emmanuel. *Kritik der reinen Vernunft*. Hamburg: Meiner, 1956.

Kern, Iso. "Die drei Wege zur transzendental-phänomenologischen Reduktion in der Philosophie Edmund Husserls," *Tijdschrift voor Philosophie*, 24 (1962), pp. 303-349.

— *Husserl und Kant*. The Hague: Martinus Nijhoff, 1964.

Kraft, Julius. *Von Husserl zu Heidegger*. Frankfurt: Verlag Oeffentliches Leben, 1957.

Landgrebe, Ludwig. "Husserls Phänomenologie und die Motive zu ihrer Umbildung," *Revue internationale de Philosophie*, 1 (1938-1939), pp. 277-316.

Lauer, Quentin. *Phénoménologie de Husserl*. Paris: Presses universitaires de France, 1955.

Levinas, Emmanuel. "Réfléxions sur la technique phénoménologique," in *Husserl* (Cahiers de Royaumont, Philosophie III). Paris: Editions de Minuit, 1959, pp. 95-107.

— *La théorie de l'intuition dans la phénoménologie de Husserl*. Paris: Alcan, 1930.

Merlan, Philip. "Time consciousness in Husserl and Heidegger," *Philosophy and Phenomenological Research*, 8 (1947), pp. 23-54.

Merleau-Ponty, Maurice. *Phénoménologie de la perception*. Paris: Gallimard, 1945.

— *Signes*. Paris: Gallimard, 1960.

Natorp, Paul. *Einleitung in die Psychologie nach kritischer Methode*. Freiburg i.B.: J. C. B. Mohr, 1888.

— "Philosophie und Psychologie," *Logos*, 4 (1913), pp. 176-202.

— *Philosophische Propädeutik*. Marburg: N. G. Elwert, 1903.

— "Ueber objektive und subjektive Begründung der Erkenntnis," *Philosophische Monatshefte*, 23 (1887), pp. 257-286.

Osborn, Andrew. *The Philosophy of Edmund Husserl*. New York: Columbia University Doctoral Dissertation, 1934.

Paton, H. J. *Kant's Metaphysic of Experience*. 2 volumes. London: George Allen and Unwin, 1961.

Picard, Yvonne. "Le temps chez Husserl et chez Heidegger," *Deucalion*, 1 (1946), pp. 95-124.

Pietersma, Henry. *Edmund Husserl's Concept of Philosophical Clarification: Its Development from 1887 to 1913*. University of Toronto: Unpublished Doctoral Dissertation, 1961.

Schütz, Alfred. *Der sinnhafte Aufbau der sozialen Welt.* Vienna: Springer, 1960.
Spiegelberg, Herbert. *The Phenomenological Movement.* 2 volumes. The Hague: Martinus Nijhoff, 1960.
Stumpf, Carl. "Erscheinung und psychische Funktionen," *Abhandlungen der königlich Preussischen Akademie der Wissenschaften,* 1906. pp. 1-40.
Thyssen, Johannes. "Husserls Lehre von den 'Bedeutungen' und das Begriffsproblem," *Zeitschrift für philosophische Forschung,* 13 (1959), pp. 163-186, 438-458.
Toulmin, Stephen. *The Uses of Argument.* Cambridge: The University Press, 1958.
Vallenilla, Ernesto. *Fenomenologia del conocimiento.* Caracas: Doctoral Dissertation, Universidad Central de Venezuela, 1954.
Van Breda, Hermann L. "Het 'zuivere phaenomeen' volgens Husserl," *Tijdschrift voor Philosophie,* 3 (1941), pp. 477-498.
Van Peursen, C. A. "La notion du temps et de l'ego transcendental chez Husserl," in *Husserl* (Cahiers de Royaumont, Philosophie III). Paris: Editions de Minuit, 1959, pp. 196-207.
Van Riet, Georges. "Réalisme thomiste et phénoménologie husserlienne," *Revue philosophique de Louvain,* 55 (1957), pp. 58-92.
Volkmann-Schluck, K. H. "Husserls Lehre von der Idealität der Bedeutung als methaphysisches Problem," in *Husserl et la pensée moderne.* Edited by H. L. Van Breda and J. Taminiaux. The Hague: Martinus Nijhoff, 1959, pp. 230-241.
Weyl, Hermann. *Philosophy of Mathematics and Natural Science.* Princeton: The University Press, 1949.
Wittgenstein, Ludwig. *Philosophical Investigations.* Text and translation by G. E. M. Anscombe. Oxford: Blackwell, 1958.

INDEXES

INDEX OF TEXTS CITED

INDEX OF PROPER NAMES

GENERAL INDEX

Absolute, ambiguity of the term, 126, 129–130, 196; givenness of subjectivity, 108–109, 123–126, 195–196, 219, 227–228; independence of subjectivity, 127–128, 195–196; time as ultimate absolute, 77, 160–162, 199–201

Abstractive, 124–125

Act, structure of, 46–51; quality of, 47–48; material of, 47–48; analysis into partial intentions, 61; differentiation of acts in stream of consciousness, 92–93; equivalent to apprehension, 50, 88; experience of, 52, 88–92, 113–114; reflection on, 14, 22–24; modifications of, 145–148; and meaning, 42–44, 53; and objects, 46–47, 54; and categorical objects, 65–68, 146; and logical forms, 15, 17, 21, 23–24, 38, 65–68, 148; and groups, 11–12, 16–17; and sensations, 48–51, 54–58, 98; see Apprehension, Noesis, Schema of matter-form.

Active genesis, 175, 193, 207

Addition and subtraction, 225

Adequateness, of subjective experience in *Ideen I*, 124–126; denied in *Cart. Med.*, 185–186, 189–190

Aesthetics, transcendental, 174–177, 182

Analogies of Experience, 215

Anticipations of Perception, 215

Apodicticity, of subjective experience, 123–126, 219; separated from adequateness, 185, 189–190

Apophantics, 167

Appearances, for sense qualities, 49–51, 79–80; for time, 79–80, 101–103; as opposed to reality, 133–134; see Representants, Schema of matter-form

Apprehension, equivalent to acts, 50, 81; of sensory data by intentions, 50–51, 54–58, 62, 79, 140, 177; and

non-intentional sensations, 110–113 time apprehensions, 75, 79–80; and objective time, 103–104; and retention, 110–113; see Act, Schema of matter-form

Apriori, of time, 108; in transcendental aesthetics, 174; before perception, 155; in genetic constitution, 171, 199; innate apriori of ego, 186

Arithmetic, foundations, of, 7 ff.; and logic, 37; and symbolic numbers, 26–27, 224

Assertion, and evidence, 153; and reason, 152

Association, does not explain symbolism, 30; and group symbolism, 29; empiricist concept of, 176; in transcendental aesthetics, 175–177

Being, absolute being of subjectivity, 127–128–228; relative and phenomenal being of reality, 128–130; 228

Belief, as normal noetic attitude, 145

Categorical acts, structure of, 69–71; and sensory data, 70; see Categorical objects

Categorical objects, described, 65; constitution of, 67–68; as result of judgment, 67–68, 170; and sensory data, 70–71; not first model for constitution, 202–203; found in *Phil. Arith.*, 6, 15, 18–22, 202; in *Log. Unt.*, 38, 139; in *Ideen I*, 146; in *Zeitbewusstsein*, 109; and reflection, 23–24

Categories, Kantian, 214–216

Causality, implied in noema of "thing," 155; needed in mechanics, 192

Cause, subjectivity not a cause of reality, 137–139, 159, 197, 199, 201; subjectivity is cause of categorical objects, 217; in genetic constitution, 170–171, 192

124–125, 186, 195, 219; not based on reality, 123–126, 185, 195; includes reality, 130–131, 133, 139, 219–220, 227; demands return to now-instant, 200; only an ideal, 185

Schema of matter-form, described, 54–58, 177; first model for constitution, 202–204; and language, 57–58; and meaning, 58–59; and objects, 60; and objective time, 102–103; and categorical acts, 69–71, 204; and immanent objects, 81, 114; as noesis-hyle, 120, 139–143, 165; not valid in constitution of acts, 91–92, 205; not valid in constitution of sensations, 94–95, 98, 205; not applicable to sensation and intentions, 98, 140, 142, 205; not valid for objective time, 104–105; limitations of, 204–206, 209–210; as psychologism, 177–178, 180, 209–210; rejection of, 177–180, 182, 186, 205–206; as pedagogical aid, 178; in Brentano, 56; in other writers, 57, 215–216; in *Phil. Arith.*, 203

Science, theory of, 37, 116–117
Sediment, of earlier judgments, 172, 182, 188, 213
Sensations, as immanent objects, 77–78, 80–82; as representants, 51, 79; content is not explained, 97–98; experience of and time, 93–98, 113–114; equivalent to states of consciousness, 96–97; not distinct from acts, 98, 178–180, 205–206; existence of non-intentional, 49, 110–113; pre-predicative, 176–177, 207, 211; and genetic constitution, 113, 177, 211; *see* Content of sensation, Sensory data
Sense, *see* Meaning
Sensory data, experience of, 51–52; apprehension of, 55–56, 141–142; and intentional acts, 48–51; as appearances, 51, 79; and content of meaning, 62–65, 149, 210–211; and logical entities, 33–36; for categorical objects, 70–71; for objective time, 102–105; *see* Content of sensations, Schema of matter-form, Sensations
Simultaneity, 25, 85
Something, concept of, 12; priority of this concept, 15; and numbers, 20
Sources, of numbers, 7–11, 15, 24 ff.; of symbolic numbers, 25 ff., 32; of symbols, 30–32; of meaning, 38, 57–

58, 174, 181–182; of noemas, 158–159; of time, 75–76, 100, 115; of logical forms, 14, 16, 23, 38, 66, 168; subjectivity as source for reality, 136–137; two sources needed for constitution, 218
Space, experience of, 183, 212; and profiles in things, 123; prior to constitution of things, 112
Spectator, fallacy of extra, 89, 91
Static analysis, 59, 71, 143, 164; surpassed, 183, 206–207
Stream of consciousness, absolute, 78; and experience of immanent objects, 89; no boundaries for, 92; as ego, 187; *see* Ego, Subjectivity.
Structure, of consciousness, 117, 119, 140–143; of logical forms, 16; of acts, 47–48, 51, 87; temporal structure of acts, 88–92; temporal structure of consciousness, 86–88, 186; of categorical acts, 69–71; of noemas, 143–144, 151–152; of time, 76, 85–86; analysis of, 52, 58, 120, 140; structural analysis surpassed, 169, 181–183, 206–207; *see* Act, Intentionality, Subjectivity, structure of
Subjectivity, absolutely given, 108–109, 123–126, 195–196, 219, 227–228; basis for rigorous science, 124–125, 186, 195, 219, 227–228; and symbols, 31; and neo-Kantian constitution, 214–215; and absolute stream of consciousness, 92; structural analysis of, 40 ff., 140
Subjectivity and Objectivity, subjectivity separable from objectivity, 102, 121–122, 127–128, 138, 164, 195–196; objectivity correlated to subjectivity, 108–109, 114, 119, 126-131, 137–138, 164, 195; objectivity transcendent to subjectivity, 133–136, 165, 196–197, 228–229; subjectivity is condition of possibility for reality of objectivity, 126–131, 137–138, 159, 191–193, 195–197, 199
Symbols, and numbers, 20, 25 ff., 224–225; and multitudes, 27; and sense data, 63; not explained in *Phil. Arith.*, 30–33, 35

Teleology, of noetic-hyletic patterns, 141–142, 171, 227; of growth of meaning, 171; of pre-predicative constitution, 175, 207
Temporality, as phenomenon, 74–75;

as process, 99; origin of, 75–76; and numbers, 24–25, 36; world time, 75, 79, 101–110; and experience of immanent objects, 80, 82–84; and experience of acts, 88–92; and experience of sensations, 93–98; pervades consciousness and its objects, 22, 143, 183, 206, 208, 222; as final absolute, 77–78, 142, 160–162, 199–201; basis of obscurity in ego, 161, 186, 190; excluded in *Ideen I*, 120, 140, 159–162; as condition of possibility, 161–162, 199–201, 210; two flows of time needed, 222

Thing, perception of, 177; constitution of in *Log. Unt.*, 54; genetic constitution of, 169, 175

Transcendence, of things is constituted, 133–136; paradox of, 134–135, 165, 227; *see* Subjectivity and Objectivity

Variation, free, 53

Ways to reduction, 132–133, 164, 196
Will, 188
Words, word meanings, 42–43; written arabesques, 31; *see* Language